SYRIA AND THE CHEMI

MANCHEStER
1824
Manchester University Press

New Approaches to Conflict Analysis

Series editors: Peter Lawler and Emmanuel-Pierre Guittet, School of Social Sciences, University of Manchester

Until recently, the study of conflict and conflict resolution remained comparatively immune to broad developments in social and political theory. When the changing nature and locus of large-scale conflict in the post-Cold War era is also taken into account, the case for a reconsideration of the fundamentals of conflict analysis and conflict resolution becomes all the more stark.

New Approaches to Conflict Analysis promotes the development of new theoretical insights and their application to concrete cases of large-scale conflict, broadly defined. The series intends not to ignore established approaches to conflict analysis and conflict resolution, but to contribute to the reconstruction of the field through a dialogue between orthodoxy and its contemporary critics. Equally, the series reflects the contemporary porosity of intellectual borderlines rather than simply perpetuating rigid boundaries around the study of conflict and peace. *New Approaches to Conflict Analysis* seeks to uphold the normative commitment of the field's founders yet also recognises that the moral impulse to research is properly part of its subject matter. To these ends, the series is comprised of the highest quality work of scholars drawn from throughout the international academic community, and from a wide range of disciplines within the social sciences.

Syria and the chemical weapons taboo

Exploiting the forbidden

MICHELLE BENTLEY

Manchester University Press

Published by Manchester University Press
Altrincham Street, Manchester M1 7JA
www.manchesteruniversitypress.co.uk

British Library Cataloguing-in-Publication Data
A catalogue record for this book is available from the British Library

Library of Congress Cataloging-in-Publication Data applied for

ISBN 978 1 5261 0471 7 hardback
ISBN 978 1 5261 0472 4 paperback

First published 2016

Typeset by Out of House Publishing
Printed in Great Britain
by CPI Group (UK) Ltd, Croydon, CR0 4YY

As long as what you are afraid of is something evil, you may still hope that the good may come to your rescue. But suppose you struggle through to the good and find that it is also dreadful?

(Lewis, 1996 [1944]: 17)

CONTENTS

ACKNOWLEDGEMENTS

Many thanks go to: James D. Boys, Robert Elias, Charlotte Heath-Kelly, Richard Jackson, Tony Mason, Alister Miskimmon, Ben O'Loughlin, David Owen, Adam Quinn, Rod Rhodes, Laura Roselle, Caroline Soper, Nick Wheeler, Caroline Wintersgill, Clare Woodford, everyone at MUP, the BISA US Foreign Policy working group (especially Andrew Futter, Oz Hassan, Jack Holland, Nick Kitchen, and Maria Ryan), the anonymous reviewers, and all my valued colleagues at Royal Holloway.

My thanks also go to Russell Bentley, whose support throughout writing this book has been incredible. This book is dedicated to him.

ABBREVIATIONS

AI	Amnesty International
AP	Associated Press
BWC	Biological and Toxin Weapons Convention
CPD	Compilation of Presidential Documents
CWC	Chemical Weapons Convention
HRW	Human Rights Watch
IR	International Relations
IRC	International Rescue Committee
IS	Islamic State
MSF	Médecins Sans Frontières
NATO	North Atlantic Treaty Organization
NTI	Nuclear Threat Initiative
OPCW	Organisation for the Prohibition of Chemical Weapons
R2P	Responsibility to Protect
SNC	Syrian National Council
SNHR	Syrian Network for Human Rights
UN	United Nations
UNHRC	UN Human Rights Council
US	United States of America
USACDA	US Arms Control and Disarmament Agency
USCIA	US Central Intelligence Agency
US Cong.	US Congress
USDIA	US Defense Intelligence Agency
USDNI	US Director of National Intelligence
USDOD	US Department of Defense
WMD	weapons of mass destruction

Introduction

BEHAVIOUR IS shaped by the forbidden. Murder, nakedness, infidelity, non-heterosexuality, and obscenity are but a few examples of the ways in which human activity is normatively constrained. Such acts are stigmatised as *taboo*. That is, these ideas exist as socially constructed expectations that actors should not engage in, permit, and in some cases even acknowledge certain behaviours that have been deemed unacceptable. In short, taboos are what we should not do. While such expectations are subject to reinterpretation, re-justification, and also Machiavellian claims that actions characterised as taboo can be considered permissible under specific conditions of use, life is framed within a series of moral and normative anticipations, or 'rules', as to which acts are socially tolerable. Likewise, this concept of the taboo extends beyond the personal and into the political arena. Within international politics the notion of the taboo is manifest in numerous issues and controversies including the legitimacy of intervention, the violation of state sovereignty, targeting of non-combatants, and – the focus of this study – weapon prohibitions, where certain types of armament are considered so excessively offensive that their possession and use are intentionally and institutionally delegitimised.

This last category includes the chemical weapons taboo – the claim that chemical arms are so odious that they should be eliminated. There is a social revulsion surrounding these devices, not least where they are considered highly destructive (signified by their frequent classification as weapons of mass destruction, or WMD) and are indiscriminate in terms of effect. These are weapons that so exceed the limits of acceptability that avoidance and proscription are requisite. Within this framework of understanding, policy reflects a normative expectation that chemical weapons use represents a grievous transgression, now evident in a number of prohibitory agreements including the 1899 Hague Convention (from which, according to Richard Price, the taboo first developed, in response to a desire for non-combatant protection from chemical shells; Price, 1995), 1925 Geneva Protocol, and 1993 Chemical Weapons Convention (CWC).

1

This normative policy structure is widely acknowledged as a 'good' thing. While not all taboos are considered in such positive and flawless terms, this is held up as a political ideal. And indeed, why not? Chemical arms are horrific weapons that can cause, and have caused, repulsive levels of destruction. Who then could object to the expectation that they should be opposed?

This book makes the provocative claim that the chemical weapons taboo is not 'good'. In fact, the taboo frequently makes things worse. It does so by skewing understanding of international security. In particular, it introduces erroneous hierarchies of thinking into arms control discourse. It creates a belief that chemical weapons are more worthy of sanction and concern than other armaments, which pushes non-chemical threats out of consideration. The taboo establishes chemical arms as an exclusive focal point, even in situations where other modes of violence inflict comparable, or even greater, levels of destruction and political damage. This unsustainable prioritisation means that conflict scenarios are misinterpreted, to the extent that they actually escalate and worsen. This is not simply a case in which the taboo distorts political thinking, but one where its knock-on effects are actively detrimental. Using the taboo as the basis of international politics in this way causes more violence, more conflict, and more destruction. The taboo is not a purely positive influence. To employ the obvious cliché, it can do more harm than good.

Critically, this is not to say that the idea that these are horrific weapons we would be better without is necessarily wrong. And indeed, this book does not seek to suggest that this is the case. Nor does it ignore the importance of the chemical arms control regime, particularly the CWC. If we are talking about doing good, then analysis cannot overlook the contribution the taboo has made here in terms of limiting chemical warfare and chemical weapons possession. What this study does demonstrate, however, is that the way in which the taboo is conventionally expressed within international politics is also highly injurious and deeply flawed (this concept of the 'conventional' will be explained more in later chapters). There is a very dark side to the taboo. This exists where the taboo has been translated into certain practical expectations, notably that the issue of chemical weapons and their elimination must come before all other threats, and that it must be pursued at all costs with no recognition of context. For some, this is extremely important. If chemical weapons eradication is as crucial as this understanding of the taboo suggests, then nothing can ever come in the way of that – otherwise we risk a situation in which the taboo is diluted and is left prey to other concerns that may detract from the issue of elimination. Yet this book contests this view to show that (a) this distinction is flawed and (b) those other concerns can be critical too. Allowing the taboo to reduce our thinking to the chemical threat alone, especially in cases where such weapons are not the only or primary threat, can only do harm. The taboo is not working.

This problem is made worse by the fact that there is no meaningful opposition to the taboo. Being such a hallowed construct, there is, it is presumed, simply no basis for criticism. Indeed, to the very limited extent the taboo has been questioned, it is typically for not going far enough in its moral condemnation of chemical devices, or calls for improved verification in terms of the taboo's manifestation within arms control regimes. The taboo itself is treated as beyond reproach. Yet more than that, this is a situation in which criticism is actively proscribed (regardless of whether or not that criticism is warranted), where it is seen to potentially damage and undermine the taboo. The taboo is presented as an essential but fragile concept, and any disparagement could cause that normative structure to disintegrate, taking away the international community's best hope for eradicating these weapons. Even if anything were inappropriate about the taboo, it is argued that it remains the most apposite option available and consequently should be protected at all costs. While the need for strong controls on chemical weapons is not disputed here, it is asserted, however, that the taboo causes serious problems, problems that cannot be overlooked any longer or justified on the basis of utility. Although the taboo may appear to embody the very best of arms control and commitments to peace, this is far from the case. In fact, it poses a considerable threat to both. Consequently, politicians, policy practitioners more generally, and academic analysts alike need to stop thinking that the taboo works within the context of international security and accept that – perversely – it is capable of doing the exact opposite.

This book makes a further claim: that policy-makers' rhetorical employment of the chemical weapons taboo is highly strategic. Its use is the calculated, constructed, and contextualised product of self-interested actors. Conventional understanding considers taboos to be intrinsic and static restraints. Specifically, taboos govern actors: they are ideas and behaviours to which actors inexorably adhere as a consequence of their social construction and which they cannot directly control. Critically, however, this theoretical position neglects the way in which taboos are not merely an issue of involuntary adherence, but an agency-centric resource for strategic discursive construction. In stark contrast to prevailing belief, this book demonstrates that taboos do not solely determine our actions, but provide the rhetorical tools for the deliberate and manipulative shaping of international debate. The same ideas and assumptions that underpin the taboo as a form of restriction can also be strategically exploited for the realisation of actor self-interest. Significantly, this is not the weak claim that taboos are simply used emotively, i.e. that the conceptualisation of a specific act as taboo, and the infringement of that taboo as an unforgiveable and immoral wrongdoing, engenders an affecting response to its violation that in turn can be played on. This is the much stronger assertion that the ideational structure of the taboo provides the rhetorical apparatus for an actor to control debate and political understanding. Actors exert considerable agency over the concepts and normative language they employ, and they can manipulate them in order to realise their own self-interested ambitions. This is not to suggest that all rhetorical acts are calculated, or that there is no genuine commitment to the chemical weapons taboo. Yet it is to demonstrate that, within this normative context, there exists considerable scope for the taboo's agency-driven strategic interpretation, where this directly influences international and foreign policy.

This is discussed in relation to Syria's civil war, specifically, the way in which Syrian President Bashar al-Assad's use of chemical weapons would come to define and dominate United States (US) foreign policy on the conflict. A year into the crisis, US President Barack Obama declared his now infamous 'redline'. This was effectively an ultimatum stating that, if Assad engaged in chemical warfare, this would cause a significant change in US foreign policy – an ultimatum that was interpreted more widely as a reference to military intervention. While Obama's exact intentions in laying down this challenge will be questioned here, it was essentially a case in which the entirety of his foreign policy came to hang on the use or not of chemical weapons. This was not limited to the issue of intervention, however. The taboo was also manifest in the later proposition of a diplomatic solution, by which Assad would accede to the CWC and agreed to eliminate all Syria's chemical stockpiles. Consequently, the chemical weapons taboo became the core focus of conflict resolution, where (a) the use of chemical weapons was seen to demand a US response and (b) the taboo formed the exclusive basis of foreign policy activity. This makes Syria a perfect example for analysis in that the chemical weapons taboo was constructed as intrinsic to US understanding of the conflict, particularly in terms of foreign policy decision-making.

On the surface, this appeal to the chemical weapons taboo would appear to be a positive. Not least because the taboo would eventually (ostensibly) underpin a diplomatic solution, so Obama would avoid military involvement, remove chemical weapons from a belligerent dictator, and place conflict resolution on a non-violent footing. There are, however, serious issues with this picture. In fact, the application of the taboo as the basis of US foreign policy has vastly exacerbated the civil conflict. It has made it erroneously appear that progress has been achieved in respect of Syria, while ignoring the reality that an exclusive focus on chemical weapons could never substantially mitigate the crisis. Indeed, all it has done is fuel the conflict further. In particular, it has achieved this by unnecessarily securing Assad's legitimacy. By engaging the dictator in the chemical weapons control regime – and specifically no other actor who could claim leadership in respect of Syria – this strengthened his position. Furthermore, by inviting him to comply with the taboo via the CWC, so this too was legitimating. He could appear to be doing the right thing (when in fact he has continued to use chemical weapons). This has unintentionally skewed the political make-up of the crisis and alienated the opposition, to the detriment of US foreign policy aims. This also plays into the strategic element of the taboo, in that Obama's deliberate engagement with it – not least surrounding the CWC negotiations – served to exaggerate these problems by contributing to the prioritisation inherent to the taboo. As this book will show, the president strategically employed the taboo to realise his own self-interest, and this act would intensify the harmful issues identified here. Overall then, this case study demonstrates something very interesting about the highly strategic way taboos are used, which changes what we thought we knew about norms and the agency that actors exert over them. Unfortunately, it also shows how the indiscriminate and careless use of the taboo can lead to major difficulties in terms of international politics and conflict. Far from helping, the taboo has constituted the most negative of all influences on conflict resolution in Syria. No other factor has been as detrimental in preventing peace.

In terms of structure, the book constitutes a step-by-step analysis of the Syria crisis and the role chemical weapons have played. The first chapter introduces the chemical weapons taboo and engages in a critical analysis that identifies the two issues at the centre of this study: that the taboo is (a) employed strategically and (b) damaging to conflict resolution. In doing so, it also outlines the theoretical framework used in demonstrating these claims. This is based on the 'strategic narratives' paradigm, which asserts that actors deliberately apply specific narratives in order to promote their political ambitions. Yet this section expands this understanding by incorporating an agency-centric interpretation of linguistic use taken from the work of political theorist Quentin Skinner – in particular, his model of the 'innovating ideologist'. While discussions in the field of International Relations (IR) and strategic language have tended to assume a socially constructed world in which actors levy only limited power over the meaning of discourse, it is shown here that narrative creation is a significantly more manipulative and manipulated process. Actors possess considerable power over the rhetoric they employ, even in relation to intrinsically restrictive concepts such as taboos.

Part I (consisting of three chapters) applies this strategic interpretation to US foreign policy on Syria, explicitly understood as a reference to Obama's redline.[1] It demonstrates that this is not the hard-line ultimatum it was made out to be, but is in fact a calculated construct that expresses Obama's own preferences concerning US involvement in the crisis. Chapter 2 starts by analysing Obama's real intentions in setting the redline to reveal that these have been misinterpreted. More specifically, that pre-existing ideas surrounding the chemical weapons taboo have caused Obama's statement to be misconstrued as a be-all-and-end-all of US foreign policy on Syria. The chapter examines the wider policy context at the time to demonstrate that this interpretation was diametrically opposed to Obama's professed position and that the redline actually constitutes a much softer and more moderate allusion to the taboo. Having established this gap between intention and convention (i.e. between Obama's reluctance to intervene and the expectation created by the taboo that he should), Chapter 3 examines Obama's rhetorical employment of the taboo as the situation in Syria progressed. Whatever his views against intervention, Obama would engage with the taboo as a core theme of his rhetoric on Syria. This is explained as a strategic move on the part of Obama; explicitly, it constitutes the construction of a strategic narrative. While his inadvertent reference to the taboo forced him towards a more interventionist stance, it also gave him the discursive tools to limit expectations for greater action to a policy that – while it did not reflect his preferences perfectly – was a significantly better fit with his desires than full-on intervention. Chapter 4 takes this a step further, to demonstrate the sheer extent to which this strategic process was agency-driven and calculated. Obama used the taboo not only to limit policy, but to actively control it. This is not merely a case in which Obama drew on conventional understandings of the taboo, but one in which he dug deep into that construct to exploit specific aspects in the promotion of his own self-interest. This was a manipulative and deliberate process, one in which Obama exercised significant control over the idea of the taboo itself. Far from the inevitable adherence to the taboo that the situation has been portrayed as, it was in fact the opposite – a case in which Obama effectively reversed that normative expectation in order to manipulate it for his own gain.

Part II (consisting of two chapters) expands this story of chemical weapons and Syria to demonstrate that the taboo has not been 'good' for the crisis. Chapter 5 analyses issues surrounding how specific weapons are perceived within a conflict, specifically where the taboo causes chemical armaments to be prioritised over others via inappropriate hierarchies of threat.[2] The way in which the taboo has dominated understanding of Syria has seen other threats ignored – notably the vast numbers being massacred with conventional devices, but also the significant biowarfare threat that exists in the country. This means that policy-makers have focused on the wrong issues in respect of Syria, a situation that precludes ever finding workable solutions to the crisis. Simply put, policy-makers are not seeing the real problems. The taboo blinds them; or rather, it applies a lens through which they can see only the chemical threat and none of the other issues driving the conflict. How then could we ever hope that these issues would be addressed? Chapter 6 builds on this to show that Syria is not simply a case of misinterpretation, but one in which the taboo has intensified the conflict. The conflict is worse and more violent as a direct consequence of using the taboo as the basis of US foreign policy. It looks at the physically and politically destructive ways in which the taboo has fed the tensions underpinning the crisis, specifically where these are identified as effects that would not have occurred had the taboo not been prioritised above all other concerns. The chapter then concludes with a more comprehensive analysis of how the taboo is detrimental to international politics and whether it should even be kept as part of IR discourse. If it is not the outstanding, necessary, and moral ideal that it is held up to be, should the taboo be dispensed with, at least in terms of its current expression? And if so, can that abandonment ever be justified? Could we really say goodbye to the chemical weapons taboo? Or does the engrained and special nature of the taboo mean we can never let it go, no matter how harmful it is?

NOTES

1   Aspects of this work are drawn from Bentley (2014a). Thanks go to Caroline Soper.
2   Aspects of this work are drawn from Bentley (2015). Thanks go to Rob Elias.

1

The chemical weapons taboo

THE ARAB SPRING effectively started on 17 December 2010, when 26-year-old Tunisian street vendor, Tarek al-Tayeb Mohammed Bouazizi, set fire to himself in protest at local government officials and police. Decrying repeated acts of intimidation, insult, bribery, and the unlawful confiscation of his merchandise, Bouazizi demanded to see the local governor to complain. After he was refused an audience he left, reportedly shouting: 'If you won't see me, I'll burn myself.' He soon returned to the governor's office, covered his body in petrol, and set himself alight in public view. Despite efforts to save him, he never regained consciousness. He would die from his injuries a month later. Bouazizi's decision to protest via an act of self-immolation is highly symbolic. Such actions are not permitted within Islam: the Quran forbids not only suicide, but also the body's destruction by fire. For Bouazizi, and for those who would follow him in similar acts of self-immolation as part of what would become the Arab Spring, this was an extreme form of protest: 'There is nothing worse they could do to themselves – it is the ultimate despair' (Darke, 2014: 43).

Bouazizi's expression of desperate frustration inspired a wave of revolutionary protests, which would not stop at Tunisia. A 'domino effect' of popular uprisings spread quickly across the Middle East, reaching countries including Libya, Egypt, Bahrain, Yemen, and – in March 2011 – Syria. Rebellion in Syria originated as mainly peaceful demonstrations against the antagonistic dictatorship of President Bashar al-Assad. An unexpected politician (his brother Bassel was due to assume power from their father, Hafez al-Assad, but died in a car crash in 1994 leaving Bashar to take the family reins), Bashar was initially heralded as a moderniser. Yet his highly neoliberal and capitalist regime, backed by mass repression and the denial of human rights, soon caused widespread discontent with his leadership. This was the trigger for the protests. The protesters' initial demands, however, were not as extreme as those experienced in other countries affected by the Arab Spring, in which many protesters had demanded a complete change in government. Instead, protesters called largely for reform as opposed

8

to Assad's resignation and replacement. Moreover, this was not intended as a violent demand; with the memory of the Lebanon civil war still fresh in people's minds, there was no desire to risk repeating that. Indeed, it was not the protests themselves that would push Syria into a state of civil conflict, but Assad's response to them.

Following the main cities of Damascus and Aleppo, demonstrations sprang up all over Syria, including the south-western town of Daraa. The protests here would make headlines after government forces carried out the arrest and torture of 15 children for writing anti-regime graffiti on a school wall. The graffiti started as a standard phrase of the Arab Spring: 'The people want the fall of the regime.' But in this case an extra line was added: 'It's your turn doctor' – a reference to Assad's training as an ophthalmologist. The actions against these children fuelled discontent in the district throughout March and April 2011, to the extent that Assad eventually decided to crush the protest with military might. Regime forces shot into the crowd, an act that only served to intensify the demonstrations further. As part of this, and in addition to the 245 killed in this initial military put-down, the Arab Spring was now to create another martyr in the revolutionary cause. During the Daraa uprising, 13-year-old Hamza Ali al-Khatib became separated from his family, and was later detained, tortured, and murdered in regime custody. His corpse was returned in a body bag: burnt, severely beaten, with three gunshot wounds to the chest, and with mutilated genitals – a warning sign to the protesters of what they risked if they chose to continue. Al-Khatib's death became a symbol for the Syrian rebellion. It was a connection highlighted by then Secretary of State Hillary Clinton (in Mohamed, 2011), who said the killing represented the 'total collapse' of Assad's willingness to listen to demands for reform. In terms of why Assad decided to react in such a repressive manner, former British diplomat Henry Hogger (2014: 5) offers this insight:

> History may take a while to reach an authoritative verdict: but the best guess is perhaps a mixture of a rather weak and impressionable personality, tough advice from those with most to lose from any dilution of the status quo – in other words the ruling elite including the Assads and their in-laws – and a sense of destiny, not uncommon among absolute rulers, equating survival of the dynasty with the safe-guarding of the nation.

Assad's aggressive response captured the world's attention. Syria's political positioning in the international community made the threat of violent unrest here especially disturbing. While all the nations involved in the uprising were of course important in respect of the political situation, international actors were more than aware that Syria has long been a lynchpin of Middle Eastern politics. As a state, it plays into a variety of controversial relationships and regional networking. Crisis here would involve, and, necessarily, has involved, numerous other states with which Syria has critical ties, not least where these have tended to be actors that are not exactly popular with the US – Russia, Iran, and the organisation Hezbollah included. Russia has long supported the Assad regime. This is a relationship that has undermined the possibility of conflict resolution within the framework of the United Nations (UN) due to Russia's Security Council veto, and, by association, that of China. Russian President Vladimir Putin has authorised the use of the veto to prevent even the international condemnation of the Syrian government, let alone any active measure against it. As well as a political relationship, this is also a heavily military one. Russia is one of the biggest suppliers of weaponry to Syria, and many of the armaments used by the government during the crisis have been identified as coming from Russian sources. Iran also maintains extremely strong links with the regime, ever since Syria's support for Tehran during the Iran–Iraq War and not least due to the extent that both states oppose Israel and the American endorsement it enjoys. The continued dispute over the Golan Heights and Iran's massive provision of arms to Syria has ensured the relationship, specifically in terms of Iran's significant interest in the continuation of the Assad regime. Syria has also constituted a key link in Iran's smuggling of arms to Hezbollah – an agreement that has seen Hezbollah become involved in the crisis in a bid to safeguard the regime. As such, it was clear from the moment the Syrian protests turned violent that a civil conflict would have implications far beyond the state itself. Syria has never just been about Syria, but what the destabilisation of the Assad regime would mean for other interested parties and their international position. It was also a situation that would intensify East–West relations, where this occurred against a backdrop of US interests in these 'proxy' countries. Within this wider context, Dmtri Trenin (2012), Director of the Carnegie Endowment Moscow Center, describes the case as one of global order:

> Syria is not primarily about Middle Eastern geopolitics, Cold War-era alliances, arms sales – or even special interests … Syria – much like yesterday's Libya, Iraq or Yugoslavia – is primarily about the world order. It's about *who decides*; who decides whether to use military force; who decides the actors for use of that force; and who decides under what rules, conditions, and oversight military force is to be used.

Assad's reign of violence escalated throughout the country as tensions grew throughout 2011. Mary Kaldor (2013: 151) has gone so far as to designate this a form of 'scorched earth' policy in order to encapsulate not just the mass killing of civilians, but also the physical destruction of rebel-held towns, housing, and infrastructure. In a similar vein, the UN Human Rights Council (UNHRC, 2015: 4) reported that 'Victims have often described the Government's strategy as that of "tansheef al bakhar", or draining the sea to kill the fish.' Admittedly, Assad would offer minimal reforms during the early stages of the crisis in an attempt to placate the strengthening opposition – such as revoking the controversial 1963 Emergency Law (which had vastly curtailed personal freedoms and permitted detention without trial), extending Syrian citizenship to the Kurdish minority, and also replacing the now highly controversial Daraa governor. Yet this was a classic case of too little, too late. And, as John McHugo (2014: 224) says, the way in which these deals were aimed at specific groups as opposed to widespread change indicates that they were merely 'signs of a government trying to buy popularity rather than reforms'. The sincerity of this is also questioned by Assad's continuation of his strategy to contain protests by violent means, despite condemnation of it. Some regime force members were so appalled that they opposed the plan and refused to comply – and were then shot themselves for failing to carry out orders. In November, Syria was suspended from the Arab League because of the aggressive nature of the regime's response. Assad's labelling of protesters as 'terrorists' did not help the situation; nor did the considerable increase in international sanctions now being placed on the state. In addition, vast numbers of refugees had started to flee violent hotspots and, if they could, the country. This caused mass destabilisation and humanitarian issues. In short, Syria was spiralling into civil trauma.

In July 2011, deserting regime officers formed the Free Syrian Army as an official opposition to the Assad regime (many had made the decision to desert explicitly because of Assad's contentious orders to open fire on protesters). A few months later, the opposition Syrian National Council (SNC) was established in Istanbul as an attempt to draw together those who opposed Assad into a coherent body. The success of this was limited, and the wider National Coalition for Syrian and Opposition Forces – commonly known as the Syrian National Coalition – would later supersede the SNC in 2012, although this too had mixed results due to internal divisions. Yet, while the opposition would continue, and remains today, as a highly fractured and internally discordant concept – to the extent that it is still impossible to realistically speak of one united opposition – this was the sign that the battle lines were now being drawn. The official mobilisation of an opposition was a key step in the escalation of the crisis. It was at this time that the International Committee of the Red Cross officially confirmed that Syria was engaged in a civil conflict. Syria was now at war, one that would bring with it many more brutal and horrific acts of violent aggression. For example, in August 2012 the Independent International Commission of Inquiry on the Syrian Arab Republic, a body established by the UNHRC, reported that:

> The commission found reasonable grounds to believe that Government forces ... had committed the crimes against humanity of murder and of torture, war crimes and gross violations of international human rights law and international humanitarian law, including unlawful killing, torture, arbitrary arrest and detention, sexual violence, indiscriminate attacks, pillaging and destruction of property. (In Blake and Mahmud, 2013: 247–8)

11

At the time of writing, the UN (2015a) had placed its most recent estimate of the crisis's fatality rate at 220,000 killed and one million wounded, with no sign of the casualties abating. As UN Secretary-General, Ban Ki-Moon (in UN, 2013a), had said two years earlier of Syria: 'After nearly two years, we no longer count days in hours, but in bodies.' In addition, the UN estimated that approximately 11 million people had been displaced, internally and externally. These statistics, however, were insufficient to involve the US in the conflict – at least not in terms of intervention. Nor was the fact that Syria had been recognised as having reached the expectations of 'manifestly failing to protect their populations' at the heart of the Responsibility to Protect (R2P) strategy (Farer, 2013: 131; Gallagher, 2014). Assad had clearly violated the terms of this international expectation, under which interventionist activity could theoretically be justified. Yet despite the sheer horror characterising the conflict, it was not until Assad had used *chemical weapons* that the US would begin to start talking seriously about its involvement. Specifically, on 21 August 2013 Assad launched a major chemical attack on Ghouta, a Damascus suburb, which killed approximately 1,400 people.

The history of Syria's acquisition and possession of chemical arms is shrouded in secrecy. Yet the decision to obtain these weapons is generally accepted as a response to Israel and an attempt to counter this enemy's conventional and/or nuclear superiority (Diab, 1997: 104; USDOD, 1997; Friedman, 2012: 402). Syria first acquired the weapons when Egypt supplied a relatively small number of chemical arms prior to the 1973 Yom Kippur War (Tucker, 2006: 227). From here, Syria began to extend its capability and develop its own programme throughout the 1970s and 1980s, not least in reaction to several military defeats by Israel and later the collapse of its patron, the Soviet Union (Nitkitin *et al.*, 2013: 4). At this stage, it was not viewed as an intrinsically offensive programme, but as the construction of a credible deterrence against Israel. In a situation where a Syrian nuclear deterrent was unfeasible, chemical weapons constituted the 'next best' option. Yet this was more a show of military strength than a weapon of actual use. Indeed, just a few years before the programme started, Syria had signed the 1925 Geneva Protocol for the Prohibition of the Use in War of Asphyxiating Poisonous or of Other Gases, and of Bacteriological Methods of Warfare. Consequently, during the programme's development, Syria had officially renounced first use of chemical warfare. Syria would not, however, join the Chemical Weapons Convention (CWC) when it opened for signature in 1993, a move that would have committed the state to the elimination of its chemical stockpiles. Yet Assad would later accede to the agreement in September 2013 as part of international negotiations surrounding the civil crisis.

In terms of what Assad was giving up under the terms of his new CWC membership, there is no solid evidence that Syria had become independent as a chemical weapons state; that is, it was not capable of running a self-sufficient programme (USDNI, 2011: 7). Technological capacity was still extremely limited, particularly relating to the construction of precursors – chemical compounds that assist in the reaction process to produce further compounds suitable for weaponisation. Yet this should not detract from Syria's success in building up considerable stockpiles, largely thanks to its extensive international network of suppliers. Support has come from a variety of sources – especially Russia and Iran, but also countries such as Egypt and North Korea (Shobam, 2005: 99). Syria has also benefited from a number of Chinese and Western private companies who were prepared to supply the country with chemical arms-related equipment, including the precursors that have proved so problematic (Lele, 2011: 753; *Strategic Comments*, 2012: 1). (These transactions had been alleged for some time, but were confirmed and made public during the famous Wikileaks publications.) Indeed, prior to accession to the CWC, Syria was named the fourth largest chemical weapons state globally and the biggest in the Middle East (*Strategic Comments*, 2012: 1). These stockpiles contain(ed) agents such as mustard gas, sarin, VX nerve agent, and unweaponised ricin. They also contain chlorine, which Assad has used in chemical attacks carried out even now, long past the CWC arms destruction deadline.

It is within this context that chemical weapons use was constructed as a starting pistol for US foreign policy in respect of Syria. It was made clear that any employment by Assad would constitute an intolerable and illegitimate act, one that would necessarily bring about a shift in the US position towards the crisis. But why chemical weapons? In a conflict characterised by appalling examples of conventional violence, why should chemical arms constitute the deciding factor? Why was this specific form of aggression insufferable when other acts of brutality – manifest in the extensive and repeated massacre of rebels and civilians – had proved insufficient to drive an interventionist foreign policy? True, there were important reasons associated with this, such as the threat of Syria's chemical weapons falling into enemy hands, not least Iran and Hezbollah. Even prior to the civil war, this had been cited as a key concern by US foreign policy-makers. There was also political anxiety regarding possible transference to, or forced acquisition by, terrorist organisations (US Cong., 2012a: 33). These risks, combined with the potential destabilisation of Syria and the subsequent loss of government control over chemical stockpiles that this may instigate, pushed chemical weapons up the foreign policy agenda. And yet, this is still insufficient to explain why it was a more important reason for involvement than mass-scale conventional deaths at the hands of the Assad regime. The reason lies within the chemical weapons taboo: the idea that chemical armaments are inherently stigmatised. The taboo is held up as a powerful normative pressure within IR – especially as an explanation for Syria where, while conventional violence has been largely ignored in preference to other political concerns (including Obama's desire to avoid becoming embroiled within a complex and contentious civil conflict), chemical weapons use could not be overlooked. It was a step too far.

The taboo

Taboos are what you are not supposed to do. They exist as socially constructed expectations that actors should not engage in, permit, and in some cases even acknowledge certain behaviours that have been deemed prohibitively unacceptable. To quote Hutton Webster (1942: 13, 17), taboos are 'prohibitions observed as customs'; 'an imperative thou-shalt-not in the presence of the danger apprehended'. They are the intrinsic 'don'ts' of society, where these are typically attached to the hypothetical or actual violation of some moral, ethical, and/or social measure – a measure that is obliged to be respected and upheld. Consequently, the socially integrated nature and 'taken-for-grantedness' of this conceptualisation have seen taboos classified as a type of norm (Tannenwald, 2007: 11; see also Price, 1998: 115; Quester, 2005: 74). To add in yet another definition: 'Norms are regarded as standards of behaviour, defined in terms of rights and obligations. In this sense norms are general prescriptions of behaviour that regulate intentions and effects' (Bjorkdahl, 2002: 13). Specifically, such behaviour can be comprehended within the terms of Peter Katzenstein's (1996: 5) conception of 'the proper behaviour of actors within a given identity'; a standard reference in the understanding of norms. Yet in the case of the taboo, action is governed not simply by normative expectation, but explicitly by expectations that identify specific behaviours as intolerable, whereby these constitute 'a particularly forceful kind of normative prohibition' based on 'prescriptions or proscriptions for behaviour' (Tannenwald, 2007: 10). Indeed, proscription is elemental to the concept of the taboo itself. Any violation is intrinsically connected to its own preclusion and/or sanction. Gary Goertz and Paul Diehl (2012) even insist that the punishment of violation is inseparable from the construction and exercise of taboos; that is, expectations of non-transgression cannot exist irrespective of their coercive enforcement. Taboos are defined and acknowledged according to the very character and requirement of their own chastisement.

In terms of expression, taboos are evident in all areas of life. The concept has been extensively applied, incorporating a diverse range of 'controversial' conducts related to, among others: sexual desire, for example incest (Turner and Maryanski, 2009); non-heterosexual relationships (Greenberg, 1990); abortion (Lumar *et al.*, 2009); bodily functions (McKinnon Doan and Morse, 2009); religious exclusions (Soderback, 2004); offensive language (Kaye and Sapolsky, 2009); and even the ability to express issues as taboo (Brenner, 2010). Somewhat confusingly, this covers a plethora of issues (although anybody who has heard of *Fifty Shades of Grey* should already possess a fairly workable understanding of what could be included under this conceptual umbrella of behavioural exclusion; James, 2012). More specifically, however, the concept has been employed within the field of IR to comprehend trends in political inter-action: for example, the killing of civilians (Sluka, 2008); creation of security regimes (Stein, 2010); use of torture (Frankenberg, 2008); and prohibitions on the possession and/or use of certain forms of weaponry. The latter includes the focus of this book – the taboo against chemical arms.

Stigmatising chemical weapons

> If in some smothering dreams, you too could pace
> Behind the wagon that we flung him in,
> And watch the white eyes writhing in this face,
> His hanging face, like a devil's sack of sin;
> If you could hear, at every jolt, the blood
> Come gargling from the froth-corrupted lungs,
> Obscene as cancer, bitter as the cud
> Of vile, incurable sores on innocent tongues,
> My friend, you would not tell with such high zest
> To children ardent for some desperate glory,
> The old lie: Dulce et decorum est
> Pro patria mori.
>
> (Owen, 1920)

Frequently (although not unequivocally) classified as weapons of mass destruc-tion (WMD), chemical arms are considered inherently horrific devices. Indeed, they are judged to be so extensive in terms of destructive effect that they have been colloquially termed the 'poor man's atomic bomb', essentially a comparable substitute for a nuclear weapon should you not have sufficient cash for the real thing. Perceptions of, and international response to, chemical weapons devel-oped primarily around their unprecedented application during the First World War, specifically the use of mustard gas, chlorine, and phosgene in the trenches. Wilfred Owen's posthumously published poem quoted above – now a staple of secondary school English Literature curricula – expresses the sheer disgust, fear, and revulsion associated with this terrifying mode of violence. Whatever other horrors the First World War battlefields would produce in terms of bloodshed and gore, chemical weapons still stood out as especially terrifying – a symbol of the very worst of the conflict, and even of conflict itself. For while the extreme nature of chemical violence had been recognised long before, it was here – at Ypres, at Verdun, at Passchendaele – that these weapons were truly branded as beyond toleration. Since then, chemical weapons have acquired a depressing history of use, most notably the 1988 chemical assault on the Kurdish town of Halabja during the Iran–Iraq conflict. Here, Iraqi dictator Saddam Hussein ordered a lethal cocktail of cyanide and other chemical agents to be used against the Kurdish minority, allegedly killing 5,000 people. Numerous photos capture the terrible scenes of bloated corpses lying in the street, many taken by photographer Sayeed Janbozorgi, who himself died in 2003 from long-term health problems caused by the attack. He is not alone. The incident has left a long legacy among the survivors of often-fatal conditions including cancer, breathing difficulties, blindness, and birth defects of survivors' children. Residents of Halabja are still calling for justice to this day.

This reputation is not limited to instances of state use. For example, equally shocking was the 1995 chemical assault by the apocalyptic Japanese cult Aum Shinrikyo on the Tokyo subway. Cult members released home-made sarin on commuter trains, using the sharpened tips of umbrellas to puncture plastic bags full of the chemical agent in order to disperse it. The motivation had been to instigate a third world war. The cult believed they were about to face a righteous 'day of judgement' style battle and thought it would be to their advantage to initiate the conflict themselves instead of allowing their enemies to select the time and place, or to destroy the cult before the fight could even occur. In total 12 people were killed in the attack, with a further estimated 4,000 seeking medical attention for suspected exposure (although how many of these were actually cases of the 'worried well' and not genuine casualties is difficult to ascertain). While this case may not have involved the extensive fatalities of the First World War or Halabja, the attack is still considered of critical importance where it ostensibly represents the risk that terrorists will employ these devices, potentially in a mass-scale attack. The debate as to whether or not terrorists would actually desire to use chemical arms to such an extent, or indeed that they are even capable of constructing or acquiring the complex weaponry necessary to do so, has been raging for decades – with no sign of consensus in either academic or practitioner circles. But this uncertainty aside, the Tokyo strike inspired a wave of concern surrounding the idea that chemical weapons could be used in a major terrorist attack – one that would kill significantly more than 12. This would be a strike that could cause substantially more damage, physically and psychologically, than a conventional assault in that chemical weapons are deemed to produce distinctly repulsive effects. Neil Cooper (2011) has captured this sentiment by referring to them as 'pariah weapons'. As such, it is hardly surprising that chemical weapons have earned themselves a notorious reputation within security discourses. In breaking down this perception, several aspects concerning the character of chemical weapons can be identified as underpinning this repulsion. Specifically, these weapons are considered especially horrific where they are massively destructive, technologically distinct, disproportionately barbaric, invisible in terms of effect (thereby creating a special sense of dread), indiscriminate in terms of effect, and fundamentally immoral (Bentley, 2014b: 7–28). In all these ways, chemical weapons have been set apart from other forms of armament, particularly conventional devices. This is a critical point: the stigmatisation is based on the idea that chemical weapons are differentiated from conventional arms in all of the above ways, and explicitly that they are seen as being worse and more horrific. These characteristics ostensibly constitute the ways in which chemical weapons are more terrible than conventional modes of violence. It is this that makes them stand out as a special concern.

Within this context, the chemical weapons taboo builds on the socially constructed revulsion surrounding these devices to label them unacceptable, specifically where avoidance and prohibition are deemed requisite in response to this. These arms are too destructive, too evil, and too revolting to permit justification. Chemical weapons are intrinsically inexcusable, where this refusal towards toleration is manifest within a wider and entrenched commitment to their elimination and proscription. Crucially, this is not simply the idea that chemical weapons are bad. This is the substantially more extensive claim that the taboo is so deeply engrained in international and domestic political thinking that it is treated a form of moral law. Actors who employ chemical weapons have not merely done something wrong; they have violated a moral principle that threatens the very security of the international community. And because of the extent of that community's commitment to the taboo, violation is not only an act against the victim, but also an act against the world. Consequently, extreme retaliation is considered permissible in the face of such a major threat.

The taboo is not uncontroversial, not least where the characteristics that supposedly identify these weapons as off-limits have been questioned. Specifically, these characteristics have been disputed as an insufficient and unsustainable basis to justify a discriminatory understanding, especially one that effectively sets chemical concerns as a priority over alternative modes of violence such as explosives or other small arms (Bentley, 2014b: 7–28). For example, the destructive capacity of chemical weapons has been widely contested, explicitly where their effects would occur on a mass scale (Panofsky, 1998; Easterbrook, 2002; Archer, 2004; Macfarlane, 2004). While these weapons exhibit the potential for extreme destruction, the actual realisation of it is far from obvious. Whatever the illusion of shady actors easily constructing killer chemical arms in their garden shed, it is extremely challenging to create a weapon capable of causing fatalities on a truly extensive scale. Even then, such an assault would likely require huge amounts of munitions to carry out successfully, which in itself may prove prohibitive if the relevant actor has no or limited access to the necessary stockpiles. Similarly, the focus on the supposedly indiscriminate nature of these devices has been criticised (Martin, 2004: 33). This is divided into two claims. First, chemical weapons may be so limited in terms of effect that their employment is capable of being used discriminately; that is, a chemical strike can be confined to a specific target. Second, other weapons are also used indiscriminately, specifically conventional devices. On the surface, this claim may seem unproblematic – does it matter if conventional modes of violence also kill in indiscriminate ways? Yet this emerges as a major issue when this supposed distinction is applied as an inequitable separation of chemical weapons from other arms. Where indiscriminate death is employed as a measure for differentiating chemical devices, the association of this characteristic with the 'other' causes that conceptual justification to fall apart. If conventional arms are also indiscriminate, then chemical weapons are not special. If exclusivity is not guaranteed, then the taboo's conceptual basis cannot hold.

Furthermore, the taboo must be balanced against claims that aversion to chemical weapons is actually the product of a more realist conceptualisation of self-interest. These arms are avoided only to the degree that this is beneficial to the user (Smith, 2006: 527–8). This is not a case of prohibitive repulsion, but a self-interested response to a given situation. An actor does not shun chemical devices on the basis that they are opposed to them, or in order to uphold some moral expectation; they do not use such devices when there is no reason for them to do so. In supporting this, some analysts have pointed to a supposed lack of military utility surrounding chemical violence. Despite chemical weapons' dangerous reputation, it does not include reliability (already alluded to above, in that their destructive effect is questioned). As such, they have been dismissed as ineffective. Consequently, security actors possess an incentive to avoid them. Moreover, a basic realist argument of deterrence can be applied; that is, the fear of retaliation in kind. Not least where chemical arms have been compared to nuclear weapons, it would then seem logical that some form of mutually assured destruction would apply. Not one as absolute as that attributed to nuclear weapons perhaps, but the sense that actors would refrain from these devices where they fear retaliation. (The conflict between this view and that of the argument surrounding limited military utility is not lost here; i.e. if they are militarily useless, why would retaliation cause concern?) In addition, the taboo must also answer to its own appeal to the need for punishment, where this could suggest that behaviour is based on realist logic as opposed to normative detestation. Do actors refrain from chemical violence in that they truly believe these devices are horrific beyond the point of toleration, or simply because they fear reprisal? As Sheri Berman (2001: 242) says: 'Ideas may be at work in both cases, but for theoretical and practical reasons it is crucial to distinguish between them. In the former, norms have been internalized; in the latter, actors engage in strategic calculation.' In this way, it has been argued that the concept of taboo is an over-complication of what is in fact adherence to realist principles. Not least within a theoretical framework that deems morals and good intentions to be a decadent luxury, why should analysis look beyond realist self-interest as an explanation for chemical arms avoidance?

It is here that Richard Price's (1995) seminal discussion on the chemical weapons taboo can be brought into play. Price's work – an impressive and detailed historical account of the taboo's development and character – is a rebuttal to this reduction of chemical weapons non-use to realist thinking. He asserts outright that a realist approach is insufficient in the absence of, or at least that this can constitute only an additional explanatory factor to, a prohibitory norm. Indeed, Price (ibid.: 75) demonstrates that no study on non-use has managed to uphold realist arguments absolutely – there remains a gap in the argument that, he maintains, can only be filled with a normative conceptualisation of the taboo. Nor has any study put forward an explanation that could not also apply in conjunction with the taboo. While factors such as deterrence are not necessarily irrelevant in comprehending a specific act of avoidance, this by itself is inadequate. This is particularly the case at the systemic level of conceptual understanding where it is *stigmatisation* that offers a more compelling explanation. In identifying the source of this stigmatisation, Price refers to many characteristics already identified above: for example, destructive effect and indiscriminate impact. Yet in a similar way to how he rejects realist explanations as the (primary) justification of aversion, Price (ibid.: 79–80) says these are also tenuous. Certainly chemical weapons are horrific devices that can exhibit these terrible characteristics. But such features only contribute to, and are not wholly constitutive of, the taboo. Specifically, because they are not exclusive to chemical aggression, they cannot form the absolute basis of the taboo. As such, while these constitute key issues in the construction and employment of the taboo, and are fundamental to the taboo's very existence, analysis cannot look only to these for a complete justification of the taboo itself.

Significantly, this is true even of characteristics that Price himself adds into the discussion – specifically, the association of chemical weapons with poison. Poison has long been stigmatised as 'an illegitimate and cruel method of warfare' (1995: 80). Indeed, the desire to control poison on the basis of its illicit nature is ancient and, according to Catherine Jefferson (2014: 647), dates back to the Hindu Laws of Manu, *c*.500 bce. Whereas other, more traditional forms of attack are seen as both noble and open – brave men advancing across the battlefield to death or glory, willing to fight resplendently for their beliefs – poison is used by the weak and devious. It is a deceitful and shameful mode of violence, which deserves prohibition as such. In particular, this association of illegitimacy has flourished through its connection to women: poison is a female weapon (Price, 1995: 81). In a depiction more suited to *La Belle Dame sans Merci*, the use of poison has been reduced to an underhanded equalisation of power in a situation where women have none, or at least none that can be deemed legitimate or morally permissible. And of course, the basic association with the feminine has hardly improved its reputation, for depressingly obvious reasons related to gender. But yet again, while Price acknowledges that this is an important and influential factor, even this alone is not enough to constitute a sole explanation for the taboo. In demonstrating this, Price refers to the historical origins of the taboo, located in the 1899 and 1907 Hague Conferences (although Jefferson,

2014: 648, claims that the first international agreement codifying a prohibition on poison weapons was in Article 57 of the Strasbourg Agreement of 1675 by French and German forces). These prohibited the use of asphyxiating shells. This is presented as a situation in which the concept of poison influenced opinion, but did not in itself cause the Hague agreements to come about, specifically in the form they would eventually take (Price, 1995: 83). Indeed, conference delegates actively rejected equating poison and the chemical shells that were the core concern, focusing instead on the threat to civilian life and creating a narrative expounding the expectation that these were unacceptable types of weaponry on that specific basis. It was this discussion of chemical weapons as an indiscriminate category of immoral devices that, Price (ibid.: 90) says, formed the conceptual foundation of the taboo at this point. As such, while the concept of poison is deemed a critical aspect of the taboo, again this is not absolute or necessary for conceptual understanding. Consequently, this adds further weight to claims that the taboo cannot be comprehended within essentialist categories.

Employing a combination of Friedrich Nietzsche's genealogical method and the theories of Michel Foucault, Price seeks to present a corrective to that static approach. Specifically, he prioritises a conception of norms as the product of historical development and ongoing social practice: 'As a result of the marriage of chance occurrences, fortuitous connections, and reinterpretations, the purposes and forms of moral structures often change in such a way that they come to embody values different from those that animated their origins' (1995: 86). History is not merely connected to the strength of the taboo in that the sheer passage of time has reinforced the very notion of proscription. This is clearly an important aspect. The Hague Conventions were vital in establishing the proscription, but it was the anti-chemical weapons provisions that came after that would normalise and solidify the taboo – the 1925 Geneva Protocol and CWC among them. Moreover, Price (1998: 114) comments that, 'Because massive chemical attacks never became a regular part of war that soldiers and civilians had to "get used to," they were never regarded as another despicable "inevitability" of warfare.' Yet this is also a case in which ideas surrounding the supposed characteristics of the taboo have had the opportunity to become engrained, even where they are not – especially where they are not – essentialist. While alone these are insufficient to uphold the taboo, their repetition in association with it has underpinned the taboo's longevity. As such, these are ideas that can be drawn upon at any given moment, where that moment exists as part of a varied conceptual history – but a valid history in spite of that variation. Instead of static conceptions, these ideas play into a fluid and contextualised understanding of the taboo, which, while drawing on them as core elements of its construction, is not exclusively defined by them.

The flexibility inherent to this understanding leads Price to conclude that the taboo is not a complete and inevitable restraint on actors, but the creation of the permissive conditions for a certain type of actor behaviour. The taboo is an important constraint, but it is not perfect as such. For example, while Price (1995: 76–7) highlights the non-use of chemical weapons during the Second World War as a critical example of the taboo at work, he accepts that different circumstances could have pushed those participating in the conflict into using chemical arms: 'Rather, the stigma against CW [chemical weapons] raised the threshold of circumstances under which one could justify a resort to CW to situations of desperation.' Beyond this threshold, there is no guarantee that the taboo would hold. Despite this, however, it remains a case in which alternative restraints would have been insufficient to prevent use in the absence of the taboo; the taboo was still a 'necessary condition' of non-use (ibid.: 75, 78). Jason Enia and Jeffrey Fields (2014: 52) concur with this more generally: 'One could still debate whether the normative aspect *entirely* explains the CW taboo, but it is recognized that these considerations were extremely influential in the normative foundations around nonproliferation and non-use.' The taboo is a behavioural guide: a one-way street perhaps, but not an inevitable choice.

Taboo strength

This flexibility is in no way seen to undermine the strength of the taboo. Price clearly views the chemical weapons taboo as an especially strong and influential norm. It has been broadly acknowledged that taboos can vary widely in terms of strength, i.e. the extent to which that expectation is accepted and internalised within actor behaviour: 'Some of these norms are very robust, while others are relatively weak and routinely violated' (Price, 1998: 105). Political life is full of taboos, but these are not all respected and enforced to the same degree. Nor indeed should they be, as Lawrence Freedman (2013: 97) highlights in his discussion of the civil rights movement as a challenge to racist taboos. As society has changed, so have the moral rubrics by which that society is run. History is replete with examples of taboos that have come, and also gone. The behavioural environment, although fundamentally constrained by normative expectation, also exists as a place in which that expectation can alter. Within these caveats of use, however, Price still upholds the chemical weapons taboo as exceptionally robust. In this case then, his identified flexibility is best viewed as a feature of conceptual use as opposed to a sign of normative weakness. Taboos are inherently vague to some extent in terms of adoption, but this does not necessarily indicate they are not substantially engrained in political thinking and behaviour.

This engrained status is so extensive in the case of the chemical weapons taboo that Price argues that even violation should not be seen to signal normative frailty either. He does not view contravention as necessarily eroding or invalidating a norm, specifically as under two conditions of use: '1) if an act is understood and accepted as an extreme and even justifiable departure from a norm; or 2) if it is treated as a violation with a disciplinary response' (1998: 116). Indeed, in relation to the second set of circumstances, Price (ibid.: 117) draws on Foucault to claim that 'violations provide the most opportune moments to define and discipline a particular practice as an aberration'. Within this context, Syria can ostensibly be seen as a case in which violation actually strengthened the norm – not least where, according to Price's logic, the incremental nature of Assad's use signposts a level of caution concerning an international backlash. That is, when an actor 'builds up' to a considerable act of violation via smaller incidents (of chemical weapons use), this demonstrates that they are aware of the taboo and are testing the waters. This is in fact an indicator of normative strength and adherence. There are, however, serious issues with this conceptualisation of violation. Effectively dismissing violation in this way is problematic in that it does not fully explain why the violator in question: (a) believed they could get away with any level of infringement; (b) was not subject to sufficient punishment at earlier stages, so that they felt safe enough to escalate their activities – which would imply that the punisher was not bound by the taboo to act accordingly; and (c) did not adhere to the taboo in the first place. While the taboo would be employed with respect to Syria, it cannot be overlooked that this was, ultimately, a response to a serious violation. The taboo was broken, indicating its irrelevance in Assad's thinking. Nor can we ignore the extent to which that response has been weak in respect of upholding the taboo, such that Assad continues to employ chemical weapons to this day.

And yet, the chemical weapons taboo has never been more prominent in international discourse than it is now, particularly in relation to US foreign policy. People who had never heard of the taboo pre-2012 are now well acquainted with its principles. Explicitly, they understand it not simply as the idea that chemical weapons are horrific, but that this view is manifest within an established political, institutionalised, and consensus-based commitment to the elimination of such arms. This is not just an ideal; it is a rule. This is not merely something you feel, but something you do; and that you should do at all costs. It is within this context that the chemical weapons taboo is upheld as especially important. It is no exaggeration to say this is one of the strongest taboos in IR. Indeed, there is a somewhat divine element to this: securing chemical weapons is presented as little short of an Eleventh Commandment. To pile on the clichés, it is the jewel in the crown of the arms control system. In particular, this is expressed in terms of the response to violation. Transgression is portrayed as unacceptable and the punishment for transgression is obligatory on the part of the international community, ideally to the point of deterrence. Few taboos carry, and are defined by, the weight of their prohibition and infringement to the extent seen in respect of chemical weapons. In this way, the chemical weapons taboo has more than succeeded in establishing itself as a fundamental part of international political behaviour.

Strategic use

It is with this theoretical framework as background that this book discusses its first major point: that taboos are inherently strategic in terms of their construction and application. Specifically, this constitutes a key point of departure from the work of Price in relation to his identified normative flexibility. What Price sees as conceptual fluidity is instead attributed here to strategic manipulation and the exercise of actor agency. This represents an opportunity for actors to exploit the principles of the taboo for the realisation of their own self-interest, even where that interest does not ultimately seek to uphold the taboo. While this is not necessarily incompatible with Price's model – and indeed Price's work provides support in that it creates the 'conceptual space' required for this claim to be upheld (i.e. the acceptance that the taboo is not absolute) – it constitutes a substantially greater assertion of agency surrounding the taboo than previously assumed. The taboo is not merely a restraint, but a premeditated resource for narrative development and manipulation. It is not just a guide, but an expectation that can be exploited in order to encourage or coerce an audience into a certain direction and logic of understanding, depending on how it is manipulated within political discourse and particularly within international narratives. The forbidden is open to exploitation.

Strategic narratives

On the surface, the claim that political actors are strategic in their use of rhetoric seems uncontroversial. However cynical this view, few would dispute that agents at least attempt to employ language in ways explicitly designed to draw support from a specific audience, or shape debate so as to best serve their interests. It would appear self-evident that politicians do such things as make emotive appeals, use oratorical tricks, and highlight certain words in order to realise their political aims. Yet, and possibly because of this assumption of self-evidence, this is a woefully under-theorised area of study. This wider failure to explore the nature of persuasive linguistics within IR, and a desire to provide new perspectives, has underpinned an increasing interest in the field of strategic narratives (De Graaf *et al.*, 2015), particularly the work of Lawrence Freedman (2006) and Alister Miskimmon *et al.* (2013) (for examples of their work being employed more widely, see O'Hagan, 2013; Natarajan, 2014; Pamment, 2014; Svendsen, 2014). In explaining the nature of strategic narratives, Miskimmon *et al.* (2013: 2) state:

> Strategic narratives are a means for political actors to construct a shared meaning of the past, present, and future of international politics to shape the behaviour of domestic and international actors. Strategic narratives provide a tool for political actors to extend their influence, manage expectations, and change the discursive environment in which they operate ... The point of strategic narratives is to influence the behaviour of others.

This theoretical structure seeks to comprehend and express how actors construct and select narratives for the realisation of political aims. The definition of 'narrative' is comprehended here as the communicative and political frameworks of understanding. They are the words, speech, and actions that allow actors to present politics in specific ways. Explicitly, they are the 'compelling storylines' by which actors strategically utilise rhetoric to craft and enact perceptions of a political situation or issue, in order to shape opinion in line with their own ambitions (Freedman, 2006: 22; see also Hajer, 1997: 56; O'Tuathail, 2002: 617; Dimitriu, 2011: 195). Actors use narratives to create a description of the world – an understanding of what politics looks like and entails – whereby they 'force' their audience to adopt certain interpretations and pathways of logic that complement the aims of the constructing actor(s). More than mere spin or framing, this is the control of political comprehension, where actors use language in order to influence how politics is carried out, and where such narratives hold together the necessary networks of communication and information required to make this popular (Arquilla and Rondfelt, 2001: 328). Unsurprisingly then, parallels have frequently been drawn with Joseph Nye's (1990) soft power (Miskimmon *et al.*, 2013: 3, 2014), as well as the concept of speech acts (Norheim-Martinsen, 2011: 521), where these also appeal to the idea that language can be taken advantage of in order to achieve something. Critically, this is understood as an intrinsically *deliberate* behaviour. Actors intentionally construct and apply narratives. The narrative is a conscious product, which is operationalised to secure a specified political purpose or benefit. While this is not to state that every act of linguistic employment is deliberate (actors do not premeditatedly consider every single word or concept they employ), the opportunity exists for the planned and persuasive expression of language, specifically via narrative structures.

In applying this paradigmatic construct, two issues must be addressed. First, that many adherents to this approach possess an extremely wide concept of what a strategic narrative relates to. Indeed, for Miskimmon *et al.*, this is very much a reference to the international narratives actors create pertaining to their state and the global political positioning of that state – to the extent that they view strategic narratives as a theory of IR in itself. Yet within this theoretical structure they also allow for more limited conceptualisations of narrative construction; specifically, what they term 'issue narratives'. This can be interpreted as the idea that narratives do not have to exist on a global scale, but that the same dynamics of political activity can be applied at other, less extensive levels of political interaction, including individual states' foreign policy. As a point of clarification, therefore, this is the specific type of narrative construct analysed here. Indeed, this study provides a useful example of how these wider constructs of understanding on strategic narratives can be applied at different levels of analysis.

Actor agency and intention

Specifically, this study demonstrates that language at this level of comprehension constitutes a fundamentally elastic construct capable of being knowingly engineered, and that evidence of this is used here to directly dispute largely static notions of language, particularly in relation to the expression of international taboos. Far from being bound by pre-existing notions of linguistic meaning, actors can modify and manoeuvre conceptual structures where necessary for compelling narrative development. Actors possess considerable power over the language they employ, and this can be exploited in order to realise their own self-interest. Significantly, this is not simply the weak claim that taboos can be used emotively – i.e. that the conceptualisation of an act as taboo, and the infringement of that taboo as an unforgiveable and immoral wrongdoing, creates an emotive response to the idea of its violation – rather it is that the ideational structure of the taboo provides the rhetorical tools for an actor to control debate and political activity. The way an actor exploits the forbidden is a highly calculated form of manipulation.

Here the analysis runs into the second issue, concerning actor agency and actor intention. There is a clash here between the idea of the taboo as a restraint and the claim that an actor possesses considerable agency over the language of their restraint. Logically, an actor cannot be entirely constrained by an expectation and simultaneously govern the meaning of it. And while Price opens up the idea of conceptual fluidity, which permits a considerable degree of flexibility concerning the absolute nature of that commitment, this cannot explain the tension between restraint and strategic manipulation in that it fails to address the nature of agency. In accepting the flexibility, Price does not fully clarify how actors deal with it or what they do with it – although his heavily Foucauldian analysis hints at a strong social constructivist interpretation. This is reflected within the strategic narratives paradigm and associated fields of discourse analysis, where analysts still emphasise the idea that language is a socially constructed restraint on actors, specifically where the claim that actors could extensively manipulate the concepts and language they employ is considered unfeasible (e.g. Doty, 1996; Milliken, 1999; Hansen, 2006; Epstein, 2008, 2013). Language is a pre-existing pressure on actors; it governs actor behaviour, not least where failing to adhere to established expectations of language would result in unintelligibility (Krebs and Jackson, 2007: 41). It is not created at whim. Even where it can still be used strategically in terms of creating persuasive speech, including narrative construction, the language available to actors restrains them in this. They cannot transcend the meaning of language in their strategic endeavours. Within this context, a taboo effectively constitutes this type of restraint in its strongest form, where it governs not only linguistic expression but also behaviour. As such, while the model of conceptual framing derived from Price provides sufficient theoretical space to engage with the issue of the chemical weapons taboo as a rhetorical resource, there still exists something of a gap between the issues of constraint and strategic use, explicitly where this relates to any control actors exert in respect of the taboo. If actors are strategic, how strategic can they be?

To resolve this, actor agency and intention must be reconsidered. Specifically, it must be reconsidered via the work of political theorist Quentin Skinner, who argues that actors possess considerable authority in respect of language. Skinner (1969) constructs ideational understanding around the intention of the actor: meaning is what an actor desired it to signify, to the extent that they can redefine words and concepts. Defining intention itself is not unproblematic, although Skinner (1972: 400–1) draws a clear line between 'intention in' (to do something) and 'intention by' (intent in doing something), where he focuses on the latter. Intention is what the author sought to convey in using a certain language, and any statement 'is inescapably the embodiment of a particular intention, on a particular occasion, addressed to the solution of a particular problem, and thus specific to its situation in a way that it can only be naïve to try to transcend' (Skinner, 1969: 50). Derived from J. L. Austin (1975) and the conception of speech acts, this is also the claim that an utterance, or the manifestation of an utterance within a text, is intrinsically 'performative' (Skinner, 1971). For example, if an actor says 'the ice over there is very thin', this may be expressed as a warning as opposed to objective observation. The intention is to highlight a potential threat; it aims to accomplish something. As the title of Austin's posthumously published book says, we 'do things with words'.

Consequently, agency becomes the central factor in comprehending linguistic meaning and use, where Skinner's approach necessitates that actors possess the capacity to control language in order to accurately express intention. Actors cannot vocalise or communicate their own intent if they do not command the language they employ. Otherwise they will simply have insufficient resources to achieve this, i.e. they would effectively be too bound by a strict and static linguistic structure that may not allow their articulation of intention. In this way, agency is key to ascertaining what an actor meant in utilising a specific language, and how the exact meaning of that plays into the realisation of an aim. In discussing this, Skinner describes any actor who engages in such behaviour as an 'innovating ideologist'. Actors select or construct linguistic interpretations in ways that serve their political ambitions, promote their own self-interest, and manipulate the political space in which they function. They influence politics through the concepts – and the specific meaning of those concepts – they choose to employ. Indeed, Skinner encourages this to the point of pure manipulation, stating that agents should be actively willing to alter linguistic understandings for their own gain. He says that the more actors are prepared to enact shifts in meaning, the more likely it is they will achieve their ambitions. It is the actors who allow themselves to be constrained by conceptual meanings already in place that will be limited in the scope of their aims (Skinner, 1974: 293).

This is not to suggest that actors are entirely free to do so. Skinner (1969: 49, 1970, 1975: 216) effectively recognises the concerns of those who view language as a pre-existing restraint by acknowledging the relevance of linguistic convention, particularly where it relates to comprehensibility. Words carry certain expectations of meaning governing the scope of their application and this cannot be easily overcome, at least not without the presence of an alternative discourse or narrative that seeks to bring about a shift in understanding. This is not, however, a case where conventions are reduced purely to an issue of restraint:

> We are of course embedded in practices and constrained by them. But those practices owe their dominance in large part to the power of our normative language to hold them in place, and it is always open to us to employ the resources of our language to undermine as well as to underpin those practices. We may be freer than we sometimes suppose. (Skinner, 2002: 7)

This notion of convention is fundamental to comprehending the taboo. Specifically, this theoretical model embodies the idea that an actor can simultaneously be subject to restriction and also capable of the expression of agency within the same rhetorical context. That even in the face of ideational and linguistic limitation, actors can still exert agency based on their intention. In this way, the use of language can be comprehended as a struggle between two forces: convention and ideological innovation. Every situation of rhetorical employment will differ as to which side is the stronger in terms of the influence on an actor and their success in developing a credible narrative. Factors such as events, the influence of epistemic communities, oratorical skill, the capacity to persuade, and the potency of pre-existing ideas will all play into this equation, as will the potential challenge from alternative discourses that other actors may attempt to put forward on the same issue. The balance between them is not some scientific formula that can be applied absolutely in all cases, but will apply contextually. Yet the key point is that agency does play a role. It may be qualified to whatever extent by the contextual circumstances and the conventional environment of its employment – not least where this relates to the rhetorical abilities of the creating actor in being able to successfully construct and communicate the narrative in question – but this still remains a necessary issue. Agency is also sufficiently robust to exert its own qualification on convention, should this be the desire of the user. Indeed, convention is effectively 'just' another construct. It may be the dominant perception – one that, in a battle of interpretations (where an innovating ideologist attempts to introduce an alternative), has a significant advantage. And yet it is still construction. Convention is not essentialist. As such, there has always been room for agency and change. Within this context, the mission for analysis is to establish how these considerations come together in order to determine the influential scope of the innovating ideologist in respect of narrative construction.

Importantly, this analytic model does not intend to say anything about non-compliance with taboos. The claim of deliberate and calculated linguistic construction could be seen to imply non-compliance to the extent that it suggests the actor is selective about what they are committed to. In short, if they are prepared to pick and choose the way they deal with the taboo, then they cannot truly believe in it (otherwise they would not be able to be selective; they would adhere to it). Yet it is wrong to assume that the strategic actor does not accept the taboo. As the joint model of context and convention identified in the previous paragraph demonstrates, the strategic actor can both internalise the terms of the taboo and see its manipulative potential. It does not automatically follow that an actor's manipulation of the norm requires that they do not respect it as a behavioural constraint, or vice versa. This is instead about appreciating a level of agency surrounding that compliance. Taboos are not absolute constraints – this we already know from Price. And it is within Price's conception of flexibility that there is scope to identify agency. Analysts may differ in terms of how far they believe that agency operates, but – as this study will demonstrate – that agency does exist *and* it has considerable impact on the use of the taboo within political discourse and narratives, even where this takes place alongside convention. Critically, this is not some basic model – that narrative construction is a little bit of this and a little bit of that. This is not the idea that actors are a simplistic binary mix of restraint and strategic expression. This constitutes a more sophisticated model, one that captures the sheer complexity of the relationship between pre-existing belief and self-interest. It is about breaking down the highly static notion of actors as effectively 'slaves' to the chemical weapons taboo and recovering the role of agency, which has been ignored. In a Skinnerian attempt to move past these overly systemic understandings, this is about bringing agency back into comprehension, not least where it reveals so much about what really occurs in respect of strategic linguistic construction.

This is also not to undermine the nature of the taboo as a restraint. Indeed, a key aspect of this discussion concerns the way in which the chemical weapons taboo is upheld as a political ideal that people have dared not break. The Syria example is a perfect demonstration of how existing ideas can be exploited without changing the terms of understanding – and where that failure to change demonstrates the exceptional strength of the chemical weapons taboo. If Syria proves anything, it is that the taboo plays a major role in politicians' understanding of chemical devices. Within this context, therefore, this study can be viewed specifically as an exploration of convention and the idea that sometimes the strongest ideational and linguistic constructs – the ones that would take great effort to modify successfully – are actually those that can be used to the greatest degree of manipulation. As Freedman (2015) has already claimed, the closer a narrative is to the real world, the easier and stronger that narrative will be; and the same can be applied not only to the real world, but to the pre-existing constructed world. That is, if you have a concept or normative expectation that many people already extensively buy into, the exploitation of it can constitute the most effective form of control. The strategic actor exploits accepted rhetoric not because of convention and restraint, but because the engrained nature of those resources can facilitate their self-interest. Adhering to established interpretations of language and behaviour is a fabulous opportunity to strategically control a given situation.

Significantly, however, this is *more than the simple reproduction of existing ideas* – which is effectively how constructivism would view the strategic process. As will be shown throughout this examination of Obama's foreign policy on Syria, the president does not significantly alter the ideals of the taboo at any point. He does, however, use those ideals in an extremely manipulative way, and for the purposes of deliberately shaping US policy in line with his own desires. Consequently, convention is actually an enabler of linguistic manipulation. In particular, this is the idea of agency-driven selection. The chemical weapons taboo may be relatively set within convention, but there is significant freedom and power in determining how, and the extent to which, it is used. Specifically, this occurs whereby characteristics associated with the taboo – although highly disputed – provide the resources for rhetorical exploitation. These are the features, already mentioned above, that require that chemical weapons be distinguished from other armaments on the basis that they are, for example, more destructive or indiscriminate. Strategic use of the taboo is not merely an emotive appeal to the idea that these devices are horrific, but a significantly more detailed and premeditated manipulation of these specific aspects of the taboo, not least where this means that the 'same' taboo can be utilised in a vast number of differing ways depending on which characteristics are prioritised as part of a given narrative. And where these features have been shown not to be essentialist, this further enables that selection. That is, the fact that they are not necessary or requisite for a successful reference to the taboo means that an actor possesses considerable autonomy concerning their application. They are not required to use any one of them, but only those that help their cause (should they wish to use any at all). The decision to base a contextualised understanding of the taboo on certain features – in choosing to play up particular characteristics and ignore others – greatly alters the presentation of the taboo and what it seeks to achieve in terms of the strategic use by an actor. In this way, convention itself provides the discursive resources necessary to carry out acts of linguistic exploitation.

Critically, therefore, this is a process in which convention is still factored in. Restraint clearly influences meaning, not least where (a) strategic use relies on the availability of the discursive tools provided by convention and (b) convention dictates the tools that can be used (i.e. an actor may exploit the idea that a chemical weapon is immoral, say, but this is only possible in the sense that convention 'decides' that this is a resource to be exploited; convention sets the terms of debate, even where that debate is inherently strategic). Yet to the extent that this constitutes an aspect of discourse that actors can choose to selectively draw upon – where policy-makers effectively cherry-pick the elements of convention they wish to utilise and dispense with others – then this remains an intrinsically manipulative act. Despite the constraining nature of the taboo, agency is still a key dynamic. Significantly, and this point cannot be emphasised enough, this is not that every act of linguistic construction is intentional, manipulative, or strategic. Even taking into account the concept of performative speech, so much of what happens linguistically occurs within accepted and 'everyday' formulations of language, to the extent that actors may not even consciously select the words and ideas they use to express themselves. That process happens automatically based on pre-existing understandings. Moreover, especially in times of crisis, an actor may choose to fall back on convention as opposed to innovation where this is deemed the safest and most comfortable option. Yet these caveats fail to negate the main premise of this argument: that language remains an innovative and malleable resource for the expression and realisation of self-interest. This opportunity for manipulation may not always be taken, and, not least in the case of taboos, actors may still feel the check of social expectation. Yet this potential exists and is regularly exploited by actors who choose to do so. Taboos are not fixed, and actors have the necessary agency to manage this to their advantage.

To summarise, this approach lies in stark contrast with available approaches to the chemical weapons taboo, and international norms more generally. It directly challenges existing understanding to argue that such normative structures are significantly more agency-centric in their use than previously assumed. At present, the taboo is comprehended as an intrinsically restrictive and static pressure within the international system, particularly where this relates to its construction as an idea within international political discourse. Actors are socialised to accept the taboo and recognise chemical weapons as prohibitively abhorrent. Yet this is disputed here to demonstrate that, while pre-existing and overriding conceptions of the taboo still have influence, those conceptions can also be applied in terms of a more agency-driven command of normative expression. The taboo should not be examined through relatively static constructivist models of language, but through agency-centric paradigms of understanding, specifically where this allows for the idea that actors deliberately construct language to ensure their own self-interest.

Admittedly, there are those who will argue that the actor intention on which this approach rests can never be recovered, at least not as an academic method. We cannot see inside another's mind (and perhaps not even our own, without a sense of self-deception) and so, therefore, it is pointless to rely on a concept of intentional agency (Wimsatt and Beardsley, 1946; Olsen, 1973: 229; Parekh and Berki, 1973: 169). If we cannot know what an actor desires, we cannot tell if and how they are strategic. In particular, Skinner has been criticised by academics such as Kenneth Minogue (1988) for failing to produce a clear model that shows precisely how intention and agency play into rhetorical and textual action. This is a decisive issue for Minogue, who asserts that, if analysts can never know how to know what has happened – if analysts do not have a method of getting inside the head of the actor they are examining in order to ascertain intention and strategic purpose – then that examination is defunct. Consequently, Minogue presents Skinner as intellectual time-wasting. Skinner (1988: 231) takes this accusation seriously: 'It is certainly unpardonable to waste one's colleagues' time.'

Yet it is worth remembering what Skinner's aim actually is in respect of this intellectual approach. Skinner does not attempt to construct a method of the type anticipated by Minogue, but instead makes an important methodological statement concerning the rejection of textualist and social constructivist assumptions as incapable of grasping the complexity of linguistic meaning. He is seeking to show that intention influences conceptual construction and employment, but against a backdrop of convention. Skinner aims only to show that convention alone is insufficient to comprehend how language is being used. Yes, there are limitations on what we can know in accepting this (although what academic method does come with a 100 per cent guarantee?), but that does not preclude that this is the way language works. It may be difficult to uncover, but this does not mean it is wrong or that we should not attempt to unearth intention and strategic purpose wherever possible. This is the sentiment adopted here. Specifically, that by applying this logic of understanding analysis is now able to address not only the ideals at the heart of the taboo, but also how those same ideals are causally exploited and not merely adhered to. Viewing the taboo in this way provides new insight into the influence it has within political dialogue and foreign policy-making. This is particularly important with respect to Syria – where the taboo is elemental to the conflict itself – in that it demonstrates that the crisis cannot be reduced to static ideas of normative belief. Analysis must abandon the current stagnant notions of the taboo and instead take into account the extent to which ideas and language can be rhetorically manipulated, especially where successful manipulation by an actor can determine whether or not foreign policy desires are realised.

A wolf in sheep's clothing

Strategic construction of the taboo also plays into the second point made in this book: that the taboo is not as 'good' as we think it is. As already stated, the chemical weapons taboo is politically very valuable. It is a line that cannot be crossed (red or otherwise). Specifically, it has been constructed as a situation in which the taboo should not be challenged or undermined. Where it is deemed of such high value to international politics, it is too important to risk criticism. Criticism would potentially weaken the concept and undo all the positive work that has been achieved in respect of controlling the possession of chemical arms and their use, both to date and in the future. Picking at problematic issues with the taboo could cause this regime to unravel, with no replacement instrument for chemical weapons control to fill the subsequent gap. Indeed, it has been argued that even where the supposedly special nature of chemical weapons cannot be proven (whereby a taboo exclusive to chemical devices necessarily requires some clear basis of differentiation from other forms of violence), there remains significant worth in the stigmatisation of these devices regardless. In discussing chemical weapons within the context of the WMD concept, for example, and even though this notion of mass destruction is considered flawed, it is claimed that there still exists considerable benefit in upholding the prohibitionary construct (Dowty, 2001; Robinson, 2004: 14). Specifically, this stigmatisation underpins the elimination of some of the world's most deplorable devices, however uncertain their capacity for destruction and damage may be. Even where the taboo is acknowledged as imperfect – even to the point of conceptual illogic – this means there is still importance attached to it. In short, something is better than nothing. And a 'something' that has attracted the extensive support and massive commitment of resources from all areas of the international community is not to be derided.

Yet this view overlooks and disguises severe problems with the way in which the idea of eradicating chemical weapons has become manifest within the international system. On the one hand it would be, at best, cold-hearted to suggest that the world would not be a better place with fewer, or preferably none, of these horrific weapons in it. Whatever the relevance of contextual arguments, such as the need for these weapons to form deterrent relationships or state rights to certain forms of self-protection, the central assertion that these weapons are 'not nice' is difficult to contest, at least on moral and humanitarian grounds. Consequently, this is not the concern that this book addresses. On the other hand, what this study does achieve is to show that the way in which the taboo has been conventionally expressed in international political rhetoric is extremely problematic. As seen in the discussions above detailing the stigmatisation of chemical weapons, the taboo is not merely concerned with identifying chemical arms as nasty. Convention and stigmatisation effectively expand this idea to state that they are exclusively so, and that they deserve prioritisation over other threats as such. Chemical weapons are not merely bad, they are worse than other types of armament – an assumption that implies that they are more worthy of attention than these, typically conventional, threats. This subsequent hierarchy is difficult to sustain, however, especially where it is (a) flawed, given the significant overlap with other weapons in terms of effect, and (b) detrimental to wider values of achieving peace, conflict resolution, and non-harm to persons. Even where it has been argued that these difficulties represent a sacrifice worth making in order to uphold the taboo, this book disputes this. Such a view may be based on good intentions in respect of chemical weapons elimination, but it ignores the sheer extent to which the taboo causes major problems – problems that are so devastating that they can no longer be ignored on the basis of utility or pragmatic politics.

The Syrian crisis exemplifies the highly negative influence that the taboo can have. At face value, the adoption of the taboo in respect of Syria would appear to be a plus. Syria is ostensibly a case in which ghastly weapons have been removed from the clutches of a dictator intent on indiscriminately killing his way to victory. Surely it would be better if someone carrying out such a vicious campaign of violence did not have access to potentially mass destructive weaponry. Yet this perception masks a Pandora's box of problems that the taboo has opened in terms of the crisis. The stigmatisation and prioritisation that conventionally define the taboo (at least in its present, dominant form) vastly distort the reality of, and response to, a given political situation. Specifically, in relation to Syria this has: both ignored and legitimated the use of conventional violence; created hierarchies that overlook other problems, including the significant biological weapons threat that exists within Syria; failed to address the crisis's core political problems; given a false illusion of progress by making it appear that something is being done to mitigate the crisis when in fact this solution could make no difference; as a consequence of this last point, prolonged the conflict and allowed it to escalate; and provided a basis on which Assad has been unintentionally legitimised and strengthened as a credible national leader, despite US efforts to the contrary.

These are issues that have not been addressed within the debate on US foreign policy on Syria in relation to the chemical weapons taboo. To the extent they have been recognised, it has instead been within the context of Obama's supposed incompetence in dealing with the crisis. In line with the conceptual situation discussed above whereby challenging the taboo is taboo itself, no one has dared suggest that these problems are directly connected to this. Criticism has not engaged with the chemical weapons taboo in this manner because, of course, the taboo can never be wrong. Yet analysis cannot appreciate what has happened in Syria – or any other conflict situation involving chemical weapons, or to which the chemical weapons taboo is applied – if it is not prepared to say that the taboo is flawed. This is even more of an issue when combined with the arguments on strategic construction. The idea that actors can use the taboo strategically for their own interests indicates they may be more concerned with what the taboo can do for them than the wider implications of it. That is, in seeing strategic value in the taboo they ignore, or choose to ignore, the damage it creates (as long as that damage is not to them and their ambitions are fulfilled). The evidence examined in this book supports this. The taboo has been extremely useful for Obama; but in placing it at the centre of his Syrian foreign policy for strategic purposes, it has also exacerbated the conflict in that applying the taboo has proved inappropriate and injurious. Strategic use exaggerates the ill effects of the taboo.

Consequently, the taboo is not the wonderful construct it is assumed to be. In fact, the presence of the concept within international political thinking and discourse can make a given situation significantly worse through its application, intentionally or otherwise. This is a controversial statement, but it is one that must be made. Because allowing the chemical weapons taboo to go unchallenged, even where this is portrayed as a necessary aspect of ensuring its survival, is extremely unsafe. Analysis can never hope to uncover the real impact of the taboo in IR if it is not prepared to be critical. And as the Syria example shows, there is considerable empirical evidence to suggest there is something to be critical of. This is not simply a case of ensuring that our explanation of IR is accurate, but also a situation in which failing to criticise the taboo has ignored major problems in respect of actual and hypothetical conflict scenarios. In Syria, these problems are causing more violence and more deaths than would have happened in the absence of the taboo as the cornerstone of US foreign policy. Within this context, can this elephant in the room be avoided any longer?

Conclusion

The chemical weapons taboo has an incredible reputation. While many taboos are recognised as particularly strong in terms of IR, this stands out as one of the most compelling. On the surface, this would seem to be a positive and a major achievement for the international community. Chemical weapons are horrific, and they do possess a potential for mass destructive effect (however disputed their actual effect may be). And to have the international community rally together to enforce this normative expectation, when it is so often devastatingly divided, would appear to be a triumph. Indeed, the taboo is protected as such. This constitutes a rare success for international politics, and, consequently, it is guarded as a fragile object – one that cannot be upset in any way for fear of breakage. Beneath the surface, however, lies a very different story. The taboo can constitute a highly negative influence within IR, one that distorts political understanding and fails to reflect the reality of a conflict scenario. This means that policy-makers' responses to that scenario become misrepresentative of the actual threat, and can actually make a situation worse – a lot worse. The conceptual presence of the taboo can detrimentally prolong and exacerbate a crisis, causing more destruction and tension than if the taboo had not been applied, at least in its conventional form. Far from the morally upstanding expectation that the taboo is assumed to be, it is a destructive and destabilising influence in international politics.

This becomes an even greater issue when placed within the ideational framework of the strategic construction of the taboo. The taboo has been presented as a significant restraint on actors. This includes the constraint created by the need to uphold the concept, i.e. the level of restriction is exaggerated because it is considered necessary for the taboo's survival. Yet the taboo is not an absolute restraint – as shown by drawing on the work of Price. But as long as it is accepted that such freedom, however partial, exists, this opens up the usage of the taboo to the idea of strategic exploitation. Specifically, this constitutes an even more extensive exploitation than that envisaged by the strategic narratives paradigm. While the nature of the taboo as a behavioural control may limit the scope of manipulation, it is still manipulation – an act that indicates agency in deciding how it should occur. Indeed, in looking at how actors deal with language over which they have limited power to change in terms of meaning, some of the most successful strategic acts actually come from the calculated use of established concepts. This has implications for the wider argument that the taboo is a detrimental conceptual force, where it logically demonstrates that actors can create the ill effects of the taboo through their strategic actions – perhaps even intentionally. It also adds considerable weight to the fundamental claim of this book: that the taboo is not what we think it is. We possess a false illusion of what the taboo consists of and how it is employed in international politics. And, most crucially, this means we have ignored not only the reality of its use, but also the damaging impact it can have on conflict resolution and diplomacy. This is a wolf in sheep's clothing. We need to be prepared to pull back the fleece and see the dangerous creature behind it – however much we would prefer to deny that it is there.

Part I

A strategic taboo

2

Setting the redline

THE CHEMICAL weapons taboo has never been so popular. Politically and publicly, Obama's narrative of the taboo as the basis of US foreign policy on Syria has catapulted the concept into the spotlight. While the horrendous nature of chemical weapons has long been recognised, the taboo has rarely received such attention. In line with Richard Price's assertion that violations can strengthen a taboo, this is what would seem to have happened here. Syria has reignited the moral fervour behind the prohibition. Yet there is a problem with this understanding: that while a clear connection exists between the Syrian crisis and the chemical weapons taboo, this was not inevitable – at least not in respect of the extremes of belief that it would be associated with. Nor were the ideals of the taboo adopted consistently within Obama's foreign policy. The taboo as a feature of rhetoric appears suddenly out of nowhere more than two years into the actual conflict, and explicitly *after* an extended period during which Obama did all he could to avoid any reference to Assad's chemical stockpiles and ambitions. Indeed, the taboo only enters presidential discourse once Obama could not ignore the issue any longer. It is only when Obama is forced to address the situation – specifically where this occurs in the shadow of his own ill-thought-through redline – that the taboo comes into rhetorical play. Consequently, references to the taboo are highly conditional. Far from representing a step in an ongoing commitment to the elimination of chemical weapons, the taboo is employed on a fundamentally ad hoc basis – when and if it is needed. This indicates something other than the straightforward application of the taboo as an accepted moral benchmark. Something else is driving use of the concept. This is not, of course, to suggest that the taboo does not exert an intrinsic value as an established prohibition. But it is to show that, within this, the taboo is not absolute to the extent that has typically been assumed, and particularly in respect of Syria. Moreover, that it is open to highly strategic use by the actors who employ it.

As evidence, the next three chapters outline the ways in which the taboo has been used in relation to the Syrian crisis. It examines how the taboo was brought into US foreign policy discourse, explicitly to highlight that this was not a preordained move but a strategic response to political need. Furthermore, it demonstrates that the development of the taboo within the wider narrative on Syria was similarly manipulated, and that the contextual longevity of the taboo was a direct consequence of how far the concept met the political desires of the actors involved as opposed to a solely moral commitment and the unconditional upholding of an ideal. Within this ideational framework, this first chapter of Part I analyses the situation from the start of the Syrian conflict through to just before the initial allegations were made of Assad's chemical weapons use in December 2012. Specifically, this covers Obama's now infamous redline statement, in which the US president stated that chemical weapons use by Assad would instigate a change in terms of US foreign policy activity. In setting this redline, the chapter asks a number of questions concerning the motivation inherent to this declaration. In the face of the chemical weapons threat posed by the Syrian dictator, was the adoption of the taboo as a basis for US foreign policy necessary? Did Obama mean the redline as the all-or-nothing ultimatum it would come to be accepted as? And what precisely was the president's intention in making such a challenge on the issue of chemical weapons, especially where this was at odds with his declared policy on Syria at the time?

Changing the equation

While chemical weapons would come to define US involvement in Syria, Assad's stockpiles were initially only rarely commented on. In discussing the conflict during his 2012 State of the Union Address – almost an entire year after civil violence had erupted in Syria – Obama (2012a) failed even to mention the chemical threat, let alone the protection of a prohibitory norm. Critically, this is not to suggest the threat of chemical weapons was ignored entirely. These armaments were highlighted as a serious concern in Obama's (2012b) establishment of a national emergency on Syria that same year, where the acquisition and development of such devices were considered 'to pose an unusual and extraordinary threat to the national security, foreign policy, and economy of the United States'. Moreover, then Defense Secretary Leon Panetta (in US Cong., 2012b: 2) famously testified at the time that the chemical stockpile situation in Syria was '100 times worse' than securing these weapons had proved in Libya. At this stage, however, this was a concern based more on the associated implications that the Assad regime's destabilisation would create in terms of the secure nature of these weapons, as opposed to a resource that would be employed by Assad himself. This was very much a debate that centred on the possibility of these devices falling into the wrong hands – al-Qaeda, Hezbollah, Iran – rather than what Assad may do with those held in his own grasp. As such, the issue of chemical weapons only infrequently appeared on the political agenda, where it was reduced to a secondary concern surrounding Assad's collapse. It was an issue that may be realised in the future, but it was not an immediate threat, nor one that related to the conventional aggression then being carried out by regime forces.

And yet the concern that Assad was willing to employ chemical weapons would intensify throughout 2012 as a consequence of the dictator's sheer and sustained brutality against both civilians and the fragmented opposition that was developing at the time. Once it was clear that Assad was not going to go quietly – that he would fight, and fight hard, to retain his leadership – US foreign policy discussions turned into a question of how extreme his already violent strategy could get. This was a man more than capable of massacre and human atrocities. Would he stop at the use of chemical weapons? Assad's preparedness, enthusiasm even, for a no-holds-barred policy of aggression would not seem to indicate a person who would respect the ideals of the taboo, at least not when forced into a corner of regime survival. In effectively trying to kill his way out of the rebellion, Assad would surely only be drawn further to methods of slaughter, regardless of the moral implications. This concern would become increasingly evident in presidential rhetoric on the crisis, with Obama (2012c, 2012d, 2013a) repeatedly stressing that chemical employment by Assad would constitute a 'tragic mistake'. This was a phrase that, in marking out weapons use as politically injudicious, connected the chemical weapons issue to sanction by the US: 'The use of chemical weapons is and would be totally unacceptable ... there will be consequences, and you [Assad] will be held accountable' (Obama, 2012d). This same sentiment would also be expressed in Obama's (2012e) infamous redline – announced on 20 August 2012 – where chemical warfare activity was identified as a 'game changer' in terms of US foreign policy:

> We have to be clear to the Asad regime, but also to other players on the ground, that a red line for us is we start seeing a bunch of chemical weapons moving around or being utilized. That would change my calculus. That would change my equation ... We have communicated in no uncertain terms with every player in the region that that's a red line for us and that there would be enormous consequences if we start seeing movement on the chemical weapons front or the use of chemical weapons. That would change my calculations significantly.

This line would come to govern US foreign policy on Syria. It apparently threw down the gauntlet to Assad and was seen as an explicit threat that the US would retaliate if Assad did not heed the warning – specifically where this would involve major intervention. Obama was seen to be issuing a non-negotiable ultimatum. And if Assad chose not to comply, this would result in serious consequences, possibly even 'boots on the ground'. Chemical weapons use was something that could not, and would not, be tolerated.

As an ultimatum, however, the redline is flawed. Using Todd Sechser's (2011: 380) criteria of a 'compellent threat' as a point of comparison – that a threat must (a) demand a change, (b) threaten military action if that change is not enacted, and (c) be made from one state to another – the redline does not comply. While the statement is clearly directed at Assad by the US, the terms of the change demanded are unclear and there are no explicit consequences attached to the failure to change, for example, military intervention. Within this framework, Obama's was a poor threat. Where a warning of this nature necessitates a strong and unambiguous presentation, so the president's proviso fails Sechser's test on numerous counts. This is also the conclusion drawn by Bruno Tertrais (2014). Complementing the work of Sechser, Tertrais has applied a similar conceptual model of effective threat specifically to the redline. He too accepts that it failed to meet the expectations of a successful ultimatum. Furthermore, he effectively expands on Sechser's observations concerning the clarity of threat to examine how a weakly presented challenge relates detrimentally to compliance. As well as acknowledging that unclear threats make adherence difficult by not setting the standards to be met, he also explores this from the perspective of the actor receiving the threat – to show that they must be made to believe both in the reality of the threat and that the issuer is prepared to see it through. This is not simply a case of expressing an ultimatum in indisputable terms, but of demonstrating that the issuer is willing and capable of upholding their challenge. If this is not communicated successfully, then the threat will not be taken seriously, leading to partial or non-compliance.

In looking at these ideas in more depth, it is worth noting that this problem of a futile redline goes back even further than Sechser and Tertrais suggest. They focus on the communication of the threat; yet the redline's inefficacy was set in motion well before the stage at which it was expressed. In particular, the explicit reference to the 'moving around' of chemical weapons is unsound in that it was well known prior to the redline that Assad was already doing exactly that. Assad had redeployed chemical arms close to rebel areas by this time, and congressional reports, as well as the *Washington Post*, reveal that both Obama and US foreign policy-makers were more than aware of this (US Cong., 2012b: 1–2, 5). Consequently, this vastly undermined the credibility of Obama's position. If your enemy is already doing what you say they cannot (where that act is constructed as a hypothetical expectation they should not violate in the future), you cannot expect them or anyone else to take that ultimatum seriously. Why would anyone have confidence in a threat that had already been violated? Moreover, an actor simply cannot comply with a demand they have broken. In expanding this, and in rejoining the work of Sechser and Tertrais on threat clarity, it must also be asked, what exactly was a 'whole bunch' of chemical weapons? It is conceptually possible that, while Assad was repositioning chemical arms into disputed regions, they were insufficient to qualify as a 'bunch', whatever that may mean. Or perhaps they were not being 'moved around' in the exact way envisaged by Obama for the redline to kick in. There was no way of knowing. Obama's lack of lucidity and precision was so great that it could not be pinned down to any specific act or event, even one that obviously involved chemical weapons. Obama would later exacerbate this confusion by attempting to redefine the terms of the threat. Soon after the redline was announced, Obama would pull back from even the weak ultimatum of his initial statement to blur the expectations of violation further. Specifically, he became vague as to what form(s) of chemical activity constituted a transgression of that line. Republican Congressional Representative for Illinois, Adam Kinzinger (in US Cong., 2013a: 35), describes this ambiguity: 'I heard what I assume the President was saying is that if you use chemical weapons, that is the red line. Now, I hear that there is a kind of shifting red line to no, no, no, we're talking about the transfer of chemical weapons, and not necessarily using them against your own people. So, it seems more like a cyan line, or a yellow line.' Consequently, there was no way for anyone to know whether the US was required to act. Likewise, it meant that Assad could not distinguish the boundaries of expected behaviour. Assad was someone who had already proved himself highly adept at testing the waters in respect of conventional violence. He had incrementally increased the level of brutality of his pro-regime campaign in order to ascertain what he could get away with without international involvement. As such, issuing such a vague challenge merely invited further incremental activity on the part of Assad in relation to chemical weapons. Where the dictator had already exploited the uncertainty surrounding the US stance to his own aggressive advantage, to effectively give him further ambiguity to play with in this way was a red rag to a bull. It would and could do nothing to restrain the type of behaviour he had chosen to engage in, and in fact threatened only to fuel it – as seen in his actual use of chemical weapons that was to come six months later.

Such threshold-challenging behaviour was additionally encouraged by a failure to outline an exact and credible punishment for crossing the redline. There was no indication as to what this would entail: for example, more extensive sanctions, air strikes, US 'boots on the ground', etc. What would the implications be if Assad chose to violate the line? Critically, it would seem that even Obama did not know the answer to this. When asked if his reference to chemical weapons use being a 'game changer' meant US military action, Obama (2013b) replied in vague and convoluted terms:

> By game changer, I mean that we would have to rethink the range of options that are available to us. Now, we're already, as I've said, invested in trying to bring about a solution inside of Syria. Obviously, there are options that are available to me that are on the shelf right now that we have not deployed. And that's a spectrum of options.

> As early as last year, I asked the Pentagon, our military, our intelligence officials to prepare for me what options might be available. And I won't go into the detail of what those options might be, but clearly, that would be an escalation, in our view, of the threat to the security of the international community, our allies, and the United States, and that means that there are some options that we might not otherwise exercise that we would strongly consider.

A short yes/no answer this is not. Indeed, his answer is specifically quoted in full here to demonstrate the sheer confusion and uncertainty evident in Obama's rhetoric at this stage. Critically, this is not a situation that can be attributed to the protection and confidentiality of intelligence; that is, Obama did not want to reveal the supposed options that could be used against Assad because it might compromise national security. While political actors have frequently appealed to a need for confidentiality in order to secure the wider defence of the country, the whole point of issuing a redline threat is that you are clear about what you are prepared to do if your adversary does not comply. Furthermore, this same issue of ambiguity was reported by an anonymous former intelligence official, who said that the entire US national security establishment was extremely confused by Obama's position, especially over whether any military-based retaliation would be considered (Hersh, 2014). In particular, it was Obama's own inability to clarify what the line was, and what the implications of crossing it would be, that was identified as the key problem in this situation. The official explicitly describes this, not as a case of confidentiality, but as a case of presidential incompetence. Ultimately, what this meant was that there was no clear disincentive communicated to Assad. While Assad may have accepted that there would be consequences, the failure to specify what those would comprise meant there was nothing concrete to deter. Assad could not make a reasonable risk calculation based on whether he was prepared to accept those consequences or not. In that position, there was nothing to restrain him and every incentive for him to push his violent strategy even further.

Moreover, there was no indication that the US would be willing to respond to violation, whatever that response may entail. Assad had already committed hideous acts of conventional aggression and had started deploying chemical arms. Yet the US had done nothing. Widespread reports of massacre, violent discrimination, and rape – among other crimes against humanity – were insufficient to provoke any tangible comeback on the part of the US. In fact, Obama seemed to be continually waiting to see if Assad would do something worse than he already had done before American involvement would be considered. Nothing was quite 'bad' enough. With such precedent in place, there was no reason for Assad to believe that crossing the redline would alter that situation. There was simply no evidence that Obama would actually respond. As Eric Sterner (2014: 408) says, this was in a case in which, 'From the Syrian government's point of view, the odds of getting away with using chemical weapons looked to be in its favor.'

Indeed, where Obama had set himself up explicitly as an multilateral president who was committed to avoiding military conflict as a form of foreign policy (discussed in greater depth below), and in the wake of his relatively hands-off approach in respect of Libya, this would hardly have strengthened Assad's perception of the redline. This is not to insinuate that Obama's wider stance was in itself weak, but that it became highly fragile when expressed through the medium of an extreme and implicitly military threat. Specifically, the conflict of those two policy approaches would create uncertainty concerning the US's willingness to follow through. Given his previous commitment to non-intervention and multilateral politics, would Obama really put troops in Syria? Was he really the type of president who would stomach such a decision? Within this context, Assad effectively bet that Obama's moderation would win out over the hawkish military option. It was a safe bet.

This created a situation in which Obama was heavily criticised for failing to put forward a credible threat, especially once evidence of Assad's use of chemical weapons became compelling. To quote Kinzinger (in US Cong., 2013b: 43) once more:

> Look, what should we do if chemical weapons are used, I am not going to advocate one way or another right now. But I will say if you are the President of the United States and you ever, ever utter the word 'red line,' I don't care if you are in the middle of a campaign, I don't care if you are in the middle of a crowded theatre on fire and the only way to evacuate it is to say the word 'red line,' you never use that unless you intend to follow through, because you are the President of the United States ... And you actually make war much more likely when you give the impression that you are not going to stand behind your word, because your enemies don't take you seriously.

Obama was seen as making threats that he was not prepared to act on. He was not only setting a redline, but setting himself up for a major fall if he did not now respond to violation. Ultimately, this uncertainty caused Obama's declaration to be heralded as something of a joke, with Tertrais (2014: 7) commenting that the redline risked 'becoming a punch line'. With hindsight, it would seem that the redline has more than lived up to expectations in this regard.

The real line

This criticism, however, has been developed on the assumption that Obama wanted to set a strong redline. He meant to issue Assad a stern and indisputable ultimatum based on the exclusive threat of chemical weapons. Specifically, this is also the assumption that there was something inherently aggressive about the threat. It was taken as a promise that the US would initiate a major intervention should chemical warfare tactics be employed. But this was not the case in either respect. In fact, the redline masks the very different strategy that Obama desired in respect of Syria – one to which the redline does not correspond, and, most importantly, was never meant to.

Many lines

At the time of its declaration, chemical weapons were not the only redline in terms of what would trigger an escalation in US foreign policy. The rationale was very much the other way around. This was less a case where the taboo caused Obama to set chemical weapons use as a benchmark in respect of Assad's behaviour; the intolerable nature of these armaments was exactly that – a point where toleration was no longer permissible under any circumstances. Instead, this was more a situation in which the president and US foreign policy-makers were analysing the increasing brutality of the Syrian regime and asking how far Assad could go before US action was needed. Specifically, the redline was constructed around a hypothetical level of brutality that included the use of chemical weapons, *but* was not exclusive to this. Chemical weapons were not the only way in which Assad could cross a line. That could also be achieved, according to Secretary of State John Kerry (in US Cong., 2012c: 2), by 'some massive massacre'. Explicitly, this would constitute a significant event where 'all of a sudden there seems to be bloodletting, not dissimilar to what prompted President Clinton to move in the Balkans' (ibid.: 39). Admittedly, Kerry would go on to discuss the problems associated with identifying such a massacre as a point of non-toleration, specifically that placing an exact number on the victims who would have to be killed for that act to 'qualify' as beyond accept-ability would be extremely difficult. Simply put, how many have to die? This is a complex and, quite frankly, stomach-churning question, and the ability to answer it is not made any easier by the fact that Assad had already succeeded in committing a number of large massacres. This effectively normalised mass atrocities to a significant extent before any limit could be established. Despite these issues, however, there was a clear acceptance that this was not solely about chemical arms. Far from the supposedly special nature of the taboo, it was not the exclusive be-all-and-end-all commitment that it would come to be understood as. Indeed, this wider approach fits in with declared policy at the time, especially where it follows a Presidential Study Directive issued by Obama (2011a: 10) the previous year, stating that: 'The prevention of mass atrocities is a core national security interest and a core moral responsibility of the United States.' This was also reflected in popular public opinion. In testimony given to Congress, Andrew Tabler (in US Cong., 2012c: 39; emphasis added), Senior Fellow at the Washington Institute for Near East Policy, said:

> [T]here is quite a bit of support in terms of the American people about issues of mass atrocities and genocide. There was recently a study, a poll that was conducted by the U.S. Holocaust Museum in which you can see that the Syrian issue itself, isolated, is

not a major political issue, but if it is combined with other Middle Eastern issues *or on genocide or mass atrocities*, it actually moves very quickly up the ladder.

This same sentiment was evident in discussions concerning Assad's loss of legitimacy. The concept of legitimacy is intrinsic to the chemical weapons taboo. A taboo act is illegitimate: it is an action that goes against the principles of established society and demands punishment. To extend this logic, it is a situation in which the actor responsible for the transgression has effectively relinquished their legitimacy, specifically where this would have otherwise protected them from sanction. The obvious parallel here is the connection between the concepts of state sovereignty and humanitarian intervention. This is the idea at the heart of the Responsibility to Protect (R2P) ideology. Here it is suggested that once a state actor has committed specified acts – atrocities, crimes against humanity, etc. – they sacrifice their rights against foreign intervention (a claim that mirrors Michael Walzer's (2006 [1977]) 'Just War' theory). They have marked themselves out as an illegitimate target and can be acted against as a consequence, regardless of the restraints typically associated with upholding sovereignty and the principle of non-intervention in sovereign territory. Indeed, it was under the auspices of R2P that the US supported a number of proposed UN resolutions that called for the condemnation of Assad, but which failed thanks to Security Council vetoes by Russia and China. This same loss of legitimacy is evident in respect of the chemical weapons taboo. Once an actor has broken the taboo, they no longer enjoy any political benefits and freedoms surrounding their legitimacy, including where it relates to continued state leadership. They have forgone their rights to such. As Obama (2013c) said of Assad's behaviour: '[A] leader who slaughtered his citizens and gassed children to death cannot regain the legitimacy to lead a badly fractured country.'

Yet this rhetoric of legitimacy was evident long before the use of chemical weapons in Syria, explicitly where this relates to acts of conventional violence. In line with the R2P anticipation that legitimacy is removed as a consequence of acts that include the conventional, the idea that Assad had forfeited his legitimate status was acknowledged long before chemical weapons use entered into consideration. The brutal conventional violence inflicted by Assad was sufficient to place him in the category of the illegitimate. He had already crossed a line. Indeed, Obama (2013d) explicitly expressed this on a number of occasions, including this one: 'And so we are going to continue to closely consult with everybody in the region and do everything we can to bring an end to the bloodshed and to allow the Syrian people to get out from under the yoke of a leader who has lost all legitimacy because he is willing to slaughter his own people [with conventional devices].' Accordingly, Obama had already accepted that Assad had breached the rules of legitimacy based on conventional aggression, and it had been publicly stated that this was the case. This view was adopted more widely throughout Obama's administration at the time, including by Pannetta (in US Cong., 2012d: 6 – 'through its repeated violations of human rights any government that indiscriminately kills its own people loses its legitimacy. This [Assad] regime has lost its legitimacy and its right to rule the country') and Kerry (in US Cong., 2012e: 1 – 'Certainly, Bashar al-Assad has lost all governing legitimacy except what he achieves at the barrel of a gun or a tank'), as well as by government advisers such as Martin Indyk from the Brookings Institute (in US Cong., 2012c: 44 – ' a regime that starts firing on its own people by definition is losing its legitimacy. It has lost all legitimacy and therefore should step aside').

So how can a regime lose legitimacy, and then lose legitimacy again? Because Obama did not mean the chemical weapons taboo in the exclusive way it would be interpreted. The chemical redline was only one part of a wider policy that sought to address a range of types of violence. Admittedly, there are two caveats to this claim. First, it is notable that conventional violence has consistently failed to inspire any change in US foreign policy with respect to Syria. The death toll is now in the hundreds of thousands and this has never proved sufficient for any escalation in American involvement. Critically, this fatality rate – however extensive – is technically irrelevant in this case where it does not constitute the extreme massacre the Obama administration identifies as a potential trigger for foreign policy activity. It is not the 'big' event Kerry says would merit a response. While this conventional redline recognised that Assad's brutality at this more general level indicated his willingness to carry out such a strike – that his past behaviour was sufficiently awful to suggest that more lethal attacks of the triggering kind were realistically possible – this was far from the idea that his actions to date were intolerable. This lies in stark contrast to the relatively immediate reaction to the use of chemical weapons. Second, the debate concerning how extreme a conventional attack would have to be before it reached a level of qualification (i.e. how many victims would have to be killed) is important, not least where there was no such debate on chemical weapons use. Weapons use alone was sufficient, regardless of the number killed. While a conventional strike would have to 'prove' its significance in fatalities, the mere employment of chemical armaments could instigate a response. While the concept of conventional massacre was highly conditional, therefore, Assad's engagement with chemical warfare was instantly recognised as demanding a reaction. Consequently, this represents an important point of distinction between the two.

And yet, this issue that both modes of violence were considered together – specifically as equals in terms of intervention – reveals that the situation is not as clear-cut as the chemical redline alone would suggest. Far from the absolute separation of chemical devices from conventional aggression implied by the taboo, there was substantial overlap. These were both horrific acts. The very foundation of the taboo as intolerable also applied to certain non-chemical forms of violence, where these too could be seen as demanding interventionist activity by the US. As such, it is impossible to detach chemical weapons from the wider debate on Assad's brutality at the time, where it explicitly incorporates non-chemical weaponry. Moreover, this was not the only redline Obama drew at the time; he also set 'redlines' in relation to other aspects of policy, for example, on the economy (Obama, 2012f). Consequently, the extent and context of this threat was conditional at best, not least where its ideational structure existed as a rhetorical trope elsewhere.

Policy disincentives to action

The interpretation of the redline as a hawkish ultimatum is also an extremely ill fit with the rest of Obama's Syria policy. More specifically, a wider analysis of his position reveals that there was no incentive to make such a major threat at the time. Indeed, the redline went against the very nature of his declared approach. In understanding the president's foreign policy thinking, analysts have been reluctant to identify a definitive 'Obama Doctrine', not least where his decision-making record has frequently been criticised as ad hoc and 'improvisational' as opposed to encapsulating a clear vision, making it difficult to pin it down to a specific ideology (Hazelgrove, 2013). Yet key trends can be highlighted, including Obama's aversion to foreign policy as military might. Despite a willingness to become militarily involved in very selective humanitarian situations – most notably Libya (albeit as part of a multilateral strategy under NATO and in which the US took a very limited leadership role) – Obama has actively sought to avoid major armed action. This selectivity has attracted severe criticism: specifically the accusation that Obama is being hypocritical by taking action in Libya then apparently sitting back on Syria (even where it has been accepted that the latter represents a different type of civil conflict from the one seen in Libya; Patrick, 2011). Despite being prepared to take action against Muammar Gadhafi, and perhaps even because of that, Syria represented an opportunity to reassert his ideological reluctance towards a military-based foreign policy. Indeed, while some have accused Obama of presidential weakness in failing to construct a coherent foreign policy strategy that treats all humanitarian situations equally, others have hailed him as the next Jefferson because of his resistance to interventionist behaviour (Iaquinta, 2011: 33). Especially throughout his second term, and despite the escalation of Syria in the background, Obama (2014) has repeatedly espoused the idea that US foreign policy would not be based on armed intervention unless absolutely necessary for the protection of the US:

> As Commander in Chief, I have used force when needed to protect the American people, and I will never hesitate to do so as long as I hold this office. But I will not send our troops into harm's way unless it is truly necessary, nor will I allow our sons and daughters to be mired in open-ended conflicts. We must fight the battles that need to

be fought, not those that terrorists prefer from us: large-scale deployments that drain our strength and may ultimately feed extremism.

Obama's shift away from military options has been linked to two key reasons: decline and détente (although it has also been understood as a spectrum between these, and not necessarily two separate ideas; Kitchen, 2011). First is the American decline argument, which states that US power is on the wane. That while the US has retained superpower status within the world since *c*.1945, like the Roman and Ottoman Empires before it America cannot sustain such an extensive level of global influence (Kennedy, 1987). Even more specifically, that the US does not now possess sufficient power to impose largely unilateral decision-making on the rest of the world, as it attempted to do in the hegemonic heyday of the post-9/11 War on Terror. Admittedly, as Adam Quinn (2011) reminds us, we have had these debates on decline before; people have been 'crying wolf' on the end of American supremacy for decades. This is not a new argument by any stretch of the imagination, and the US has repeatedly disproved these ongoing predictions of its demise, often increasing its power in the process. Yet Quinn also cautions to remember that, in the children's story, the wolf did show up in the end. Just because the US retains its international status does not guarantee that this will continue to be the case. Or that, even where it does remain a superpower, this could not also be a situation in which the US is significantly less influential in relative terms, i.e. the gap between it and other major states could narrow, or even close. Within this context, Obama's pullback from highly aggressive and hegemonic behaviours surrounding the use of the military can be seen as a response to international systemic pressure. It is the recognition of his more conditional power, and the maintenance of some degree of international status by avoiding overstretch. Despite his outright refusal to accept the notion of decline, and his persistent references to American exceptionalism and American power, Obama can be seen as responding to a shift in state position, one that simply does not permit extensive armed action.

This argument, however, has relevance even for those who remain unconvinced of the decline thesis. For even if America is still strongest, the idea that it can take on every single crisis in the world is optimistic at best. Whatever we would like our hegemon to be capable of, total assurance of world peace is beyond feasible – at least in terms of military enforcement. Particularly around the issue of humanitarian intervention, there have long been questions about who should intervene and whether this must always be the US given the significant burden that role entails (Brown, 2004; Pattison, 2010; Wheeler, 2010). As such, Obama's reticence can be interpreted as an acceptance that, decline or no decline, the US simply does not have the military might to intervene effectively in all humanitarian scenarios, and that this requires a more selective strategy towards military employment overall: 'Whether the United States is in a condition of resurgence or decline at any given moment, it seems undeniable that its responsibilities, ambitions and pretensions in the global order make it difficult for the US leadership to set priorities and adequately attend to the domestic sources of American strength' (Allin, 2014: 166). This plays strongly into Obama's wider commitment to multilateralism, where this constitutes another key trend in Obama's foreign policy approach (Kaufman, 2014: 443). This idea is famously expressed in Obama's own book, *The Audacity of Hope* (2006), and it constituted a major aspect of his electoral promises in 2008 for which he, some would say prematurely, was awarded the Nobel Peace Prize shortly after entering office (Homolar, 2012: 104). This multilateralism has also been termed the 'responsibility doctrine' (Hachiguan and Shorr, 2012), in that it seeks to encourage other states to take on at least part of the burden of global security and lessen the pressure on the US. The US must reach out to the rest of the global community – or at least, carefully chosen allies – otherwise it risks an unsustainable position of over-commitment. Within this context, Obama has been called a pragmatist and/or a realist in that he appears to be adapting rationally to this global power situation, one in which hegemonic expressions of military strength are no longer possible (e.g. Huber, 2015). Obama has readjusted foreign policy in the face of circumstance; indeed, Donnette Murray (2013: 155) has explicitly described this as a 're-characterisation of US leadership'. And again, we see in this the same idea of Syria effectively representing a test case for this new foreign policy thinking. Whatever the pressures created around Libya, this has not precluded Obama's move away from old models of understanding, and particularly the heavily militaristic approach of his predecessor, President George W. Bush. Indeed, Libya has only created an impetus to try even harder to avoid the massive armed involvement that Obama shunned in respect of Syria.

Second, it is argued that foreign policy reticence on Syria is an issue of détente. This is expressed as the idea that unilateral or select coalition action is not appropriate; that the world is inherently multipolar and not structured around the whim of the US – an idea that has overlap with the concept of multilateralism discussed above (Kazemzadeh, 2010: 194). This is not simply the case that other nations must 'step up' in terms of sharing responsibility, but that they should be allowed to contribute without domination by the US. Global politics is exactly that: global. And the structure and character of international political action should reflect this. More specifically, this is a response to what Obama has perceived as the excesses of Iraq and his desire to avoid a similar conflict occurring on his watch. It is hardly controversial to state that the 2003 invasion will not go down in history as one of America's finest hours. Within that context, Obama has frequently highlighted this policy as something not to be relived, explicitly where this has been taken to represent the immoderation of US unilateral intervention; was related to a lack of credible evidence; and had made the world 'weary' of conflict (Obama, 2013e). In relation to this last point,

Obama would add: 'And I assure you, nobody ends up being more war weary than me.' Why then would Obama wish to risk another major foreign policy scandal, especially so close to the last? At the very least, Iraq cast a dark political shadow that could undermine any intervention as long as the Iraq invasion was still fresh in political memory. As Obama (2013f) admitted outright: 'I have resisted calls for military action because we cannot resolve someone else's civil war through force, particularly after a decade of war in Iraq and Afghanistan.' Not least where Obama had declared that part of his foreign policy was to rehabilitate the somewhat battered reputation of the US following action in Iraq, why would he consider a strategy in Syria that could potentially repeat the same mistake that was made in 2003?

Some position this within less pragmatic terms, instead presenting it as a case in which Obama had been burned by previous military engagements and was now scared of attempting the same, irrespective of his own personal brand of foreign policy (Hamid, 2013). As such, this so-called policy of 'leading from behind' has been discussed as resulting from a fear of controversy, not a more rational politics (Chesterman, 2011). Placing this within a wider context, parallels can be drawn between President Bill Clinton's experience in Somalia and his subsequent refusal to intervene in the 1994 Rwanda genocide, where this also represents a case in which the failure of prior humanitarian action influenced a willingness to engage in future activities. Clinton was so stung by the negative reaction to problems experienced in Somalia that he shied away from engagement in Rwanda, fearing a similar backlash. Critically, this comparison continues in terms of the response to Clinton's aversion. Just as Clinton was criticised for standing on the genocide's sideline, Obama's reserve over Syria has been condemned on the same grounds (e.g. Stevenson, 2014: 121). Obama too has let massacre occur because he is afraid that his actions in preventing it will be condemned. This opinion is reflected in analysis of Obama's multilateralism, which has been derided as a mask for anti-involvement. As Daniel Drezner (2011: 58) argues, Obama's multilateralism is 'designed to curtail the United States' overseas commitments ... and shift burdens onto global partners', an approach that has 'delivered underwhelming policy results'. Even for those who are not willing to write off the strategy as a failure, this is lukewarm at most (Skidmore, 2012).

Whatever the reason for Obama's policy stance, however, it is clear that the president saw no incentive to intervene in Syria at the time. Intervention would have gone against everything Obama had declared he was committed to, whether that came from conviction or fear. His ad hoc approach has caused wider confusion, in that, when looking at his time in office overall, it appears the president has been randomly discriminatory on intervention. Yet in relation to Syria, Obama never demonstrated anything other than a wish to avoid war. Intervention was never his desired policy. Consequently, the idea that he would start issuing extreme ultimatums is inconsistent with this declared position. Why would Obama place himself in a situation where there now existed a trigger for intervention when he had not been prepared to take that action in the first place? Where Obama had so blatantly pursued a non-military and multilateral strategy, why would he then choose to make such a hawkish and unilateral statement of intent, one more worthy of the Bush administration before him?

In addition, the redline was issued during a period in which prevailing political opinion was that the Assad regime was close to collapse. Throughout most of 2012, it was largely assumed the Syrian dictator was on borrowed time and that the growing opposition would soon bring about the regime's destabilisation, as had happened in several other states involved in the Arab Spring where revolutionary activism had challenged the existing government, for example, Tunisia and Egypt. Obama (2013d) explicitly declared: 'I'm confident that Asad will go. It's not a question of if, it's when.' Within this context, why would Obama believe that he needed any sort of ultimatum? If Assad was to fall, why would Obama think there would be any need to act? Indeed, there would soon be nothing to act against. While reminding Assad of the international expectation against chemical weapons use was important, there is nothing to suggest that this was understood as an aggressive prompt for intervention. Consequently, the redline was not an all-or-nothing commitment. In fact, to the extent that Obama was merely marking time on the Assad regime, there was every reason *not* to get involved – redline or no redline – and let events take their course without risking controversial intervention by the US. While Obama would accept that certain acts (among them chemical warfare) would significantly influence his position, this was fundamentally a waiting game as opposed to an offensive strategy. If the US could sit it out, there was no need to even talk about taking action.

Questioning the taboo

Consequently, a gap starts to emerge between the taboo and an active commitment to its preservation in that (a) the taboo itself is never mentioned at this initial stage, and (b) Obama's wider comprehension of the chemical arms situation in Syria did not reflect more orthodox expectations of the taboo. Specifically, in not referring explicitly to the taboo – instead using different forms of exclusionary and discriminatory language, i.e. the redline – this 'other' language was not confined to the chemical weapons threat. Within this context, Obama believed that chemical weapons use constituted a critical issue that would justify a shift, as yet undefined, in US foreign policy. But then so did other, explicitly conventional threats. This sheds a very different light on Obama's intention in drawing the redline, and even whether this can be accurately termed a 'redline' within the framework of the concept's typical understanding. No evidence exists to demonstrate that Obama was constructing an absolute ultimatum, one that replicated the taboo as a necessary reaction to intolerable behaviour. There is nothing to suggest Obama meant this as anything more than a recognition of the severity of the chemical weapons threat; indeed, there is nothing to suggest he could not equally have made the same statement about extreme forms of conventional massacre, where this would remain in compliance with the policy Obama had chosen to adopt. Indeed, the idea of an absolute and exclusive redline is conspicuously inconsistent with the rest of his expressed beliefs concerning Syria at the time. Here, Obama had gone out of his way to avoid any clear and binding commitment to intervention, preferring a policy of possibilities that would avoid backing himself into a specific commitment. Within this wider policy context, why then would Obama suddenly take a strong stand that diametrically opposed his existing position and which he believed to be unnecessary in the political circumstances?

To the extent that Obama's redline can be viewed as a type of major threat, it was a moderate deterrent at most. It was a warning that chemical weapons use would change the situation from the perspective of foreign policy. And in the age of the taboo, how could it not? Indeed, that there was a redline of any description on the use of chemical weapons was a recognition that this was an act that could not be ignored. Yet it was not a commitment to massive intervention, and it was not one that would be acted upon only in the case of chemical weapons use and not in cases of conventional forms of violence also. This was instead a case in which Obama was actually attempting to gently invoke the taboo as a limited form of deterrent, and in which Assad too would be bound by this normative expectation, especially if it had the weight of the US behind it. This was not the taboo as an all-out promise of future military action, or a case in which the strength of the taboo had overridden the previous policy desires Obama had set. This was instead a reminder of an expectation Obama believed Assad had at least some commitment to. As such, it constituted a significantly more subtle interpretation of the taboo – one that focused substantially more on the principles of the taboo as opposed to the element of punishment. Obama accepted that there was something intolerable concerning chemical weapons use that would demand specific political attention, even if it were not explicitly vocalised as the taboo. But this should not be confused with the taboo as a form of crusade.

As Skinner says, conceptual meaning is something that takes place within the intentions of the actor. And Obama intended something very different from a more orthodox construct of the taboo. While Obama clearly acknowledged the taboo's presence, the detail of acting on it and the president's own comprehension of what this should mean, however, was more complex and individualistic. Consequently, Obama's redline rhetoric can be revisited. This includes the way in which he was criticised for redefining the terms of the redline after its declaration. Far from the interpretation of the shift as an inherently flawed and weak threat, it was in fact a situation in which Obama strategically revised the line in order to manage expectations regarding his more moderate approach, and where this itself demonstrates that moderation. By blurring the criteria for violation, Obama's construction of the redline precluded interventionist demands because the trigger was unclear: if policy-makers did not know whether the line had been crossed, they could not insist on response. Obama could control foreign policy via this ambiguity, expressly in respect of evading military involvement. Obama's restatement of the line was not a 'bad' threat, but the act of someone trying to remove himself from a commitment he had never intended to make and which conflicted with his intention. He was endeavouring not only to change the terms under which intervention would become necessary (specifically to raise the threshold from something as limited as the movement of chemical weapons, which itself was already occurring), but also to push foreign policy expectations onto a softer footing that was more consistent with his own ambitions. Obama was effectively resetting the terms of debate in his favour.

The extreme backlash against this move, however, is testament to the strength of the taboo. The irony, therefore, is that the taboo played less of a role in guiding US foreign policy under Obama and more of a role in creating an unintended hype around the redline as an expression of the taboo (understood in conventional terms). Particularly once allegations of Assad's chemical deployment started to surface, Obama's statement inadvertently snowballed into a major commitment to retaliation. The prevalence of the taboo at the international level, combined with the expectation that violation was inherently connected to decisive punishment, meant that this would become something much more than Obama had ever intended. The situation took on the principles of the taboo as the ideal it is typically held up to be within general international discourse, and not in the terms envisaged by Obama. Of course, in line with the wider arguments here in terms of strategic use, such invocation of the taboo was sometimes manipulative in itself. For example, former Republican presidential candidate, John McCain (2013: S3288) – a major supporter of intervention in Syria – would regularly and loudly cite the redline as evidence that Obama was not living up to either his word or the actions anticipated by the taboo, which he claimed that this commitment directly called upon. In this sense, the taboo was a tool for both criticising Obama as a foreign policy leader and also stealthily promoting the interventionist cause. Yet it remained a more extensive construction in addition to these acts of strategic exploitation. The taboo embeds certain ideas and normative expectancies. Where these ostensibly represented an absolute refusal to accept the use of chemical weapons, so this was the expectation unintentionally evoked by Obama's redline statement.

Like Skinner's convention, this was a case in which pre-existing beliefs came to the fore. Within this theoretical context, the redline can be seen as a case where Obama was specifically not an innovating ideologist. As such, convention proceeded to overwhelm him. With no attempt by the president to control the

convention via rhetorical presentation, this effectively drowned out his introduction of a more modest understanding of the taboo. In effect, this inadvertently became a conflict of two narratives – Obama's more moderate stance, on
the one hand, and the expectations of the unconditional taboo, on the other.
In failing to address this other, predominant narrative, Obama could not skew
opinion towards his own interpretation. The idea of the taboo as convention was
so strong that it would effectively subsume any other conceptualisation of it, in
a case where there was no attempt to facilitate Obama's own interpretation. And
not least where Obama's redline threat was perceived as so uncertain in terms
of its construction and content, so this provided a perfect situation for others
to interpret Obama's statement within their own framework of understanding.
Obama's failure to establish and clarify his own personal comprehension of the
taboo among what was effectively his audience created the conceptual opportunity for others to cognise it in conventional terms. Consequently, Obama makes
an excellent case for the adoption of a Skinnerian perspective. He has shown
what happens when an actor ignores the complex intersection of convention
and agency: their own narrative collapses, and they get caught in the quicksand
of convention. In failing to view rhetoric as a conflict between these factors (as
per the theoretical model outlined in Chapter 1), Obama was unable to appreciate the necessity of presenting his softer interpretation of the taboo in innovating terms. Ignore Skinner at your peril.

In discussing the problems associated with the redline as an effective form
of threat, Sterner (2014) says that Obama misinterpreted events and the reality
of deterrence in issuing the warning that he did. There is a lot of relevance to
this statement, and yet, ultimately, this was not the main issue. This was primarily a case in which the president had underestimated the taboo. It was not
Obama's commitment to the norm that would see him trapped in a policy he
had never made, but his ignorance of its conceptual strength and reputation as
convention. Consequently, he involuntarily walked into a policy that he had not
intended. In respect of this, there was a joke at the time that his painting of the
redline had only painted him into a corner. Just as Tertrais had warned, Obama
was truly now a punchline.

Conclusion

Syria is an excellent example of the importance of the taboo in foreign policy
thinking. It is clear that Obama and other US policy-makers believed there
was something distinct, if not exclusive, about chemical weapons that had the
capacity to change an international political situation and the stakes inherent to that. Whatever the clarifications and caveats this book seeks to place
on the redline, it does not seek to undermine the idea of the taboo as a considerable influence on political actors. The taboo has major sway in respect of

international relations, with the power to shape the foreign policy discourses relevant to it. Yet what this chapter does demonstrate is that this influence is more complex and less absolute than its reputation would make out, to the extent that adherence to the taboo cannot be seen as inevitable – at least not in the extreme terms within which it has been conventionally portrayed. Looking at Obama's reaction to the escalating situation in the early days of the Syrian conflict, it was far from a situation in which the chemical weapons taboo dominated his thinking. In fact, it was a relatively minor aspect of his foreign policy calculation. While he knew the use of chemical weapons was indeed a 'game changer', it was not quite the rewriting of the rules that Obama envisaged. Indeed, the strength of the taboo is more apparent in the political and public reaction to his redline statement than in his own thinking on the Syria crisis. Obama was merely expressing a policy of redlines – specifically 'redlines' as plural, since it also included forms of extreme conventional massacre as an impetus to foreign policy escalation. This was not an issuing of a major ultimatum. Yet convention surrounding the taboo saw it taken this way. Consequently, it was not Obama's commitment to the taboo that would entrap him in this policy, but his failure to realise what citing the taboo would mean, explicitly in the absence of ideological innovation in promoting his own more moderate interpretation of the situation. And as Obama was about to discover, innovation would only get harder in the face of the taboo's violation. Assad was about to demonstrate this all too clearly by actually using these terrible devices, and ensnaring Obama even further in the chemical redline.

3

Ghouta and ideological innovation

A s 2012 WOUND down it was clear that Obama could not eschew his unintentional commitment to the redline. And yet, as nothing had transpired in terms of chemical weapons use by Assad so far, this was of no major significance. An ultimatum had inadvertently been set, but there was no evidence that this had been violated. With hindsight, this was a sword of Damocles hanging over the White House. But this was also a time in which Obama did not believe that the Syrian dictator could hold on to power and would soon be deposed, let alone that he would actually engage in chemical warfare. In this sense then, it did not matter that the redline had become exaggerated through false expectation. As long as Obama was not tested on it, there would be no issue.

But this is exactly what happened. Obama's position would soon clash with Assad's very real employment of chemical arms. While discussions of Assad's chemical activity tend to focus on the Ghouta attack of August 2013, it had become an issue long before, with allegations starting to emerge at the very end of December 2012 (definitely not what Obama had wanted for Christmas). These reports would multiply over the coming months, placing increased pressure on the US to act. And while Obama would initially attempt to delay having to face his own ultimatum by denying that the attacks had taken place, or by qualifying the evidence of chemical warfare as insufficient to justify a crossing of the redline, he would eventually have to accept the overwhelming proof that Assad had broken the taboo. It is here that the rhetoric of the taboo appears in Obama's foreign policy discourse. While the taboo had been decidedly absent from Obama's language prior to this, it was now a prominent aspect of the Syria narrative; after Ghouta, the taboo would find itself at the very front and centre of political discourse. This creates a question as to why. Why did this highly emotive rhetoric suddenly emerge within foreign policy statements? Was this simply a continuation of the trap that Obama had found himself in with respect to the taboo? That is, in being forced to accept the taboo, would Obama also then employ its associated rhetoric? This would seem the logical conclusion, not least within the context of a hard social constructivist argument. Yet this is an overly simplistic way of analysing the conceptual situation, one that ignores the role of actor agency and the strategic construction of narratives. As already stated in Chapter 1, language lies at a complex intersection of convention and agency – and this case is no exception. The innovating ideologist remains at the heart of understanding, even where it ostensibly relates to a situation of conventional restraint and/or the limited ability of an actor to be strategic. This is explored here from the first allegations of chemical weapons use by Assad, on to the now infamous chemical attack at Ghouta, and right through to Assad's agreement to accede to the Chemical Weapons Convention (CWC) and give up his chemical stockpiles for destruction.

Denying the evidence: before Ghouta

Allegations surrounding Assad's use of chemical arms first emerged in December 2012. These related to an incident on Christmas Eve in the western city of Homs. At the time of the attack, Homs was an opposition stronghold – dubbed the 'capital of the revolution' and held under bloody siege by regime forces. In terms of the allegations, news organisation *Al Jazeera* was first to report the use of chemical weapons as part of the offensive. It stated that seven people had been killed in the al-Bayyada district of Homs after victims had 'inhaled a "poisonous gas" used by government forces' during an attack (Al Jazeera Syria Live Blog, 2012). This was later claimed to have been a military chemical named Agent 15, which affects the nervous and respiratory systems. *Al Jazeera* cited their sources as activists in the region. One of them, Raji Rahmet Rabbou, told reporters: 'The situation is very difficult. We do not have enough facemasks. We don't know what this gas is but medics are saying it's something similar to Sarin gas' (ibid.). This eyewitness testimony was also the first evidence to emerge from medical and humanitarian staff in the area that it was a chemical strike. Based on the condition of victims they had treated, they expressed confidence that it had not been a purely explosive assault. Furthermore, the report contained a video that was by then already circulating virally on the Internet – a disturbing shot of an adult male victim being treated for severe respiratory difficulties resulting from chemical gas inhalation. The man was shown writhing and moaning in pain, choking violently while medical staff attempted to control his breathing.

Further confirmation of the attack came the next day from Major-General Abdul-Aziz Jassem al-Shallal, previously the chief of Syria's military police. After secretly working with the opposition for some time, he had chosen to publicly defect to the rebellion, citing Assad's aggressive and violent treatment of rebels and civilians as the reason for his defection. In a video posted on *Al Arabiya* news he said: 'I declare my defection from the regime's army because of its deviation of its fundamental mission to protect the nation and transformation into gangs of killing and destruction' (in *Al Arabiya*, 2012). Yet as well as constituting a high-profile defection, the video captured political interest as al-Shallal also stated that Assad forces had employed chemical weapons. Not least because of the redline, this was instantly picked up on as a signal that US policy could be about to change. Indeed, US diplomats would inform the White House that the Homs attack had almost certainly been chemical. While publicly the US government had gone out of its way to avoid addressing the issue, a diplomatic cable document signed by the US consul general in Istanbul, Scott Frederic Kilner, and leaked online in January 2013 via *Foreign Policy*, admitted that the evidence of a chemical strike was 'compelling' (Rogin, 2013). Critically, this did not confirm outright that chemical weapons had been used, but the recommendation clearly suggested that it was the likely explanation. Senior US government officials were quick to qualify the claim, instead attributing the event to an unfortunate use of riot control agent. It was supposedly a case in which a riot control agent might have been employed in a densely populated and contained area, which meant that the chemical could not disperse properly. As such, this had caused a few people to become accidentally overwhelmed by an extremely high concentration of the agent. This contradicts evidence in the cable itself, however, which cites evidence from neurologist Dr Nashwan Abu Abdo, who was in Homs at the time of the attack. Here he said the attack was an act of chemical warfare: 'It was a chemical weapon, we are sure of that, because tear gas can't cause the death of five people.' Despite this, the official line maintained there was insufficient proof that a chemical attack had taken place. White House National Security Spokesman, Tommy Vietor (in *Reuters*, 2013), explicitly stated that media reporting of the incident 'had not been consistent' with US intelligence on Syria's chemical weapons programme, although he also reinforced Obama's message that Assad's use of chemical weapons would constitute a 'tragic mistake' and that the dictator would be held accountable should any such action take place.

This tactic of denial would become a regular feature of the Obama administration's response to the increasing accusations of chemical warfare. In the case of Homs, the unreliability of evidence became something of a theme, or at least the idea that the evidence was sufficiently unreliable in terms of intervention. This is understandable given Obama's concerns about US military intervention in the post-Iraq era. A major aspect of the Iraq controversy was the way in which evidence was deliberately concocted to justify an otherwise prohibitively contentious policy. It is now widely accepted that the Bush administration falsified claims concerning Saddam Hussein's possession and stockpiling of weapons of mass destruction (WMD) in order to carry out the 2003 invasion (Easterbrook, 2002: 22; Murphy, 2003: 609; Kaufmann, 2004: 20; Kellner, 2007: 622–3; Sunstein, 2007: 36–7; Thrall, 2009). Admittedly, Bush still maintains he believed the threat to be genuine at the time – a claim he asserts repeatedly in his autobiography (Bush, 2010: 102, 235–7, 240). And yet the consensus is that this was not the case. The supposed WMD were an excuse. Specifically, the existence of WMD was a more tangible and credible excuse than the very vague idea that – as an evil dictator who had defied America multiple times in the past – Saddam was a natural target for removal via US foreign policy action. Indeed, Deputy Secretary of Defense, Paul Wolfowitz (in Cirincione, 2007: 150), effectively admitted this when he said that the WMD threat was merely a convenient reason for invasion: 'For bureaucratic reasons we settled on one issue, weapons of mass destruction [to justify the Iraq mission], because it was the one reason everyone could agree on.'

The infamous WMD that never were will not be quickly forgotten. Within this context, it is hardly surprising that Obama would be reticent about relying on information that was not 100 per cent guaranteed, not least where there were concerns over the allegations' reliability in respect of chemical weapons in Syria and so, in effect, the extent to which the taboo had been broken. Obama did not want another Iraq. And in particular, he did not want another incident in which the US intervened, all guns blazing, only for it to turn out that the evidence was flawed – or even worse, made up. He did not want anyone to be able to accuse him of putting US security at stake on the basis of inaccurate information:

> And I'm very mindful of the fact that around the world – and here in Europe in particular – there are still memories of Iraq and weapons of mass destruction accusations and people being concerned about how accurate this information is. Keep in mind, I'm somebody who opposed the war in Iraq, and I am not interested in repeating mistakes of us basing decisions on faulty intelligence. (Obama, 2013g)

Yet this was also a tactic of avoidance and delay. In short, if the line had not been crossed then there could be no expectation for Obama to react. And the best way to ensure this was to simply shut one's eyes to the redline. It was easier to focus only on the unreliability of the evidence and, therefore, effectively deny that the line had been violated by failing to sustain or accept the proof that it had. As part of this, it can be noted that Obama's concerns over Iraq were highly opportune. While Obama had long expressed the view that Iraq was an unjustifiable strategy, this assertion also now provided an excellent means of strategically supporting his claims relating to the role of evidence within foreign policy decision-making processes on Syria. A reminder of the chaotic and distressing situation that had emerged with respect to Iraq was particularly handy in stating that the US could not act in Syria without indisputable proof – especially where this allowed Obama to evade calls for intervention. The logic was clear: unsubstantiated evidence was a key problem in the Iraq scandal. Consequently, why then would the US risk repeating this in Syria by jumping in recklessly without explicit proof? Not doing so was presented as the practical and pragmatic option. It was also one that facilitated Obama's strategy of denial.

Obama would soon have much to deny. Two months after Homs, further allegations hit the headlines regarding a chemical weapons attack in Aleppo – Syria's largest city, and often cited as the oldest city in the world. Twenty-five people were reported dead and approximately 110 injured in a sarin attack on the Khal al-Assal neighbourhood on 19 March 2013 (Pita and Domingo, 2014: 392). The area was government controlled at the time of the strike, yet rebels had recently made significant incursions, including taking the local police academy just a couple of weeks earlier. It was later alleged that regime forces had targeted the chemically armed missile used in the attack at the police academy itself, but that this had missed and hit a civilian area instead. Crucially, the chemical nature of the strike was not in dispute this time. Indeed, the Syrian government was the first to identify it as such, specifically where they attributed responsibility to the opposition (*Strategic Comments*, 2013a: 1). The regime would also publicly call on the UN to investigate it specifically as a chemical act. (The matter was deemed to be of UN concern as the Organisation for the Prohibition of Chemical Weapons (OPCW) could not be involved at this stage since Syria was not then a member of the CWC.) In support of its claims, the government circulated photos and videos of the strike and also encouraged news organisations to publicise them, alongside interviews with survivors. One such interview by the Syrian Arab News Agency was with a young girl awaiting treatment in a nearby hospital. She said: 'My chest closed up. I couldn't talk. I couldn't breathe ... We saw people falling dead to the floor. My father fell, he fell and now we don't know where he is' (Holmes and Solomon, 2013). This fits in with other eyewitness testimony collected at the time, as UN investigators outline:

> The interviewed witnesses reported on experiencing or observing the following symptoms: irritation of skin, miosis, impaired vision, foaming from the mouth, weakness, convulsions, shortage of breath and loss of consciousness. One survivor stated that 'the air was static and filled with a yellowish-green mist and filled of a strong pungent smell, possibly resembling sulphur.' (UN, 2013b)

The relevance of the government propaganda lies in the way this was constructed as an attack by the opposition. The chemical character of the strike was played up only as long as the Assad regime could attribute blame to alleged rebel activity. In line with this book's theme of strategic narratives, the Syrian government was creating a negative image of their adversaries as immoral and unnecessarily violent. Consequently, Obama was far from the only strategic actor in this game: Assad too was using narrative construction in order to uphold his threatened regime. Assad, moreover, was not alone in this effort. Also quick to make their point was Russia, who instantly came to the support of the Syrian government by backing up their claims that it had been the opposition who had carried out the attack (*Russia Today*, 2013). In a blatant show of support for the regime, Putin publicly maintained Assad's innocence and asserted that evidence obtained by Russia clearly indicated rebel responsibility. Yet denials would also come swiftly from the opposition itself, and there soon began a tense battle of blame as to who had carried out the strike in question. Each side would vehemently protest their innocence in the matter, blaming the other for the assault instead.

Ultimately, the UN would officially lay that blame at Assad's door, although the investigation into what had happened in Aleppo would take time to complete. This was thanks, first, to bureaucratic wrangling over what exactly should be investigated, as Assad would attempt to limit the inquiry to Aleppo, whereas other member states were keen to see the investigative remit extended to other allegations of chemical weapons use; and second as a consequence of Aleppo becoming sidelined in favour of a focus on events that would later take place at Ghouta. In the end, however, and much to Syria's chagrin, UN involvement in investigating the event went considerably beyond Aleppo and would eventually report on a long – although not comprehensive – list of other chemical incidents. As well as Homs and Aleppo, it included: Salaquin, 17 October 2012; Darayya, 13 March 2013, Otaybah, 19 March 2013; Adra, 24 March 2013; Jobar, 12–14 April; Darayya, 25 April 2013; Saraqueb, 29 April 2013; Sheik Maqsood, 13 April 2013; Qasr Abu Samrah, 14 May 2013; and Adra, 23 May 2013. It would also cover Ghouta, as well as a number of events after that incident: Bahhariyeh, 22 August 2013; Jobar, 24 August 2013; and Ashrafiah Sahnaya, 25 August 2013 (UN, 2013b: 3–6). Overall, this evidence was taken to indicate that the Assad regime had undertaken a systematic programme of chemical warfare. Not only had Assad used chemical weapons, but these arms had been employed as an embedded aspect of the government's wider military strategy.

The growing evidence that would feature so prominently in the UN's report made the situation extremely difficult for Obama, who was now uncomfortably ensnared within an ultimatum that he had never desired. The proof was mounting up faster than he could deny it. It was now increasingly unrealistic and unfeasible to claim that chemical weapons had not been used. Consequently, US policy instead shifted towards the idea that, while usage had clearly occurred, it could not be fully ascertained *how* the chemical weapons had been employed and, critically, *who* had employed them. A new uncertainty was played up: if not over use, then over the details of use. Obama (2013b) said: 'We have evidence that chemical weapons have been used. We don't know when, where, or how they were used.' In a further response (again cited in full in order to demonstrate the sheer extent of prevarication characterising his discourse at this time), the president said:

> With respect to chemical weapons, we intend to investigate thoroughly exactly what happened. Obviously in Syria right now you've got a war zone. You have information that's filtered out, but we have to make sure that we know what we can prove. So I've instructed my teams to work closely with all other countries in the region and international organizations and institutions to find out precisely whether or not

this red line was crossed. I will note, without at this point having all the facts before me, that we know the Syrian Government has the capacity to carry out chemical weapon attacks. We know that there are those in the Syrian Government who have expressed a willingness to use chemical weapons, if necessary, to protect themselves. Everybody who knows the facts of the chemical weapons stockpiles inside Syria as well as the Syrian Government's capabilities, I think, would question those claims. But I know that they're floating out there right now. The broader point is, is that once we establish the facts, I have made clear that the use of chemical weapons is a game changer. And I won't make an announcement today about next steps because I think we have to gather the facts. (Obama, 2013a)

Once again this was constructed as a situation in which the available knowledge was insufficient to justify a pro-interventionist stance. Allegations of opposition use could be exploited in order to sustain the argument that the evidence had yet to reach a point at which action could be considered acceptable, or that an indisputable target for US foreign policy could be ascertained. Moreover, this was a way for Obama to counter the idea that he was not taking action. Obama (2013b) explicitly stated of his administration: 'We're not waiting. We're not standing by.' This was not a case in which Obama was refusing to act, or that his commitment to chemical weapons use as a game changer would not apply. Instead, it was an unavoidable situation in which he did not yet possess the necessary evidence to intervene at that point. A violation had taken place, but, without evidence as to the identity of the violator, the retaliation inherent to the principles of the taboo could not be enacted. The fact that this complied with Obama's resistance to intervention was, of course, purely coincidental.

Similar disclaimers were more widely applied to US intelligence. On 25 April 2013, Miguel Rodriguez, Assistant to the President and Director of the Office of Legislative Affairs, sent intelligence information to Senators John McCain and Carl Levin indicating Assad's use of sarin, albeit with the caveat that further evidence was required. This was specifically the claim that uncertainty concerning the 'chain of custody' (i.e. whether the opposition could have acquired chemical weapons from regime stockpiles, or whether these were too highly secured for that to happen) precluded the intelligence communities from confirming 'how the exposure occurred and under what conditions' (in Nitkitin *et al.*, 2013: 12). While these claims of sarin use were far from assured, therefore, it was clear that the evidence was intensifying. Indeed, only the day before these intelligence letters were sent, there were new reports from opposition activists that Syrian forces had employed chemical weapons at the town of Adra, north-east of Damascus. One of many chemical attacks that would be launched against the Damascus area over the coming months, it was a significant assault that 'left men foaming at the mouth and dogs twitching in the street' (Shachtman and Lynch, 2013). It also represented a key point in the growing criticism of Obama's apparent inaction, specifically the idea that Assad was effectively baiting the US through chemical weapons use. Muhammed Saed (in *Syria Direct*, 2013), a physician working at the Adra field hospital at the time of the attack, said: 'The [Assad] government is testing the Western countries every day by using chemicals on different levels.' The net was closing in on Obama.

It is here that Obama started to explicitly adopt the language of the taboo, albeit on a highly limited and selective basis. The exact detail of this employment will be explored in greater depth in the next chapter, but the key point at this stage of the analysis is that the rhetoric of the taboo now emerged as a clear aspect of US foreign policy discourse relating to the Syrian crisis:

[W]e have established international law and international norms that say when you use these kinds of weaponry, you have the potential of killing massive numbers of people in the most inhumane way possible, and the proliferation risks are so significant that we don't want that genie out of the bottle. (Obama, 2013b)

We have to act prudently. We have to make these assessments deliberately. But I think all of us, not just in the United States, but around the world, recognize how we cannot stand by and permit the systematic use of weapons like chemical weapons on civilian populations. So this is going to be something that we'll be paying a lot of attention to, trying to confirm, and mobilize the international community around those issues. (Obama, 2013d)

Admittedly, this was not yet the dominant narrative it would become after Ghouta. Before this, Obama still upheld the redline as a fundamentally unspecified concept, as opposed to an immediate trigger: '[T]his is not an on-or-off switch. This is an ongoing challenge that all of us have to be concerned about' (ibid.). Moreover, it was not until 13 June 2013 that the White House officially conceded that Assad had employed such devices 'on a small scale against the opposition multiple times in the last year' (in Nitkitin *et al.*, 2013: 2). And even then, in terms of the redline, the president did little to react aside from authorising a relatively minor expansion of military assistance to opposition forces in Syria. Yet this still represents a new discursive recognition of the taboo, one not previously evident within Obama's rhetoric. Even in setting the redline, the taboo was not a conceptual framework that was ever drawn upon previously. Consequently, this represents a considerable change in terms of foreign policy narrative construction. The idea of an inherent and international expectation against these contentious armaments was now a part of Obama's rhetorical expression. And it was one that would become even more prevalent after the terrible events at Ghouta that would occur that summer.

Chemical! Chemical!

One year and one day after Obama declared the redline, Assad carried out the most vicious chemical weapons assault of the Syrian civil conflict. On the morning of 21 August 2013, a major sarin strike took place in Ghouta during which an estimated 1,400 people were killed and over 4,000 injured. This was the deadliest chemical assault since Saddam's bombardment of Halabja in 1988. The Syrian military had been attempting to expel rebel forces from the densely populated Damascus districts – and indeed, as the previous section demonstrates, this was far from the first, or the last, chemical attack against this area. Yet Ghouta stands out because of the sheer number of fatalities caused, especially where so many of the dead were non-combatants. Lawyer and activist Razan Zaitouneh (in *Democracy Now!*, 2013) said: 'We couldn't believe our eyes ... I haven't seen such death in my whole life.' It took over 16 hours to bury the first wave of the dead as there were so many corpses to deal with. In particular, the high number of children killed made this incident of significant international concern. After investigating the attack, the UN (2013c: 1) expressed with 'profound shock and regret ... the conclusions that chemical weapons were used on a relatively large scale, resulting in numerous casualties, particularly among civilians and including many children'. The report explicitly declared that this was a war crime and a violation of the 1925 Geneva Protocol.

The attack was a two-pronged strike against the Zamalka district in the east of the Ghouta region, and the Moadamiya district to the west. Zamalka was attacked early in the morning, between 2 and 3 a.m. Moadamiya followed a few hours later at 5 a.m., shortly after morning prayers. Once again, the Assad regime was swift to deny its involvement, with strong international support from Russia. Russian Foreign Minister, Sergei Lavrov, in particular was extremely vocal concerning supposed evidence discovered by Russia that this had been a rebel-organised attack. One of the most prominent pieces of proof he put forward was the 50-page testimony of Lebanese Carmelite nun, Mother Agnes Mariam de la Croix, challenging the reliability of video evidence and suggesting the attacks had been carried out by the regime. These videos started appearing on YouTube immediately after the strikes had taken place. These would quickly become viral because of the shocking images of the dead and dying, as well as hospitalised victims. Indeed, the scenes of hundreds of corpses lying in rows, wrapped in white sheets, are now emblematic of the slaughter that took place. Yet Mother Agnes – a well-known supporter of Assad – disputed the credibility of the videos, making the claim that the entire attack had been a fabrication by the opposition (Jalabi, 2013). Most controversially, she said the children who had supposedly been killed and left lying in rows – whom she termed 'angels', because of their subjection to the manipulative whim of the opposition – were not dead, but drugged and made by rebels to lie still as photographs were taken of them (Mother Agnes de la Croix, 2013: 3). She stated that the opposition had artificially created these scenes to falsely accuse the Assad government of chemical assault. There were even accusations that the US had been involved in the charade, that the alleged deceit was a bid to create a 'false flag' event in order to justify intervention in the civil conflict (Levesque and Choussudovsky, 2013).

Despite this, however, there was no doubt expressed by the UN that it was Assad who was responsible for the strike, and that it was chemical in nature. Witness accounts clearly demonstrated that victims had experienced a range of symptoms associated with chemical warfare, including 'shortness of breath, disorientation, rhinorrhea (runny nose), eye irritation, blurred vision, nausea, vomiting, general weakness, and eventually loss of consciousness' (UN, 2013c: 6). In addition to eyewitness testimony, scientific analysis of the target site detected sarin at the scene of the attack, as well as in biological samples taken from victims. It was also argued that the very nature of the attack's effect signalled a chemical strike. There was very little evidence of physical destruction – and certainly not enough to have caused the reported number of fatalities by conventional explosives alone. There would have been considerably more physical damage to local buildings and infrastructure if explosive force by itself had been the cause.

These claims are supported by a Human Rights Watch (HRW) report on the event, which confirmed regime forces as the aggressor. HRW (2013a) states it could find no evidence that the rebels had acquired such weaponry, and that the explosives employed were identical to those held by the Syrian army. The report provides an in-depth account of the types of weapon used in the strike. Two types of armament were employed. First was a surface-to-surface missile of approximately 330 mm in diameter, a weapon that the Syrian army was known to have produced and stockpiled. Second was a 140-mm surface-to-surface rocket, which had almost certainly come to Assad from the Soviets. Both were equipped to deliver the nerve agent sarin. Particularly with regard to the 140-mm rockets that were used at Moadamiya, only three types of warhead have been designed for such missiles: high explosive fragmentation, white phosphorous, and a chemical warhead containing 2.2 kg of sarin (ibid.: 5). As there was no evidence that an explosive warhead did the damage experienced at Ghouta, since the extent of the physical damage was extremely small, HRW maintains that logically it must have been a chemical assault. This is backed up by eyewitness accounts:

> One rocket hit around 5 a.m. We were praying in the mosque near the turbi area 400 meters away [from the strike site]. We heard the strike and went to the site to help the wounded. We thought it was a regular rocket but when we got there someone was screaming 'Chemical! Chemical!' The rocket fell in the first floor of a four-storey apartment building. Everyone in the building died in their sleep. It didn't cause a lot of destruction ... It made an opening in the wall. After the person was screaming, people covered their faces, with shirts dunked in water. We didn't smell anything, but people were fainting. I covered my face with a shirt dunked in water and was rescuing people and taking them to the medical center ... If anyone entered the building where the rocket fell they would faint. (Ibid.: 4)

The same applied to Zamalka, where 330-mm missiles were used. Again, nothing in the witness accounts or the resulting evidence could be seen to support a solely explosive incident. As Zamalka resident, Um Hassan (in Mahmood and Chulov, 2013), recalls:

> We were in a panic to take the children and run out of Zemalka to any nearby villages. People who were sleeping in their homes died in their beds because they could not feel the effects of the attacks. I still feel sick and drowsy with all the smoke I breathed. As we were trying to [leave], I could see people coming out of their homes but they would fall down. We tried to help some of them but they died before we got them to the hospital. We picked up a woman with her two kids, the rocket had hit their house but ... they all died. I could see the foam coming out of their mouths and noses.

Invoking the taboo

After Ghouta, the chemical weapons taboo became a staple of Obama's foreign policy discourse on Syria. During an interview with PBS one week later, on 28 August, Obama discussed the attack; while he would still display caution in unconditionally attributing blame to Assad, a major change in his rhetoric was evident, wherein it was explicitly and strongly framed within the context of the taboo. In answering a question as to whether military action would now be used, he said:

> But what I also said was that if the Assad regime used chemical weapons on his people, that that would change some of our calculations. And the reason has to do with not only international norms but also America's core self-interest. We've got a situation in which you've got a well-established international norm against the use of chemical weapons. Syria has one of the largest stockpiles in the world of chemical weapons ... So what I've said is that we have not yet made a decision [on military intervention], but the international norm against the use of chemical weapons needs to be kept in place. And nobody disputes – or hardly anyone disputes that chemical weapons were used on a large scale in Syria against civilian populations ... We have concluded that the Syrian government in fact carried these out. And if that's so, then there need to be international consequences. (In PBS, 2013)

This rhetoric would escalate over the next few days, including in Obama's key Rose Garden speech on 31 August. This speech was important in that it outlined Obama's response to the crossing of the redline. He declared his acceptance that, given this ultimatum, some form of comeback was now required. Admittedly, this was a highly qualified response. Obama announced that he intended to launch air strikes against Assad in retaliation for the breaking of the taboo, *but* this came with the caveat that he would seek congressional approval for such action before doing so. While stating that this was not politically necessary and that he possessed the executive power to enact air strikes regardless of Congress, this was a case in which he was not prepared to go forward unless he had the clear backing of the US government. This statement was framed within the terms of the taboo. While announcing his proposed action, Obama (2013h) said of Ghouta: 'Now, this attack is an assault on human dignity ... It risks making a mockery of the global prohibition on the use of chemical weapons.' He continued: 'What's the purpose of the international system that we've built if a prohibition on the use of chemical weapons that has been agreed to by the governments of 98 percent of the world's people and approved overwhelming by the Congress of the United States is not enforced?' The same rhetoric was employed elsewhere at the time:

> This norm against using chemical weapons that 98 percent of the world agrees to is there for a reason, because we recognize that there are certain weapons that, when used, can not only end up resulting in grotesque deaths, but also can end up being transmitted to nonstate actors, can pose a risk to allies and friends of ours like Israel, like Jordan, like Turkey, and unless we hold them to account, also sends a message that international norms around issues like nuclear proliferation don't mean much. (Obama, 2013i)

Between the Rose Garden and Obama's annual address to the UN on 24 September less than a month later, all of Obama's speeches on Syria and chemical weapons condemn those weapons as intolerable. Of these speeches, 57 per cent (16 out of 28) explicitly mention the taboo, or chemical weapons use as a violation of international law (63 and 27 per cent, respectively). In terms of statements on Syria more generally (i.e. irrespective of chemical weapons; 36 statements), this means a considerable 44 per cent of presidential statements at the time appealed to the taboo as the basis of future foreign policy.

Obama, the innovating ideologist

In the wake of Ghouta, Obama's strategy of denial could no longer hold. The evidence was simply too compelling, and the scale of the attack too great, to continue the illusion that the redline had not been violated. Subsequently, this also meant that the interventionist expectations that had developed around the violation could similarly not be sidestepped. If the line had been crossed, Obama had to act. The extent to which Obama had (not) genuinely intended that obligation to uphold the chemical weapons taboo in Syria was irrelevant. Where the redline had been interpreted as an all-or-nothing commitment, and as long as he failed to reconceptualise that understanding in accordance with his real intentions, then Obama had to stand by his inadvertent policy – even if that opposed what he had envisioned the redline to mean and what he desired as a foreign policy resolution to the crisis. Obama was effectively told: put your money where your mouth is (even if your mouth never meant to say it in the first place).

If anything, this was a simple case of credibility. Obama's reputation was at stake, as was that of the US. To not act on the redline would have been an ostensible sign of weakness and extremely poor leadership. This applied both in terms of Obama's position as president and America's ability to exert power on a global scale. It would have been political suicide for Obama not to respond, not least where failure to respond could be seen to effectively sanction the use of chemical weapons. Specifically, by indicating that violations would go unpunished, Obama would have sent a message that the taboo could be broken and there would be no comeback or consequence to this, hence removing any disincentive for actors to engage in chemical warfare. Consequently, Obama was painted as a central figure determining the taboo's future – with the redline the key decision point and where proponents of the chemical weapons control would not tolerate a weak conclusion. As Brad Sherman, Democratic Congressional representative for California, said of this matter:

> Now Assad has crossed that red line, it is America's red line. If we do not act, Assad will use chemical weapons many times in the future. They may be decisively successful for him, and dictators for decades to come will learn from Assad's lesson that chemical weapons on civilians used on a mass scale can be effective and that the 1925 protocol against their use is a dead letter. (In US Cong., 2013c: 25)

John Kerry added, as part of the same set of congressional hearings:

> [W]e have no chance ... if we back off and give him [Assad] a message of impunity. We will have said to him, nobody cares, gas your people, you do what you need to stay in office, and we are backing off. That would be – I honestly find – I mean, that would be one of those moments in history that will live in infamy. And there are some of those moments: Munich; a ship off the coast of Florida that was sent back filled with Jews who then lost their lives to gas because we didn't receive them. There are moments when you have to make a decision, and I think this is one of those moments. (Ibid.: 32)

Consequently, the redline was a policy restraint. Indeed, the likelihood of some form of intervention at the time was described as 'inevitable' because of the expectation that Obama must respond (*Strategic Survey*, 2014: 182). Furthermore, it should be noted that these discussions were taking place just weeks before the twelfth anniversary of 9/11 – hardly the best time to risk looking like a frail and feeble president, especially on matters of international security. As such, Obama could not remove himself from the commitment that the redline had placed upon him. Within such a context, it would be extremely easy to reduce this to a case of rhetorical entrapment as well. Obama had become caught in the redline, which would then logically lead to his adoption of the language associated with it. In having to engage with the issues of the taboo (however inadvertent that engagement was), the president would also employ the rhetoric that accompanied it. The chemical weapons taboo is extremely prominent and the rhetoric surrounding it highly established. Even where this is understood as a political construction as opposed to the expression of an essentialist understanding, it is clear that linguistic convention in respect of the taboo is both pervasive and deeply engrained within political thinking. Consequently, it could be argued that it is simply not possible to talk about the taboo without applying the linguistic framework that defines it. Obama was just as trapped in rhetorical convention as the convention of the taboo itself.

But this explanation barely scratches the surface. The highly one-sided perception of Obama as utterly defenceless against a tide of normative expectation is theoretically convenient, certainly, but it fails to capture the complexity of what was happening. Critically, this is not to dispute the way in which Obama was initially overwhelmed by the taboo – a clear case of convention winning out in the absence of any counter rhetorical innovation by the president. Obama went into the situation of Assad's chemical weapons use pre-constrained by the redline and its associated convention. This did not, however, preclude his ability to strategically construct narratives consequential to it. While this example demonstrates the sheer complexity of the intersection between agency and existing understandings, it is not a case in which the hard social constructivists win. As Skinner seeks to express with his comment that 'we may be freer than we sometimes suppose', language is not a prison. Convention may constitute a serious constriction on narrative construction, but there remains room for the innovating ideologist.

At the centre of this was Obama's exertion of control over the terms of his entrapment. If he was now facing a situation in which intervention was seemingly unavoidable (despite his best efforts to deny that the redline had been crossed), then he needed to ensure that intervention occurred under the best possible circumstances. As already stated, Obama was extremely concerned about the prospects of another Iraq, something he had previously tried to evade by refusing to intervene. Yet if the option of avoiding intervention was now off the table thanks to Assad's use of chemical weapons, then the situation had to be reframed in terms that could not permit comparison with Iraq. If Obama could not escape the redline, he could at least make it more palatable should intervention prove to be the only way out. In response, portraying the situation as one in which a hideous and unforgivable contravention of international moral values had taken place created a valuable narrative. The taboo was an ideal way of turning Syria into the most worthy of humanitarian crises. While this would also have the unintended consequence of supporting the argument for intervention by playing up the moral need to respond, this was less of a concern in a political environment where some form of intervention appeared inescapable. Indeed, Obama had at this stage proposed air strikes, which – although not the extreme 'boots on the ground' of Iraq – required an excuse to carry through. The proposition of air strikes was not uncontroversial and Obama was set to face serious opposition within Congress on the matter. In this way, Obama was using the taboo to set out his justification surrounding the congressional vote on air strikes, and also as preparation for any escalation in military action against Assad. If Obama was effectively being forced into pushing the button on greater US involvement, he could at least push it in a flattering light.

71

And the taboo is extremely flattering. Not least where it is defended as a necessary and upstanding aspect of the international political system, supporting the taboo is unlikely to do an actor political harm in terms of reputation. In fact, it could present Obama in extremely positive terms. This included looking like a strong and righteous president – where this occurs in the sense of Obama seeking to show that he had the leadership strength to make a decision and stand by it, as well as the added bonus of appearing as a moral and humanitarian leader. The aura of upholding the taboo is a particularly becoming one. This was a case not merely of being the 'good guy', but of constructing a political image of Obama as a powerful, virtuous, and honourable force fighting for what was right in international politics. It was also an image of protection. Chemical weapons are highly feared. Whether seen as a genuine threat or the constructed product of stigmatisation, these are horrific devices that inspire extreme dread and anxiety. Within this context, Obama was a knight in shining armour. He successfully constructed himself as the one with the power to stop chemical attacks and to take control on behalf of the international community. Obama would secure the world from dictators wielding chemical arms. Amid criticism that Obama was being weak on Syria, this was a very timely way of improving his profile, both nationally and internationally.

Consequently, Obama's employment of the chemical weapons taboo was a strategic narrative in that it deliberately fulfilled certain political needs. The president was constrained, but this was not a case in which he had nothing to work with in a strategic sense. Obama has not been heralded as a great rhetorician for nothing. Despite the conflict between the redline and his preferred policy, there was still scope for him to identify the strategic benefit in the idea of convention, even where this exceeded what he was initially willing to commit to. While 'making the best of what you have' is not an ideal expression of the situation, it certainly gives a sense of what had occurred. The redline may have ensnared Obama, but what he did next – specifically in coping with this unexpected policy commitment – was a rhetorically strategic act. Obama engaged with the taboo in a way that would best serve his interests and give him the best possible advantage. As such, Obama's actions constituted the calculated adoption of an available narrative construct, not merely a falling into a rhetorical trap.

In understanding this, Skinner's work is again relevant – specifically his claim concerning ideological innovation and the idea that the ideologist who is willing to challenge and change existing ideas is more likely to get what they want. In this sense, Obama 'gets' something by being strategic. He does not get exactly what he is after, however. Because he did not change the convention of the taboo, he only gets a bit of what he desires. The implication being that, if he had succeeded in terms of ideological innovation when the redline was first set, he could have overcome the constraint that would follow. Yet while Skinner encourages the modification of language for the purposes of achieving self-interest, this does not necessarily make the actor who adheres to convention any less of an innovating ideologist; a less successful one perhaps, but still an agent of rhetorical manipulation. That is, convention can be used for deliberate and exploitative purposes – that convention itself is a facilitator for ideological innovation – but also the strength of convention can be integral to its strategic value. Convention can be an extremely powerful concept. It can be so resilient that it offers value to the user when applied in its current state. The emotive and strategic pull associated with it is so intense that using it in its existing form can be equally, if not more, manipulative than seeking to change it, not least where the latter would have to be accompanied by a complex narrative capable of suc-cessfully reframing that idea. Within this context, the chemical weapons taboo stands out as a particularly effective linguistic resource, ripe for manipulation. It could be used to shape debate precisely because that framing was so extensive. It was because people had already bought into the concept that they were forced into compliance with Obama's narrative. As such, there was every reason for Obama to allow himself to be constrained by convention where it provided an ideal basis for a strategic narrative, one that was largely guaranteed to be effec-tive because of the potency of the convention behind it.

Critically, this is not to suggest that Obama's commitment to the taboo was purely strategic. Given the social pervasiveness of the taboo and the horrific nature of the chemical attacks carried out in Syria, it would be inappropriate to assume that Obama did not possess any inherent or genuine aversion to the use of chemical devices. Yet this does not preclude the acceptance that those same ideas can be applied strategically. Fears – no matter how sincerely felt – also provide an opportunity for the manipulation of policy, not least where their emotive character makes them particularly effective as rhetorical devices. The chemical weapons taboo was an excellent rhetorical tool for achieving Obama's aims within the limited context of the redline, and his strategic move in using it should not be masked by an over-simplistic comprehension of linguistic entrap-ment or social construction.

The CWC solution

This strategic employment of the chemical weapons taboo would also underpin what happened next, or rather what did not, i.e. the air strikes. The congres-sional vote did not take place. Instead an alternative solution was, accidentally, put forward. Speaking at a news conference soon after Obama's Rose Garden speech, Kerry inadvertently outlined a potential diplomatic solution based on Assad's official elimination of chemical weapons. In response to a question on whether there was anything Assad could do to avoid air strikes, the Secretary of State replied: 'Sure, he could turn over every single bit of his chemical weapons to the international community in the next week – turn it over, all of it without delay and allow the full and total accounting [of it], but he isn't about to do it and it can't be done' (in Mohammed and Osborn, 2013). While Kerry would later claim that the idea of eliminating Assad's chemical weapons had been discussed behind the scenes by the US and Russia the previous week, it was largely accepted that this statement was unintended. In fact, it was initially described as a major gaffe on the part of Kerry in having spoken out of turn. Gaffe or not, it quickly turned into something of a political coup. Why wouldn't it work? If the proposed air strikes were specifically a response to chemical weapons, why could the situation not be resolved by removing those chemical armaments from the equation? The unsustainability of this argument will be discussed in later chapters, but at the time this appeared to be a logical solution, not least at a point where Obama was more than willing to discuss any alternative that would preclude the militaristic activity he had never wanted in the first place. If Assad could be required to accede to the CWC and submit to both the official inspection and destruction of his stockpiles, then this would get the redline off Obama's back. It was not as if Syria claimed to hold any basic objection to the concept of the CWC. It was a signatory of the 1925 Geneva Protocol, which banned first use of chemical weapons. The rationale for failing to support the 1993 agreement had always been linked to Israel rather than any conceptual hostility. Syria had long maintained that it would be willing to sign the CWC if Israel agreed to sign the Nuclear Non-Proliferation Treaty and disbanded its nuclear programme. Within this context, Syria's accession was always understood as highly conditional, but not written off. Where the threat of US retaliation could be used to effectively override the Israel issue, the CWC provided a way out of the air strikes stand-off.

The US was not the only country that saw this political opportunity. Russia too expressed support for it, and on 9 September Putin issued a proposal to Syria for it to accede to the CWC. While air strikes were not technically taken off the table (despite Syria's attempt to make this conditional on the removal of that threat), it was understood that the deal would stave off all military action by the US and that the congressional vote would be withdrawn. With Assad's initial consent secured, negotiations took place over the following week. This led to a joint framework arrangement for the disposal of Syria's chemical weapons by the US and Russia, which was released on 14 September. It demanded that Assad accede to the CWC, release full details of his stockpiles and facilities, and grant immediate and complete access to chemical weapons sites by UN inspectors and relevant bodies. Assad agreed.

Assad's subsequent disclosure of what was in his stockpiles appeared to match US estimates. It had been assumed that Syria had approximately 1,300 tonnes of chemical agents, including 300 tonnes of sulphur mustard (a blistering agent associated with mustard gas), as well as sarin and VX. The number of sites identified was significantly lower than US intelligence had suggested, but this was attributed to the policy of consolidation that Assad had carried out following the start of the crisis, whereby he had concentrated his chemical stockpiles at key installations instead of leaving them dispersed across the country. There was, however, one surprise for the US: Syria voluntarily disclosed that it also secretly possessed ricin, albeit unweaponised. But in many ways, this was a welcome declaration in that it seemed to represent Syria's willingness to comply. Assad was apparently being honest and conforming to international expectations. Indeed, there was considerable positivity at this stage concerning the progress that was being made. Mark Fitzpatrick (2013: 109) commented: 'This [the CWC agreement] is remarkable, considering that a month earlier, Assad was still denying he even had CW.'

On 27 September, the framework agreement was simultaneously submitted to the UN Security Council and the executive council of the OPCW, passing through each successfully (Crocker, 2015: 13). Only days later, on 1 October, a team of OPCW and UN officials arrived in Syria to begin the destruction of the country's chemical weapons stockpiles and facilities. The timetable for elimination was highly compressed, allowing only one month to destroy all production equipment and nine months to eliminate the full chemical stockpile. As such, not everyone was convinced by the proposed solution; in particular, the extremely tight timetable was viewed as optimistic at best. Libya had possessed significantly fewer stockpiles at the time of its elimination programme, and this had taken far longer than the time allocated to Syria. Furthermore, the agreement assumed an extremely high level of compliance by Assad (*Strategic Comments*, 2013b). If Fitzpatrick highlighted how 'remarkable' this transformation in Assad's diplomacy was, others would say it was too remarkable. Assad was not exactly known for his cooperative engagement with the international community. Why then would anyone realistically think the dictator would suddenly change his entire diplomatic approach? As American expert on chemical weapons Amy Smithson (2013) wrote in a piece entitled 'A Phony Farewell to Arms', published on the day the OPCW entered Syria to begin the dismantling process: 'barring a miraculous personality change, Assad should not be expected to lay down his chemical arms meekly.' Despite these concerns, however, the CWC option was still a vastly more attractive option than air strikes were for Obama. In that respect, it was at least worth trying.

Obama presented this process within the context of the chemical weapons taboo:

> My goal is to maintain the international norm on banning chemical weapons. I want that enforcement to be real. I want it to be serious. I want people to understand that gassing innocent people, delivering chemical weapons against children is not something we do. It's prohibited in active wars between countries. We certainly don't do it against kids. And we've got to stand up for that principle. If there are tools that we can use to ensure that, obviously my preference would be, again, to act internationally in a serious way and to make sure that Mr. Asad gets the message. I'm not itching for military action. (Obama, 2013j)

The use of chemical weapons anywhere in the world is an affront to human dignity and a threat to the security of people everywhere. As I have said for weeks, the international community must respond to this outrage. A dictator must not be allowed to gas children in their beds with impunity. And we cannot risk poison gas becoming the new weapon of choice for tyrants and terrorists the world over. We have a duty to preserve a world free from the fear of chemical weapons for our children. But if there is any chance of achieving that goal without resorting to force, then I believe we have a responsibility to pursue that path. (Obama, 2013k)

Once again, the taboo was not applied here out of a sense of continuity and restraint, but for strategic purposes. The taboo was still important in terms of convention; indeed, it would seem logical that the very reason Kerry came up with the CWC solution was thanks to this. That is, in engaging in a debate defined by the discourse of the taboo, it was unsurprising that such an idea could emerge out of it, even as – especially as – an accident. Yet again, however, there is a strategic element. Even where this was a fundamentally different situation from the one outlined in the previous section – in that the air strikes which the taboo had previously been employed to justify would no longer take place – it was still a case in which the taboo was beneficial. Explicitly, it supported the very notion of this diplomatic agreement as an answer to the crisis. This was not merely playing up the importance of controlling chemical weapons, however, where this would provide validation for this avenue of policy; that is, because upholding the taboo is a recognised aspect of international politics, this solution should be enacted. In an even more valuable addition to this, it emphasised the importance of the CWC – and so effectively equated it to the strength of air strikes, as well as potentially even more intensive forms of military involvement. It made the CWC a sufficient measure to place on Assad, one that fit the international 'crime' of chemical weapons employment. On the surface, signing an agreement was unlikely to be seen as being as drastic as air strikes, not least where the civil conflict would continue. But in presenting the CWC in these specific terms of the taboo, it was a reassurance that it was enough to deal with the situation. It was a big enough stick with which to beat Assad for his actions. And, ultimately, the employment of the taboo gave Obama his all-important escape route out of military action in Syria. Consequently, this may not have been the perfect policy in his eyes. But the narrative of the taboo gave Obama a substantial degree of control over the situation, not least where he could then avoid air strikes and military intervention. The CWC was the way out. Invoking the taboo was a way of ensuring that.

Conclusion

Despite the theme of entrapment that emerges in respect of Obama and US foreign policy on Syria, this cannot be reduced to the inexorable employment of the taboo. Issues such as convention, conceptual expectation, and continuity in respect of the taboo all apply; that these factors create restraints on an actor is not disputed here. Yet the diminishment of this situation to pure constraint threatens to disguise the role that strategic narratives play in the expression of foreign policy, particularly as expressed by the innovating ideologist. Taboos are not merely expectations to which actors slavishly adhere. They are also the resources for strategic narrative construction. They are ideas that can be exploited in order to shape debates and facilitate the realisation of actors' self-interested aims and desires. Yes, they constrain. By their very nature, they govern actor behaviour and threaten punishment if they are not complied with. But placing this at the centre of analysis vastly skews understanding of what agents actually do with language in respect of international politics. The example here demonstrates this. Obama exerted considerable power and agency over the narratives he employed. Even though the situation was not of his making, it was still a case in which he could engage in ideological innovation, albeit to a limited degree. Moreover, the constraints of convention were not merely boundaries on the extent of that innovation, but the very facilitation of it. The chemical weapons taboo was an extremely effective strategic resource, but specifically one where the engrained nature of its understanding made it so valuable. In this sense then, convention is not merely restraint, but the very basis of the calculated construction of language. It is a tool of the innovating ideologist.

Critically, this argument can be taken even further. Obama's strategic manipulation of the chemical weapons taboo goes far beyond the mere idea of the norm itself. Obama was an even greater innovating ideologist than this alone suggests. In terms of strategic use and the manipulated construction of narratives, this chapter represents only the tip of the iceberg in terms of evidence. For those social constructivists who remain unconvinced by the argument of agency, there is a substantial weight of evidence to come. This will be the focus of the next chapter.

4

Obama's taboo

O BAMA'S CHEMICAL weapons taboo was a strategic narrative. While it would be remiss to suggest that he did not buy into the basic principles underpinning the taboo, it was also a highly convenient and effective ideational tool for addressing the problematic redline commitment. Yet this is far from the end of the story, specifically in terms of the sheer extent to which taboos are used strategically. The Syria example represents a much more detailed, extensive, and calculated level of discursive employment. While drawing on the general repulsion inherent to the chemical weapons taboo constituted an important way of dealing with the redline once it became unavoidable, this was likewise a situation in which the detail of the taboo also possessed significant rhetorical value – explicitly as a form of strategic exploitation. Obama's response was not a straight adoption of the taboo, but a case in which its innermost ideals were engineered to reflect and facilitate political interests. Obama did not merely apply the wider conception that 'chemical weapons are bad', but dug deep down into the specifics of the taboo for rhetorical ammunition. In particular, the taboo was used to force an understanding of foreign involvement in Syria as an intrinsically international issue as opposed to a purely US concern, thereby promoting the multilateral approach Obama had craved all along. By drawing on the very exact perception that the taboo's validity is manifest in its global support – just one of many features that 'make up' that normative expectation – Obama could manipulate understanding of the crisis in line with his own foreign policy ambitions. Similarly, morality (a key aspect of the taboo's construction) was also used to frame and exacerbate the threat posed by Assad ahead of possible US intervention as a form of pre-justification. Finally, this strategic construction of chemical weapons also related to their status as weapons of mass destruction (WMD). Obama's biased application of the WMD concept was used to control both international and domestic expectations concerning intervention, as well as diplomatic efforts concerning Assad's accession to the Chemical Weapons Convention (CWC).

As such, this chapter constitutes an exploration of the extent to which taboos can be used strategically. This cannot be reduced to a case in which actors are entrapped, or merely draw on emotive ideas that certain weapons are unacceptable in order to influence the scope and direction of debate. The level of strategic construction is significantly more extensive and pervasive. In relation to Syria, it was a rhetorical act that went far beyond convention to become a highly particularised and agency-driven discursive tool capable of redefining the US position on the crisis. It constituted an exceptionally manipulative strategy, one that did not stop at attempting to influence people via allusions to the proscribed nature of chemical devices, but also sought to actively change and govern US foreign policy at a very explicit level. Obama did not simply utilise the taboo in order to pull provocatively at the heartstrings – he used it to tell the head what to think as well.

The devil in the detail

The previous chapter examined the extent to which Obama deliberately applied the taboo within political discourse as a strategic narrative, not least where this employment was highly conditional and was only brought into rhetorical play once Obama could no longer avoid the issue of Assad's chemical weapons use. Specifically, this explains why Obama suddenly started to talk about the taboo well into the Syrian conflict despite never having mentioned it beforehand. This cannot, however, be limited to a case where the taboo dictated Obama's foreign policy. That is, one in which Obama, through invoking the ideals of the norm, would become irrevocably tied to its protection, which explains the taboo's rhetorical prominence. While Obama may have painted himself into a corner, it was not a situation in which he then sacrificed agency over the ideas that put him there. Indeed, to the extent he became entrapped within a certain narrative, Obama also sought to control and selectively employ it for his own strategic purposes. Explicitly, this was a case in which the fundamental ideals that conventionally constitute the chemical weapons taboo were utilised in exploitative ways in order to shape debate in line with Obama's foreign policy interests. Strands of understanding that have become connected to the taboo – even where this connection is not essentialist – were individually exploited for the achievement of given political aims.

To begin to place this in context, the most straightforward example of manipulation was where Obama drew attention to the horrific physical and psychological consequences associated with chemical weapons. Such a basic model of manipulation may not immediately seem to apply to the complexity of the innovating ideologist. Yet when compared to Obama's earlier rhetoric on the matter, the deliberate and strategic employment of this language becomes evident. Prior to Ghouta, Obama failed to discuss the repugnant effects of chemical

79

warfare. It was simply not mentioned. To whatever extent the chemical threat had been referenced before, for example, as a potential threat following the expected destabilisation of the Assad regime, it was not a discourse that incorporated any understanding or expression of what weapons use would actually look like in terms of effect. Even to the point at which such understanding can be taken as implied – where the destruction caused by these devices is so frequently considered intrinsic to the taboo itself – there still remains a clear distinction between the supposed implication here and the explicit and highly emotional description of chemical weapons' effect that would appear within the president's post-Ghouta narrative construction. Indeed, the incentive had previously been to downplay this aspect of chemical weapons employment. Where the strategy had been to deny the evidence surrounding attacks such as those at Homs and Aleppo in a bid to avoid enacting the ultimatum of the redline, so the greatest advantage came from not talking about the actual destruction and slaughter caused, nor alluding to the extreme damage chemical weapons can hypothetically create. But now, in tandem with the escalation of Obama's rhetorical use of the taboo after Ghouta, this aspect of chemical warfare developed into a significant and evocative feature of the Syria narrative. Very suddenly, the conceptualisation of effect was now central to political dialogue.

This is especially evident in Obama's focus on child fatalities. While the killing of adults was also acknowledged as grotesque, it is specifically the deaths of children – the most innocent within a conflict – that are highlighted (Obama, 2013f, 2013h, 2013k, 2013l). The concept that children are the 'ideal victim' in terms of emotively constructing an event is nothing new (Hoijer, 2004). It has long been acknowledged as an effective tool in the manipulation of opinion, especially where this relates to matters of security. It is unsurprising, therefore, that immediately upon confirming the US's acceptance that Assad had carried out the strike at Ghouta, this became a key aspect of Obama's narrative construction:

> As you've seen today we've released our unclassified assessment, detailing with high confidence that the Syrian regime carried out a chemical weapons attack that killed well over 1,000 people, including hundreds of children. This follows the horrific images that shocked us all. This kind of attack is a challenge to the world. We cannot accept a world where women and children and innocent civilians are gassed on a terrible scale. (Obama, 2013e)

This was a strategic reference, particularly where this tactic was directly employed as an instrument for gaining congressional and international support. This apparent need to avenge Ghouta was specifically pinned to the provocative murder of children, where this would seem to demand that the political community stand behind Obama on the Syria issue. As Obama (2013h) bluntly stated: 'Here's my question for every Member of Congress and every member of the global community: What message will we send if a dictator can gas hundreds

of children to death in plain sight and pay no price?' There is certainly little sub-
tlety to work through in considering the deliberately affecting pull of this sen-
tence. In contrast to the impassive discussion of chemical weapons prior to this,
Obama was now willing to lay the emotion on with the proverbial trowel, specifically in order to win political backing. While these were not the first children to
be killed by chemical weapons (or indeed of any form of armament, including
the conventional) in the Syrian crisis, US foreign policy discourse now revolved
around a vivid and value-laden description of Assad's actions. It was now a case
of the more detail – the more gore – the better, at least insofar as it could be
exploited to garner political endorsement for Obama's position.

Obama (2013f) also referred to the explicit videos of Ghouta that were
widely circulated on the Internet: 'The images from this massacre are sicken-
ing: men, women, children, lying in rows, killed by poison gas; others foaming
at the mouth, gasping for breath; a father clutching his dead children, implor-
ing them to get up and walk.' The way in which Obama drew on video evidence
stands out as another highly emotive form of political communication. This is an
evocative technique that requires the audience to 'relive' the images they have
seen, forcing them to reconsider in graphic detail the terrible destruction that
was caused. Again, this is well recognised as an effective tool in constructing an
audience's understanding of an event – demonstrated in terrible clarity by the
notorious beheading videos by Islamic State (IS) (Hawkins, 2014). Here, the terrorist organisation (which itself would become a major faction within the crisis)
widely publicised grotesque videos of the killing of hostages and 'non-believers'.
These then found viral fame both online and in the wider media. While it may be
inappropriate to describe this tactic as a success, it cannot be denied that it has
proved an extremely effective strategy in promoting the group on a global scale.
It has also constituted a major resource in terms of recruitment. As such, it provides an excellent example of the strategic potential of videos, where their effect
can influence an audience, specifically one to be convinced of a certain framing
of events. In applying this to back to Obama's strategy, the president was press-
ing home the awful images at a time when he needed political and public actors
to be as disgusted by the strikes as possible.

In this way, therefore, the taboo came to constitute a rhetorical – and indeed
now visual – cornerstone of US foreign policy. Insofar as the destructive effect
of chemical weapons is considered intrinsic to the taboo, Obama was exaggerating this aspect of normative comprehension in order to frame the situation
in his favour, or at least create circumstances that were amenable to any form
of involvement he might have to consider. Just as he had deliberately failed to
engage with such rhetoric prior to the confirmed use of chemical weapons by
Assad (where this was an issue that a non-interventionist would have been
keen to downplay), so Obama now threw himself into it where the strategic
and evocative exploitation of the threat suited his modified ambitions. Yet the

key point here, and which this chapter is devoted to making, is that this was not simply a basic manipulation of an emotive idea. It constituted a substantially more strategic and detailed act of rhetorical and narrative construction. Obama was reaching into the taboo for whatever aspects of its understanding would be most valuable to him. He effectively deconstructed the taboo in order to deliberately select and highlight vital aspects that could assist him within the context of discursive manipulation. This was a strategic resource, not merely a reference to the detail of events or an expression of the general principles of the taboo. Obama was engaging with an ongoing dialogue as an innovating ideologist – not to the extent that he was directly altering conventional meaning of the taboo, but where he was using convention at a highly strategic and calculated level and for the realisation of his own self-interest. As such, Obama's sheer selectivity and calculated presentation of these ideas within a constructed and emotive context were more than worthy of Skinner.

An international problem

This trend is even more apparent in the way Obama has employed the taboo to construct intervention as an international responsibility. Despite his focus on the US – not least where he had proposed specifically American air strikes, the official ratification of which would come from Congress as opposed to a multilateral body – statements were framed in ways that manipulated the global context of the taboo in order to complement the president's self-interest. The chemical weapons taboo is heavily constructed around its supposedly universal application, especially where this relates to its expression within political fora. So many actors are perceived to buy into the taboo that this common acceptance has become a self-sustaining expectation as well as a sign of its legitimacy. In this somewhat paradoxical sense, then, actors adhere to the taboo *because* it is legitimate, but its legitimacy comes *from* that adherence by actors. It is strong because people support it, but people support it because it is strong. Within this context, this two-sided reinforcement of the chemical weapons taboo demonstrates the substantial degree to which the idea of normative compliance on an international scale has become inherent to a conventional understanding of the taboo, particularly where this concerns upholding the taboo against violation. It is this idea that was core to Obama's strategic construction.

   This strategic act started with another paradox: Obama used the taboo to divorce himself from the controversial redline. Where the redline was now unavoidable, Obama sought to create a sense of distance between himself and this commitment. The commitment may remain (specifically as beyond Obama's immediate control), but he could strategically modify the nature of it in order to redefine his associated responsibility. This was achieved by constructing policy rhetoric around the idea that the common nature of the taboo translates into, and constitutes, an international norm. By highlighting the taboo as a world-wide concept, one that exists only via collective international consent, Obama reconstructed the redline as a self-evident and pre-existing ideational pressure. The unacceptability of chemical weapons use was not 'his' idea. This was not a policy exclusive to the US, or even to the Syria crisis. It was a common belief already manifest within the international system. As Obama (2013g) stated: 'I didn't set a red line, the world set a red line ... that wasn't something I just, kind of, made up.' Obama presented himself as merely drawing on a norm that had long existed in the very fabric of international thinking – who could blame or chastise him for that? Any state would, and should, have done the same. Indeed, Obama was quick to highlight the idea that not only was the taboo an intrinsically global commitment in terms of character, but it also existed as a very real and tangible political obligation that states had unequivocally signed up to. This assertion of the taboo was persistently reinforced by Obama's (2013c, 2013f, 2013h, 2013i, 2013m) framing of debate within the institutional context of the CWC, and his reiteration that 98 per cent of states were committed to this prohibition (a reference to the number of states that had endorsed the convention). This percentage comes up again and again in presidential rhetoric at this time – a reminder that the vast majority of states, and not just the US, had put their name to this normative ideal. The world had effectively signed on the dotted line, and so this could not be deemed exclusive to US foreign policy. Upholding the norm was explicitly identified as the 'obligation' of the world (Obama, 2013e).

The relevance of this is seen in how it plays into *who* was responsible for maintaining the taboo. Specifically, this allowed Obama to push that responsibility onto the shoulders of the international community. If Obama was not the sole architect of the idea, then he also could not be expected to accept full liability for it. Regardless of its hegemonic status, why should the US carry the can for a policy that was adopted at the global level? Consequently, insofar as the case for Syrian intervention was successfully constructed as an international concern, the responsibility to act and/or for acting lay with all states and not only the US. Obama essentially applied a global lens in a way that reduced the pressures both on himself and the US surrounding intervention, in that he was (a) no longer the sole focus of interventionist activity and (b) removed from any accountability associated with carrying out a response to violation, or at least no more accountable than any other nation. By highlighting the common adherence to the taboo, Obama spread out the accountability associated with it. In expanding this point further, this was also yet another strategic expression of the president's concern that intervention could become perceived as another Iraq. By deliberately constructing chemical weapons use as an international issue – one in which accountability for any response should be shared globally – Obama could preclude a situation in which US action would be considered within the same controversial framework of the War on Terror. The US logically could not be held solely accountable. If Syria was clearly established as a world responsibility, then it could not become another US foreign policy scandal. Assad's chemical weapons could not become Saddam's WMD stockpiles.

This strategy was also a commitment to multilateralism. As already discussed in Chapter 2, Obama repeatedly stated his preference for a multilateral solution in Syria as opposed to unilateral US action. Within this context then, and by constructing the Syrian question as an international responsibility, Obama's rhetoric forced (at least the perception of) an inter-state approach. Establishing the taboo as global ensured that Syria was 'not just an American problem, this is a world problem' (Obama, 2013b). It was 'not going to be something that the United States does by itself', or where it would 'bear that burden alone' (Obama, 2013n, 2013c). Critically, this construction of multilateralism did not necessarily imply a physical contribution to military action (although this is not to say this would not have become the case had air strikes been carried out at this time and, subsequently, escalated), but placed the liability for those actions – even if enacted by the US – within the international system. If the taboo was global, US action could not be opposed insofar as it directly sought to uphold normative expectations of chemical weapons non-use.

Backing US policy in this way constituted a significant aspect of the multilateral narrative. In decrying what he viewed as the catch-22 position of the US with respect to intervention – where the US is both expected to solve political crises and criticised for over-involvement in those same issues – Obama (2013j) said:

> [T]hey always look to the United States. Why isn't the United States doing something about this, the most powerful nation on Earth? Why are you allowing these terrible things to happen? And then, if the international community turns around when we're saying it's time to take some responsibility and says, 'Well, hold on a second, we're not sure,' that erodes our ability to maintain the kind of norms that we're looking at.

Through such rhetoric, the international community was not only held accountable for and via the taboo, but was also impelled into a situation where that responsibility required it to support whatever course of action Obama pursued. Whatever the US chose to do in the name of the chemical weapons taboo, the rest of the world would have to not only accept it, but endorse it. There could be no room for criticism, as there had so clearly been in relation to Iraq (due to the fact that the US had not established unambiguous international support prior to invasion). As such, other states were compelled into acquiescence, if not perfect compliance, with the US as a consequence of Obama's logical and strategic construction of the argument. The way in which Obama had structured the discursive situation forced international state actors into a very precise logic of thinking that effectively gave the US free rein on Syria, as long as the activity in question could be framed as upholding the taboo.

Obama took this notion of global accountability so far as to explicitly assert that any failure relating to chemical weapons use in Syria would be the fault of the international community. In a guilt-laden ascription of future blame, states were sternly warned that the responsibility for any collapse or weakening of the taboo would be theirs, not least where such failure would, insisted Obama (2013j), most likely occur as a result of inaction by an international community that 'is paralyzed and frozen and doesn't act'. Further emphasis was placed on this where failure was associated with dire consequences for security more widely, in that it would send a dangerous message that the world was prepared to let norm violations go unpunished:

> Make no mistake, this has implications beyond chemical warfare. If we won't enforce accountability in the face of this heinous act, what does it say about our resolve to stand up to others who flout fundamental international rules? To governments who would choose to build nuclear arms? To terrorists who would spread biological weapons? To armies who carry out genocide? We cannot raise our children in a world where we will not follow through on the things we say, the accords we sign, the values that define us. So just as I will take this case to Congress, I will also deliver this message to the world ... we will insist that an atrocity committed with chemical weapons is not simply investigated, it must be confronted. (Obama, 2013h)

Critically then, this established a justification not merely for intervention, but also non-intervention. Whatever happened, or did not happen, was thanks to the international community and not US foreign policy decision-making. In this way, the sheer extent of the chemical weapons threat was rhetorically tied to the commitment and obligation of the international community. And by emotively emphasising the consequences of failing on Syria within this constructed framework of global accountability, so Obama (2013g) could again push away sole responsibility for the taboo: 'My credibility is not on the line, the international community's credibility is on the line.' By this very logic, any resolution of the Syrian crisis would have to be pursued (or not) by multilateral means, and Obama was off the hook for the consequences. Obama had used this very precise aspect of the taboo to construct a win–win situation for the US.

Moral decisions

Likewise, Obama also exploited the chemical weapons taboo as an issue of morality. The perception that chemical weapons are immoral constitutes a major aspect of the taboo, largely in that they are considered indiscriminate killers – particularly where a contrast is drawn with conventional weapons, which are seen as more targeted in terms of effect (Stern, 1999: 3, 12). Playing into the classic rule of war distinction between targeting combatants and non-combatants, this is the idea that chemical weapons' inability to distinguish who they kill is impermissible, immoral, and leaves them subject to an illegitimacy of use not applicable to

conventional arms (Hashmi and Lee, 2004). This last point in particular is supposedly manifest in the construction of specific international arms control regimes
that establish the distinct illegality of chemical weapons employment, including the
CWC. Yet this approach is problematic. For one, as Susan Martin (2004: 33) demonstrates, chemical weapons can be used discriminately. As such, there is little
to differentiate these devices from other forms of weaponry, not least where it is
also difficult to maintain that these other forms – including conventional armaments – cannot also cause damage indiscriminately. Analysis has only to point to,
say, the Second World War Allied aerial bombing raids on Dresden to demonstrate
this. Similarly, landmines constitute an example of weaponry widely accepted to
be indiscriminate (Roth, 1998: 2; Walsh and Walsh, 2003: 665). Asmeret Asefaw
Behre (2005: 375) encapsulates this specifically where he terms them 'weapons
of indiscriminate mass terror' – a twist on the concept of WMD. Consequently, a
conceptual distinction based on indiscriminate effect is flawed. This is not to argue
that indiscriminate effect does not play a role in the construction and understanding of chemical weaponry – it is an important factor. Yet it cannot be considered
essential to that comprehension, only as a political construction – which in turn
cannot constitute an absolute basis of distinguishing chemical arms.

Similar issues apply to morality more generally: it is 'hard to see a moral
distinction between being killed by gas and being blown up' (Easterbrook,
2002: 22). As such, attempting to establish a moral hierarchy of weapons based
on effect is difficult, if not downright repugnant. Whatever the pragmatic needs
of classification, many would take issue with the idea of deeming one violent
death worse than another purely on the basis of what caused the fatality in
question, and irrespective of the circumstances involved or the levels of pain
inflicted. Furthermore, and going back to the CWC regime that supposedly sets
these arms apart as taboo, John Sislin (1998: 456) highlights that conventional
armaments are also subject to a comparable illegitimacy of employment, where
this translates into a conception of immoral use, for example, protections against
landmines, UN arms embargoes, the 1980 Inhumane Weapons Convention, and
the 1139 crossbow ban. There is nothing exclusive about the idea that chemical
weapons are so immoral that they require special prohibition. Indeed, they have
been considered *less* immoral than conventional devices in the past. Circa the
First World War, it was argued in some quarters that chemical weapons were
actually more humane than conventional forms of assault in that they avoided
the physical destruction of infrastructure as well as 'battlefield blood and gore'
(Guillemin, 2005: 6; also Haldane, 1925). Although this represented only one
aspect of debate at the time, it is clear that some actors deemed the tactic of
chemical warfare to be the more moral option. Consequently, analysis needs to
reflect that, while chemical devices are terrible weapons capable of unspeakable
acts of aggression, the supposed exclusivity of immorality inherent to those acts
is too uncertain to constitute an absolute distinction.

Yet again, however, morality remains imperative to the understanding of chemical weapons and the taboo that defines them, even if this is not essentialist or guaranteed. While the characteristic of immorality is highly disputed, it remains a prominent association, albeit to the extent this is recognised as contingent (Price, 1995: 80). Indeed, it is a major strategic factor in respect of Syria. Morality has influenced perceptions of Assad's capacity for chemical warfare. This started during those very early discussions over the potential future extent of Assad's brutality in 2012, when it was argued that his extreme acts of conventional violence indicated he did not possess the necessary moral values that would inhibit a resort to chemical warfare. Leonard Spector (in US Cong., 2012b: 38), Deputy Director at the Center for Nonproliferation Studies, said as part of congressional hearings:

> [W]hat they [the Assad regime] have done just recently in terms of the wholesale [conventional] slaughter in some of these cities indicates that they are pretty prepared to take extremely harsh and coercive measures. And so you wonder how big a threshold they perceive they would be going over if they were to take this additional step [chemical weapons use]. I think there has been enough international focus on this to at least etch the threshold a little deeper than it might otherwise be, but I don't think there is any kind of moral compunction.

That is, it was not just Assad's previous actions but *what these actions said about his moral disposition* that was important. It was not merely a willingness to massacre that suggested he would use chemical arms, but the idea that this demonstrated a specific lack of moral fibre. Using chemical weapons was not merely a question of killing, but a question of character. Obama would later pick up on this strategically, specifically in order to exaggerate perceptions of Assad as an intolerable actor within the international system. Regardless of the immorality or not of chemical weapons, it was in Obama's interests to portray Assad in the least flattering of terms. Not least as pressure for intervention grew as a consequence of the redline, it was to Obama's advantage if his adversary were thought to be unacceptable. This construct of morality provided an ideal model for doing so.

This is nothing new in respect of US foreign policy. Chemical weapons have long been used as a way of constructing and undermining dictators who were seen to threaten America. During the 1990s, this constituted a major discursive resource in constructing the threat of Saddam Hussein, where this drew explicitly on the taboo and its characterisation as upholding the moral over the immoral. Under President George H. W. Bush, this was the idea that Saddam had already used chemical weapons (at Halabja) and so had demonstrated his immoral preparedness to use even more destructive weapons, specifically arms also conventionally classified as WMD: 'Saddam has used chemical weapons of mass destruction against innocent villagers, his own people. Each day that passes brings Saddam Hussein further on the path to developing biological and nuclear weapons and the missiles to deliver them' (Bush, 1991: 11). As such, Saddam's character in using chemical weapons (and potentially other mass destructive weaponry) was highlighted as a sufficient reason not merely to justify, but to demand US intervention within the Middle East. His willingness to carry out evil acts was key, explicitly where the extent of that evil was connected to the nature of the weapons involved. Where the taboo allowed chemical weapons to be set apart as especially abhorrent, this could be employed to play up the inexcusability of Saddam's values. Anyone who wanted to use such horrific weapons must logically be bad and, subsequently, a target for removal. Clinton also drew upon this same narrative during his administration, and expanded it to refer to Saddam's supposedly ridiculous and unreliable nature. Clinton (1998: 26) would compare Saddam's development of chemical weapons to the dictator's wasting of national resources 'building lavish palaces' instead of acting as a conscientious political leader, in that his acquisition of these devices was part of that same selfish and frivolous behaviour. Saddam was not a 'safe' actor within the international system. He could not be trusted to possess chemical weapons, and he could not be trusted *because* of his possession of them, not least where the latter revealed the unacceptable disposition of his personality and political position. Once again, therefore, the chemical weapons threat was an intrinsic component in the construction of US foreign policy and foreign policy discourses. The calculated emphasis on Saddam's mass destructive potential as taboo was strategically fundamental to both Bush Senior's and Clinton's structuring of a certain conception of threat and the successive justification of US foreign policy in the region. This is what Obama was also seeking to achieve in terms of wider perceptions of Assad. Given this previous utility in using chemical weapons as a strategic rhetoric device, Obama could appreciate that it was a proven method. Even despite the later controversy of Saddam's non-existent stockpiles during the Bush Junior administration, the chemical weapons taboo and the ideas inherent to it remain highly effective as strategic resources, and have been so for some time. The chemical weapons taboo is a strategic narrative with significant pedigree.

Morality also framed Obama's conceptualisation of the conflict where this links back to fears surrounding the Iraq scandal and the president's belief that critics would view intervention in Syria as a morally corrupt act. To return to the work of Price (2013), it was highlighted at the time that 'Plenty of observers would interpret any U.S. attack in the region as being motivated by less than morally agreeable objectives.' In consequence, deliberately playing up the supposedly moral nature of intervention – where this constituted the punishment of a particularly horrific violation – was an extremely attractive rhetorical tool. In stark contrast to the controversy of Iraq, the US was now seen to be upholding the most noble of causes and directly attacking immorality within the international system. (A somewhat ironic approach, perhaps, given the construction of the 2003 Iraq invasion in largely similar terms.) The application of the taboo created the perception that action within Syria would comprise an altruistic response to a moral need, as opposed to an act of self-interest. As Obama (2013g) responded when asked by a news reporter if it was appropriate that a Nobel Peace Prize winner should go to war: 'I would argue that when I see 400 children subjected to gas, over 1,400 innocent civilians dying senselessly in an environment in which you already have tens of thousands dying, and we have the opportunity to take some action that is meaningful ... then the moral thing to do is not stand by and do nothing.' In this way, Obama used the conception of morality as a barrier against criticism. Regardless of his own opinion on intervention, the expectations resulting from his inadvertent setting of the redline meant that increased involvement had to be constructed as a plausible option. Should Obama be pushed into taking that involvement further, he needed to ensure that it was not seen in self-interested terms – not least where it was taking place under the long shadow cast by Iraq. As with his employment of the taboo to promote a multilateral approach that would sanction the viability of any form of interventionist activity in Syria, so Obama similarly utilised the conception of morality to justify whatever might come next and put himself in the strongest, most favourable position possible going forward.

Weapons of mass destruction

This is again evident in a further strategic construction of policy, relating to the classification of chemical weapons as WMD. Price (1995: 100) says the WMD label significantly reinforces the taboo, in that it extends an illegitimacy associated with mass destructive armaments (particularly nuclear weapons) to chemical devices also. As such, the WMD concept has proved an important aspect in understanding their stigmatisation. Yet this is a label that itself has been associated with strategic use, specifically where actors have selectively employed the WMD concept in order to realise political ambitions. Indeed, the inclusion of chemical weapons within this classification has, historically, proved far from assured; their mass destructive status has instead been largely dependent on the contextualised needs of policy-makers rather than any definitive definition (Bentley, 2014b). That is, chemical weapons are only WMD when it is beneficial to an actor for them to be so. Not least where the WMD concept has frequently been used as a way of designating weapons as suitable for elimination, the categorisation (or not) of chemical devices as WMD has considerable implications in terms of wider security and international policy. Consequently, this lack of essentialist understanding leaves their rhetorical construction as WMD open to manipulation and reconstruction. Thus the WMD concept would provide Obama with an effective discursive resource in respect of foreign policy on Syria – or, more accurately, his failure to apply the concept would do so. For Obama only very rarely referred to chemical arms in Syria as WMD. Assad's chemical weapons were not weapons of mass destruction.

This conceptual absence is a strategic expression of Obama's policy caution towards Syria. Given his significant hesitancy over intervention, why would he then apply such politically inflammatory language? As seen in relation to, and now because of, Iraq, the concept of WMD is a highly evocative one. Labelling a threat 'WMD' has significant implications: as soon as a threat is identified as mass destructive it becomes a priority issue, specifically one sufficient to justify even full military invasion. Even where it is now accepted that Saddam Hussein did not possess WMD stockpiles, and given the widespread condemnation of US foreign policy around WMD as an excuse for intervention, that language – which evoked such fear and dread prior to the 2003 invasion – still means something in the post-Iraq era. To whatever extent that language has been rejected or discredited, its use does not now take place in a conceptual vacuum where previous expectations and emotive associations no longer apply. If the US went into Iraq for WMD, surely it would then also be obliged to go into Syria for the same reason, if Assad's chemical arms were acknowledged as mass destructive devices. Indeed, the failure to locate WMD within Iraq and the controversy associated with it is effectively irrelevant within this context, in that it does not, and did not, negate the principle at the heart of that strategy, i.e. that unacceptable WMD possession by a 'bad' actor provides sufficient justification for intervention. That ideal still holds regardless of its problematic application in relation to Iraq. In fact, it remains today, specifically at the centre of the chemical weapons taboo itself, where the moral and physical protection of these arms is fundamental. Yes, it may have been misused by the Bush administration, but even this act highlighted a moral ideal that exists irrespective of its manipulation. Once again, there are echoes of Price's argument that violation can actually strengthen a taboo, or – perhaps more accurately given the nature of the overall argument presented here – its strategic value as a taboo. Subsequently, Obama's extreme care in steering clear of the language of Iraq and WMD was not solely due to a desire to avoid making a link between that case and Syria, but also because using this specific concept would have vastly increased the pressure to intervene. By not employing the WMD concept, Obama was attempting to reduce expectations surrounding intervention and inhibit any escalation of the situation by using language that would seem to demand action.

Critically, this is not to say Obama avoided the concept entirely, but his use of it is extremely rare, heavily contextualised, and – importantly – connected to the realisation of specific policy ambitions. For example, Obama briefly mentions WMD at times when intervention is raised as a likely possibility, both after the first wave of chemical weapons allegations and following US confirmation of their use at Ghouta in August 2013. In relation to the former, Obama employed the phrase in his initial response in which he discusses chemical devices as distinct from conventional forms of aggression, specifically in that this distinction could then be justified as a policy trigger in a way that conventional massacre was not. In a joint statement with King Abdullah II of Jordan at the time, Obama (2013d) said:

> But I meant what I've said, and I will repeat, that it's obviously horrific as it is when mortars are being fired on civilians and people are being indiscriminately killed. To use potential weapons of mass destruction [chemical] on civilian populations crosses another line with respect to international norms and international law.

This statement can be viewed as the strategic creation of the discursive conditions for interventionist policy. While such action was ultimately avoided at that stage, it was accepted that this could be interpreted as an infringement of what had come to be understood as the redline. Knowing this to be a possibility, Obama hardened his language in preparation for a potential response. He drew on the WMD concept's emotive associations – where these effectively represent a process of prioritisation over conventional violence, one capable of validating an interventionist foreign policy – in that these afforded him certain political freedoms, or at least a freedom to pursue particular options if he so chose. He used the WMD concept to prepare the political field should intervention become necessary. Indeed, his speech with King Abdullah II was made at a time when Jordanian support for US policy in Syria was uncertain. Within this context, a stronger rhetorical approach was diplomatically beneficial in ensuring compliance. By highlighting the new seriousness of the political situation in Syria engendered by the allegations of chemical weapons use, increased pressure could be exerted on Jordan to toe the US policy line. Note, however, that Obama referred to chemical arms only as *potential* WMD, where the idea of potential exists as a form of qualification. Obama used the threat of WMD, but in a way that still left him significant liberty on the issue in that they were not necessarily WMD yet. The statement hinted at WMD (where this supported his hard line with Jordan and pre-justification of greater involvement in the crisis), but the implied 'maybe' built into the construct in no way tied Obama down. He was still being cautious. Intervention, however, did not occur, and once Obama had decided against a military reply without further evidence of chemical employment at that stage, the reference to WMD was very quickly dropped. Once it served no strategic value, it was abandoned in favour of a return to the former, more pragmatic rhetorical approach of avoiding the contentious term.

This same discursive trend is evident in respect of Ghouta, in relation to which Obama, in announcing US acceptance that Assad had used chemical weapons, stated (2013e): 'We have currently rules in place dealing with the proliferation of weapons of mass destruction. We have international norms that have been violated by certain countries, and the United Nations has put sanctions in place.' Interestingly, however, in Obama's famous Rose Garden speech the following day, during which he declared that he would seek congressional approval for air strikes, WMD were not mentioned at all. Assad's chemical stockpiles are not discussed within this conceptual frame of reference. Context provides an answer as to why, in that while firmer language was initially attractive in setting the stage for possible intervention, once Obama's policy became concerned with gaining congressional support for a more limited policy of air strikes, he faced a substantially more delicate political situation than the pushing through of intervention or coercing hesitant state partners. In consequence, Obama's rhetorical framing returned to one of caution and restraint. While Obama certainly did not hold back in emphasising the seriousness of Assad's chemical weapons use, there remained an incentive to avoid the evocative language of WMD where his policy approach now played into intensive partisan negotiations within Congress. Why rock the boat? This trend would become even more apparent in relation to the alternative plans that would emerge in preference to air strikes based on Assad's accession to the CWC. Consequently, in a case where military options had now been (at least temporarily) taken off the table and replaced with a fragile diplomatic strategy, there was again an incentive to avoid hard-line language such as WMD. Where this has become the language of decisive intervention – a heavy-handed approach that could have destabilised the precarious diplomatic process that was now developing – it was deemed more prudent to remain focused on a rhetoric designed to persuade and encourage Assad's compliance with the CWC.

Dealing with certain other actors required a stronger discursive approach, however – as seen in Obama's exchanges with Putin. In a statement following joint talks, the US president said: 'Failing to respond to this breach of this international norm would send a signal to rogue nations, authoritarian regimes, and terrorist organizations that they can develop and use weapons of mass destruction and not pay a consequence. And that's not the world that we want to live in' (Obama, 2013j). Russia was always going to be a point of opposition in respect of US foreign policy, thanks to the strong relationship between Putin and the Assad regime. It is unsurprising then that, right from the start, Russia made it clear that it would not commit to any action that threatened the regime, or that even sought to condemn it for the brutality it was waging against its own populace. It was also clear that its veto power at the UN Security Council – and the veto of China – would prevent any major forms of involvement or intervention from taking place via that forum. Putin had effectively established himself as a roadblock: a diplomatic barrier on Assad's behalf. Both in terms of diplomacy and more military forms of intervention, Putin was the obstacle. Given the fundamental role Putin has played in the Syrian crisis, therefore, and the extent to which Russian support for American action was considered strategically important, convincing Putin to cooperate with (or at least not significantly oppose) the US constituted a significant aspect of Obama's policy. Consequently, Obama selected a muscular linguistic approach – one that included the WMD concept – in order to compel Putin. By highlighting the gravity of Assad's act of chemical weapons use via its classification as mass destructive, Obama could more successfully portray this as a situation demanding a response. If it was an act of WMD use, it was necessarily a priority issue that entailed a stern reaction. Debate was framed in such a way that refusal to act would be seen as failing to address the severity of Assad's actions, even from an ally. In this way, the WMD concept was a rhetorical tool of coercion applied to specific policy-makers in order to shape a reply to the chemical attack. Its employment provided a sense of political leverage, strategically utilised in order to influence – herd, even – international support for US foreign policy.

The strategic nature of this is also evident in comparison to other foreign policy discourses on WMD. Specifically, Obama has been more than happy to talk about WMD elsewhere. For example, Obama (2009a, 2009b) has repeatedly spoken of North Korea's nuclear weapons as a WMD capability, where that classification has allowed him to portray the state as a major concern. In a move similar to Bush's identification of the 'axis of evil', in which hostile states were specifically characterised as such by their supposed acquisition of WMD, the concept has been employed to highlight North Korea as a primary risk and constitutes a core justification for making it a priority of US foreign policy. It is only in relation to Syria, therefore, that Obama demonstrates avoidance, proving that his failure to employ the concept does not stem from a wider aversion to it, but is strategically limited to the Syria question. Indeed, even more telling than the North Korea example, there are cases where, while Obama discusses threats such as chemical arms proliferation and terrorism explicitly as WMD concerns, when moving on to consider Syria, even within the very same statement, the president never calls these chemical weapons by that name (e.g. Obama, 2013o). The concept effectively disappears from rhetorical use halfway through, once the context of the statement has changed to Syria. This selectivity shows that the employment of the WMD concept is a fundamentally strategic act in Obama's rhetoric. He cherry-picks the cases to which it is applied depending on its strategic value, even within the same speech.

The WMD concept as a strategic tool has also been used with regard to the political situation in Iran (Obama, 2011b). Indeed, on the very few occasions when Obama has employed the term in respect of Syria, it has related mainly to Iran. This tactic was utilised for two strategic purposes. First, it provided a way of demonising a country holding a key position within the wider political context of the Syrian crisis, specifically a position that was anti-US. The close relationship between Iran and Syria remains of significant concern to US foreign policy-makers. Highlighting Iran as a 'rogue' WMD threat was intended to undermine and discredit Iran as a player in the conflict. Second, Obama has used Syria as a springboard to steer foreign policy debate towards Iran, whereby exploiting the association of Assad's chemical weapons with the WMD concept permitted an ostensible link to other hostile regimes deemed a mass destructive threat, and explicitly to Iran's nuclear ambitions. Establishing Assad's chemical weapons as mass destructive focused attention to this other issue; as Obama (2013f) put it: 'a failure to stand against the use of chemical weapons would weaken prohibitions against other weapons of mass destruction and embolden Asad's ally Iran, which must decide whether to ignore international law by building a nuclear weapon or to take a more peaceful path.' Obama strategically manipulated the conceptual association inherent to the WMD term as an umbrella classification (one that incorporates a range of weaponry) to force a focus on Iran and its alleged nuclear capabilities. By drawing on concerns related to Syria in this highly calculated way, Obama could engage with, and highlight the seriousness of, Iran – itself a core tenet of his foreign policy agenda, and one that Obama was relatively more comfortable with than his inadvertent involvement in Syria. As an additional point here, the wider rhetoric of the chemical weapons taboo is not employed in respect of Iran (or other issues such as North Korea), despite the reference to WMD; it is exclusive to Syria. This too is contextual, again indicating strategic use. As such, it provides yet more evidence of the highly manipulative way in which the ideals of the taboo were applied at the time. This was not a straight application of the taboo to a conflict scenario, but the innovative, creative, and manipulative exploitation of those ideas for the realisation of Obama's self-interest.

Strategic taboos

Thus, the sheer extent of Obama's strategic exploitation of the chemical weapons taboo to influence the scope and direction of US foreign policy is evident. By selectively employing these specific ideals in order to set strategic priorities – where this application could be used in respect of emphasising certain threats (i.e. Assad's chemical weapons) as a primary concern at pertinent points of the Syrian crisis – Obama could control comprehension of, and response to, that conflict. As such, this demonstrates further that normative and ideational constructs are not merely constraints, but strategic resources for anyone willing to act as an innovating ideologist. The taboo constituted a linguistic frame around which Obama could shape foreign policy and decision-making processes. Obama exploited very detailed perceptions and fears associated with the taboo to facilitate his pursuit of certain actions. Via this strategic construction, Obama effectively established certain discursive boundaries of understanding, for example, the construction of Syria as an international concern, where this could not necessarily have been achieved without the associated framework of comprehension provided by the taboo. In particular, this relates both to logic and an emotional pull that would force policy-makers into specific pathways of decision-making. Obama had utilised the ideals of the taboo to set the terms of discussion and action, where the deliberate and calculated employment of the ideas conventionally associated with that taboo constituted the key tool in realising this.

In presenting this as strategic, this rhetoric was, at least initially, exclusive to Obama; the taboo does not feature to the same extent within foreign policy discourses put forward by other national leaders. Putin, for example, did not refer to the taboo, even when discussing the CWC as a diplomatic solution. This is hardly surprising in that his support for Assad meant there was no strategic value in the taboo's rhetorical application, at least not in the way presented by Obama. Given that the taboo had since been constructed as an effective tool for undermining Assad and promoting certain policy options consistent with Obama's interests, it was not beneficial to Putin. Putin's stance did, however, give impetus to the adoption of such rhetoric by Obama in order to counter Russian demands in support of Assad and imply an international norm that 'should' override Putin. If the taboo was global, then surely it applied to Putin also – thereby enhancing the US's position and undermining Russia's. Thus the highly contextual nature of the taboo's use demonstrates its strategic application. Critically, however, Obama's rhetoric would subsequently be picked up within other discourses relating to Syria. Obama created the narrative, but given that it was designed to convince others of the US's position, it is unsurprising that the narrative would become mirrored elsewhere, and this constitutes a sign of Obama's success in promoting it. For example, the primary UN report confirming Assad's usage of chemical weapons at Ghouta stands out in that, despite not using such language previously in related reports, it now adopted the same narrative constructs as Obama had employed in respect of the taboo. In the early pages of the report, the UN explicitly states that chemical warfare is confined by normative restrictions surrounding chemical weapons, which echoes Obama's morality rhetoric: 'The international community has a moral responsibility to hold accountable those responsible and for ensuring the chemical weapons can never re-emerge as an instrument of warfare' (UN, 2013c: 1). The fact that this rhetorical trend emerges *after* Obama's narrative construction with respect to Ghouta suggests that the UN was engaging with this wider rhetoric to the extent that Obama's dialogue had become relevant, especially where US foreign policy played such a major part in these discussions. Thus, Obama can be seen as effective in his rhetorical construction, since this discursive replication occurs in other contexts of use.

Even in a position of restraint, therefore, actors possess agency over the narratives they employ, where the use of such narratives facilitates the achievement of their strategic aims. They can take control of language even where it appears to be defined by normative constraint. This would seem to constitute a fundamental contradiction between the dynamics of agency and social construction, but in fact it plays right into Price's idea of an inherent flexibility within the context of the taboo's expression: that it is not a perfect commitment, but a behavioural influence. The taboo is a guide, but the guide is not always followed – like the instructions for flat-pack furniture. Within this frame, taboos are not absolutes, but potential resources for strategic language, particularly where their socially and politically engrained character makes them so attractive as such. But this is not merely limited to the taboo as a general idea. Ideological innovation goes significantly further than this. This is a case in which an actor can be highly strategic and selective in the aspects of language they use. This is particularly important here in that it shows the extent to which Obama was being an innovating ideologist. To the degree that he uses the taboo, it could still be written off as convention and restraint. Yet, demonstrating here that it was not simply an adherence to convention, but an extremely strategic process in which selected aspects of the taboo were used for exploitative reasons, shows that convention alone is not a sufficient answer. The evidence here is too compelling to argue that Obama's use of the chemical weapons taboo was merely this. The selective nature of the taboo's employment – where specific aspects of the taboo were prioritised over others, and these aspects were used in respect of explicit political aims in a very targeted way – shows that something more is going on. Specifically, this was strategic and agency-driven.

Conclusion

The language of foreign policy is not innocent. While the chemical weapons taboo may, at least in part, represent a genuine and socially engrained commitment to preventing the employment of these horrific devices, this normative expectation also comprises a set of political resources open to rhetorical manipulation and exploitation. This is what Obama has done in respect of the taboo within the political context of Syria, and also in terms of the WMD concept. To the extent that chemical weapons use, intentionally or otherwise, became a catalyst for US policy in Syria, Obama sought to control subsequent discourse via a biased linguistic application of the established normative ideals associated with, if not essential to, the taboo. Critically, this was not merely a general appeal to the basic emotive construct of the taboo; that is, the idea that these weapons are abhorrent to the point of prohibition and prescription. It was a highly detailed and calculated strategy that sought to dissect the taboo itself and draw on the most compelling aspects of that construction in order to achieve strategic aims. By using specific elements of the taboo to force policy-makers into a certain mindset, so Obama was able to directly shape the intervention debate. The same applies to the classification of chemical weapons as WMD, where that label is connected to strategic employment. As a highly evocative concept, one closely linked to the justification of intervention, it could be selectively utilised in order to emphasise, or indeed downplay (via its absence), explicit aspects of policy. Consequently, the fears, repulsion, and stigmatisation inherent to the taboo were not just policy drivers in the sense that they engendered pre-existing frames of understanding, but they also provided the rhetorical resources necessary for the strategic control of that policy. They were the tools of an innovating ideologist.

Part II

A failed taboo

5

Chemical weapons and false hierarchies

RITICISM HAS not been in short supply vis-à-vis Obama's foreign policy on Syria. This has included the issue of chemical weapons, where Obama has been challenged over his commitment and response to the redline; the way in which chemical weapons use became the lynchpin of America's foreign policy regarding Syria; and Assad's continuing use of the chemical agent chlorine in violation of the Chemical Weapons Convention (CWC). What stands out about the criticism, however, is the lack of reference to the chemical weapons taboo. Specifically, whatever failures have been identified with respect to Obama's stratagem, the taboo has not been questioned or subject to censure. Of all the criticisms made of Obama, his application of the taboo is not a concern that he has had to respond to. Why? Because nobody wants to be seen to say anything negative about the taboo, even where this does not directly seek to contest the basic idea that chemical weapons should be eliminated. As already established throughout Part I, the idea of the taboo within international politics is extremely influential. But more than this, the expectation is considered a necessary, valued, and moral aspect of the international system; it is politically sacrosanct. Consequently, any argument that could be seen to undermine or destabilise the taboo, specifically in the sense of questioning its validity, is, in turn, deemed sacrilegious. Where the taboo is upheld in such extreme terms, any criticism of it becomes 'othered' as the opposite extreme and is considered not in terms of its critical analysis, rather that the interlocutor in question is defying the commitment to the removal of chemical weapons. Within this binary context of polar positions, they are portrayed as effectively stating they support chemical warfare. In this way, the matter has been reduced to a simple good/bad debate, one in which any critique automatically falls into the latter category. This is the focus of the next two chapters, which will not only outline the major problems with Obama's foreign policy strategy and its focus on chemical weapons, but will also specifically discuss this in relation to the taboo.

101

This chapter starts the next section by examining the ways in which the taboo has distorted comprehension of the Syria crisis. As conventionally understood, the taboo exudes the stigmatisation of chemical weapons: the idea that these weapons are not just horrific, but distinctly more horrific than other forms of armament. In this way, the chemical threat is set apart as a priority concern. Yet this conceptual structure has caused severe problems, explicitly in respect of Syria. Underpinning this argument is an analysis of how chemical weapons have skewed understanding of the wider conflict, especially in terms of the non-chemical threats involved. While removing chemical weapons would have proved a plus (if Assad had not continued to use them), the push to eliminate chemical weapons has fundamentally warped US policy-makers' broader response to Syria and caused them to ignore critical issues relating to the use of conventional weapons, as well as other types of weapon associated with WMD – specifically biological armaments. The taboo creates false hierarchies that overstate the relative importance of chemical weapons and overlook core threats inherent to the crisis. This is an issue that goes way beyond chemical weapons alone to undermine the whole resolution process. Expectations surrounding the taboo are so pervasive and invasive that they have undercut the entirety of US foreign policy on Syria.

The wrong solution

From the moment Obama confirmed that Assad forces had employed chemical weapons at Ghouta, the entire conflict was effectively reduced to this one issue in the eyes of US foreign policy. The redline, in combination with existing expectations surrounding the taboo and Obama's employment of them as the basis of his strategic narrative, would see the whole of the US's engagement in the crisis focused on this single concern. Chemical weapons were presented as the core problem in respect of US foreign policy regarding Syria, and they would be the solution to it also. The focus on chemical weapons was so intense that it came to constitute the US's sole interest in respect of the civil conflict. Little else mattered. This is not, of course, to say that non-chemical threats mattered previously; Obama had paid scant attention to other threats prior to this, including the mass-scale conventional killings carried out by the regime. But to the extent that the US was now considering greater involvement in Syria, it was on the basis of chemical weapons only.

This can be taken a stage further, to assert that the taboo creates an exclusionary lens through which a conflict is viewed. Conceptually distinguishing chemical armaments as requiring special consideration engenders their acceptance as the dominant threat within a given situation. This is not merely a matter of prioritisation, which causes other threats to be devalued relative to chemical violence. It is that these threats cannot be 'seen' in cases where the taboo is applied. It is a lens that shuts out all issues not related to chemical weapons. The taboo places the political spotlight on chemical weapons alone: they become the primary issue, while others are forced into the shadows. The hierarchical understanding of conflict imposed by the taboo – where chemical weapons necessarily take precedence over alternative forms of aggression as a consequence of their stigmatised status – does not simply marginalise these other threats, but removes them from consideration. They are deemed irrelevant. This has distorted the wider perception of what is actually happening in Syria. Because the conflict is reduced to terms of chemical warfare, other factors – the massacres, the conventional aggression, etc. – are removed from consideration. In effect, the chemical weapons issue becomes detached from the rest of the conflict, and the entirety of that conflict becomes understood within the limited conception of chemical risk. This is not merely a situation that misrepresents the civil conflict, but one that actively distorts the perception of and response to it.

The difficulty here is that chemical weapons constitute only a fraction of what has happened in Syria. Specifically, chemical warfare in Syria has been a tactic – a horrific and deplorable tactic admittedly, but only the military expression of a political crisis and not the crisis itself. Of course, this is not to suggest that chemical weapons cannot significantly shape how a conflict transpires. It is also not to suggest that chemical weapons are incapable of constituting the basis of a crisis, in which the elimination or removal of such armaments from that wider situation would be sufficient for its resolution. But this is not the case in Syria. The civil crisis there is not, and has never been, about the presence and employment of chemical arms. As already outlined at the start of this book, the outbreak of conflict was an act of political rebellion against the repressive policies of the Assad regime, one that challenged the imposition of an unacceptable dictatorship on the state. Viewing the conflict in terms of any specific category of armament, therefore, should take into account the regime guns that were fired into crowds of protesters by government forces, causing the initially peaceful demonstrations to erupt into civil violence. Consequently, because the political and violent upheaval in Syria is not based on the chemical threat, the way in which the taboo reduced US interest in the conflict exclusively to chemical warfare is inappropriate and may preclude further efforts towards resolution.

Critically, this is not to suggest that addressing chemical weapons in Syria has not been beneficial. Whatever the arguments put forward here concerning the constructed and problematic nature of the taboo, chemical arms are terrifying (albeit not exclusive in the terror and destructive effect they inflict) and their removal from a fragile conflict scenario can only be a positive. It is surely uncontroversial to state that eliminating chemical arms within Syria – or indeed any violent situation – is preferable to having them in it, not least where they are held by a dictator more than content to massacre on an extreme scale. Moreover, the taboo attributes special status to chemical weapons in respect of what they can achieve, where this relates to the expression of actor motivation. Chemical weapons ostensibly allow for the realisation of certain aims and aggressive actions that may not be possible with solely conventional means. For example, the perception of extreme destruction linked to chemical weapons underpinned the argument that Assad's continued possession of such arms would have provided him with a potential 'knock-out' blow, not only against the opposition but also in respect of any possible US military intervention (US Cong., 2013d: 45). That is, chemical weapons are deemed to be so decisively destructive that they possess the capacity to provide a clear and overriding advantage on the battlefield (the clash between this and the arguments that chemical weapons are militarily useless, outlined in Chapter 1, has not gone unnoticed here). Within this context, removing, or at least significantly degrading, Assad's stockpiles would have a major impact on the scope and trajectory of the conflict by eliminating that ability. Similarly, there have been specific concerns that chemical weapons would be employed explicitly for the purposes of genocide and the ethnic cleansing of key Sunni areas in Syria, which areas Assad would then turn into an Alawite state (Steven Bucci in US Cong., 2012b: 35). While it was acknowledged that conventional weapons were also effective in carrying out genocide, testimony given to a US Congress committee warned that chemical weapons could do so more quickly, and more efficiently, and that this ease of use may actively encourage genocidal behaviour by limiting the effort required to do so (ibid.: 25). In this sense then, there would seem to be an exclusive role for chemical weapons. Consequently, the focus on chemical weapons could be upheld as important, even if such weapons constituted only a relatively minor part of the overall political and conflict situation.

Yet these arguments do not overcome or justify the *exclusive* focus on chemical weapons, particularly where this focus has been effectively applied to the rest of the crisis also as a consequence of prioritising the chemical threat over all other concerns. What was supposed to be an historic starting point for negotiation and the cessation of the civil conflict has proved little more than a brick wall. As Republican Congressperson Ileana Ros-Lehtinen (in US Cong., 2014a: 2) said:

> So far, the administration's approach to resolving the Syrian conflict leaves much to be desired by any metric. Unless the administration addresses the underlying root causes for this humanitarian disaster, we are likely to be here again next year and in the years to come asking the very same heart-wrenching questions. Getting chemical weapons out of Syria is a vital step forward, but more importantly, we must be working together to ensure that Assad leaves power so that his reign of terror ends.

This was repeated on the Democrat side. House Representative David Cicilline (in US Cong., 2013e: 5) said: 'In our efforts to come up with a solution regarding chemical weapons we have largely lost sight of the other ongoing humanitarian issues surrounding this crisis.' Within this context, Assad's accession to the CWC was the diplomatic equivalent of moving the deckchairs around on the *Titanic*. In a similar resort to analogy, former US State Department adviser, Frederic Hof (in Fitzpatrick, 2013: 107), likened it to excising the appendix of a patient with untreated cancer: the operation may be successful, but the patient is still suffering and dying. Consequently, the CWC was little more than a distraction. The idea of bringing Assad into a diplomatic agreement was attractive, specifically one that ostensibly dealt with the horrifying threat of chemical weapons. Yet because this threat took attention away from the other issues underpinning the Syrian crisis, and this distraction was disguised by the application of the taboo, it misrepresented what was actually happening. Policy-makers could not see the real situation. Whether they wanted to take on the wider conflict or not was irrelevant given that the taboo meant they could not even comprehend what was involved.

Hierarchies of violence

Within this context, it is important to go back to the Syria crisis and consider what was not 'seen'. What has been missed as a consequence of the taboo?

Conventional weapons

The school building was seriously damaged. There were pools of blood and dead bodies were scattered everywhere. Many students were trapped and buried under rubble. He kept looking for his children among the dead bodies and severed body parts, trying to identify them by their clothes. He could not find them so he rushed to Omer Abd Al Aziz hospital. To his shock he found his son, [redacted], seriously injured in the head, bleeding heavily but still breathing. He rushed to get a car to transfer him to Turkey for medical treatment. He asked a friend to accompany him and then continued to look for his other son ... His friend called him a little while later and told him that [redacted] did not make it to Turkey, as he had died upon reaching Bab al Salama border crossing. (UNHRC, 2014a: 11–12)

Chemical weapons are potentially devastating armaments, as demonstrated all too clearly at Ghouta. Yet a chemical attack is not the only – or indeed the main – way in which violence has been carried out in Syria. Significantly more people have died as a consequence of conventional massacre, carried out with weapons such as guns and explosive devices, than from chemical assault. While the eyewitness testimony, quoted in previous chapters, that details the terrible effects caused by chemical warfare is horrific, the evidence surrounding conventional attacks is equally harrowing, as the above quotation demonstrates. This is an already familiar issue in the debate on chemical arms, specifically where such weapons are supposedly distinguished from other forms of weaponry on the basis of destructive effect and where this underpins conventional understanding of the taboo. Here it is argued that the distinction of chemical aggression is unsustainable, not least where it relates to destructive capacity and the types of physical effect caused. As Ronald Higgins (2002: 3) comments: 'However dreadful, a death from poison gas ... is not obviously more horrific than a fiery death from napalm or through multiple lacerations from antipersonnel mines or carpet-bombing.' Similarly, Stephen Walt (2013) wrote in the *New York Times*: 'Does it really matter whether Assad is killing his opponents using 500-pound bombs, mortar shells, cluster munitions, machine guns, icepicks or sarin gas? Dead is dead, no matter how it is done.'

In response, advocates of the taboo counter that chemical weapons remain the deadlier threat. Conventional arms can do terrible things, but the wider capacity of chemical arms for mass destruction still separates them as a higher concern. Even where this is reduced to potential threat as opposed to the evidence seen in reality – i.e. the theoretical ability, however unrealised, of chemical arms to cause extensive hurt – it remains sufficient for some to draw a line (Braut-Hegghammer, 2013). As Sohail Hashmi and Jon Western (2013), for example, state:

> Nobody doubts that conventional weapons can and do kill in large numbers – Hutu extremists in Rwanda demonstrated the lethality of even simple machetes and hoes. But nuclear, biological, and chemical weapons are labelled weapons of mass destruction because they have a higher potential to kill or wound very large numbers of people compared with other weapons. If used to full capacity and under the right environmental conditions, chemical weapons are more lethal than virtually all kinds of conventional weapons.

Yet the idea that we can/should draw a distinction between different types of killing – where one is prioritised over the other as being more obscene – is elsewhere recognised as inappropriate, if not simply offensive. Even where chemical weapons are associated with vile effect – the invisibility of the attack, the invasion of our bodies, the idea of chemicals that we do not understand taking control of us – it is hard to maintain that they cause a more terrible death. To play devil's advocate: would you rather die in your sleep from chemical poisoning or from being tortured in agony for days with conventional devices? These are never easy comparisons to make, and they can easily be manipulated – as the intentionally biased nature of the previous question demonstrates. But some (like Higgins and Walt) would ask why we have to make comparative distinctions in the first place. Why should the taboo impose this hierarchy of pain? Not least where the destructive effects of chemical weapons are so heavily contested – to the point at which it is neither essentialist or guaranteed, but based on contextualised political construction – how can the taboo be upheld so absolutely, to the exclusion of all other forms of violence?

Events in Syria add weight to this argument. The hideous atrocities of the conflict are widely known, not only those carried out by the Assad regime, but also those by the opposition and the Islamic extremist organisations that have since become involved in the conflict, such as IS. Critically, these acts of aggression are often considered to be on a par with the violence that is portrayed as being exclusive to chemical arms. For example, in terms of forcibly clearing out population areas as a method of punishment or ethnic cleansing, Assad's policy of conventional destruction has proven more than successful in achieving such aims (Chulov, 2014). While there will always be the hypothetical threat of a major chemical attack capable of killing thousands, or tens of thousands, the reality on the ground is that taking chemical weapons out of the equation has had no mitigating impact whatsoever on the extent of the killing, or on any aspect of strategy. In fact, the violence has escalated (discussed more in the next chapter).

Moreover, this concept of conventional violence is not limited to acts such as bombing, but also includes other forms of physical and psychological harm, specifically cases of human rights violation. Despite the lifting of emergency law by the Assad regime, the issue of torture has been conspicuous on the list of international concerns surrounding Syria (AI, 2012). Human Rights Watch's report on the Syrian regime's 'torture centers' includes testimony such as the following:

> They hit the bottoms of my feet with a stick. There was a thick belt tied around my legs so that I couldn't move them. I was lying with my face on the ground and my feet up. There were two people beating me with a silicon stick. One was standing on my neck. You prefer death. You hope to die. The entire time I was in detention my family knew nothing about me. They didn't know whether I was dead or alive. (Fadi in HRW, 2012a: 3)

Reported torture methods in Syria include:

> [P]rolonged beatings, often with objects such as batons and wires, holding the detainees in painful stress positions for prolonged periods of time, often with the use of specially designed equipment, the use of electricity, burning with car battery acid, sexual assault and humiliation, the pulling of fingernails, and mock execution. (Ibid.: 2)

Critically, this programme of torture has shown no respect for age: torture victims as young as one year old have been reported (Dardagan and Salama, 2013). It is hardly surprising then that the UNHRC (2014b: 30) has concluded on this basis that 'Syria has become the world's worst humanitarian catastrophe'.

Torture has been described as 'systematic' within Syria, with specific reference to the Assad government (HRW, 2012a: 10). It is not considered merely a by-product of conflict – something that is employed as part of waging a wider military campaign – but the systemic, planned, and deliberate construction of a dedicated network, encompassing an 'archipelago' of torture and detention centres coordinated across Syria. These have frequently been established in large institutional buildings previously used for civilian means, such as hospitals and schools. Critically, this has happened in part because the programme has expanded so extensively that existing torture facilities were simply insufficient to cope with the vast numbers of people being put through the system. Indeed, torture in Syria has very quickly become something of a franchise, with new facilities being set up anywhere that can meet the programme's space and incarceration requirements. Despite this expansion, however, the huge numbers of those being tortured mean that there is still a major problem in terms of overcrowding, lack of food, and insufficient medical attention. Cells are so full that, it has been reported, detainees have no room to sit and are forced to remain standing for extended periods of time, with prisoners having to take turns sleeping. While the maximum cell occupancy under the Council of Europe's Committee for the Prevention of Torture is five detainees to a cell four by five metres square, at a military intelligence branch centre in Damascus there were 70 people held in such a space (ibid.: 15). As well as constituting a form of torture in itself, this demonstrates the sheer extent to which the programme is engrained in Assad's strategy. Significantly, it is a programme that also incorporates torture as the concealment of death, in that there are numerous reports of the Assad government claiming that suspected and actual rebels have died of natural or unavoidable medical causes while in the programme, whereas their friends and relatives insist they have unjustly been murdered by the regime. For many, the number of such deaths is now sarcastically perverse, if not merely suspicious. As one Syrian (in UNHRC, 2014b: 5) commented sardonically: 'It seems now everyone in Syria has had a heart attack.'

Evidence from the Syrian torture centres also adds weight to arguments that rape should be classified as a weapon (e.g. Bergoffen, 2009; Cannon, 2012) or, as others prefer to term it, an 'instrument of terror' (Meger, 2012). Not least where rape is itself a core aspect of the Responsibility to Protect (R2P) (Trahan, 2015: 50), the systemic nature of the sexual violence that been used in torture and detention is emblematic of the extent of the Syrian conflict (HRW, 2012b; Legagnoux, 2014).

> They took me to an interrogation room in the basement. The office said 'bring Khalid' ... I was at the back so couldn't see Khalid well, but they pulled down his trousers. He had an injury on his upper left leg. Then the official raped him up against the wall. Khalid just cried during it, beating his head on the wall. (AI, 2012: 24)

> He pushed a rat in her vagina. She was screaming. Afterwards we saw blood on the floor. He told her: 'Is this good enough for you?' They were mocking her. It was obvious she was in agony. We could see her. After that she no longer moved. (In Proudman, 2013)

Rape and sexual assault have been employed throughout the Syrian conflict, to such an extent that it has been compared to the rape campaigns of Bosnia. The Bosnian conflict of 1992–95 is notorious not just for the genocide that was carried out, but also the intensive strategy of rape that was implemented by Serbian fighters, in which approximately 20,000 women were attacked (Hansen, 2000: 56). Consequently, Bosnia has long been a byword for the horrors of mass sexual violence. It is within this infamous and extremely telling context that Norwegian Foreign Minister Espen Barth Eide (in Wolfe, 2013) stated his opinion that what happened in Bosnia was 'repeating itself in Syria right now'. In 2013 alone, 38,000 Syrian refugees approached the UN for help in response to acts of sexual assault or gender-based violence – a figure that, given the stigma associated with sexual violence and the difficulties in accessing help, is likely to represent only a fraction of the problem (Miles, 2014). This has been a major feature of the conflict. For example, the aggressive regime clampdown on protesters in Daraa at the start of the conflict involved not only shooting into the crowds, but also the organised rape of local girls by government forces (Kahf, 2014: 559). In this way, rape was part of that impetus towards civil crisis. Janet Benshoof (2014: 146) considers rape so important in this respect that she has termed it the 'other red line'. Rape has been so extensive that, as revealed in interviews with Syrian refugees by the International Rescue Committee (IRC, 2013: 2), it was the primary reason why many Syrians were fleeing the conflict. Investigations also exposed a further problem created by the prevalence of rape: a massive increase in reports of early and/or forced marriage of women and girls. Refugees were (a) so afraid their daughters would be sexually abused that they would rather marry them off as soon as possible in the hope that this would protect them, and (b) attempting to marry females who have been raped as the only way of ensuring their honour, despite the extremely young age of many of these brides (Greenwood, 2013). There are even cases in which women have been killed to 'protect' them from rape. The IRC (2013: 7) reports one incident of man who shot his daughter as they were approached by armed troops in order to prevent her dishonour.

Assad is not the only one to authorise rape as part of the civil violence. On the rebel side, Islamic cleric and Salafi sheikh, Yasir al-Ajlawni, declared it a legal fatwa for rebels to 'capture and have sex with' Alawites (of which Assad is one), as well as other non-Sunni and non-Muslim women (in Chumley, 2013). Similarly, this has also proved a major issue in terms of the rise of IS in the region (Ahram, 2015). It has been widely reported that the group has abducted women to be sold into sexual slavery (Pinheiro, 2015) and forced marriage with IS fighters, often multiple times (Peresin and Cervone, 2015: 502). One 14-year-old girl was sold/re-sold 15 times to various IS fighters. She said (in Susskind, 2015): 'The worst moments were when one man would sell me to another. And I would have to hear them debating what my life was worth.' There are also reports of young women being coerced into recruitment as brides and to provide sexual services to IS, both in order to boost morale within the organisation and to encourage recruitment (Zawaiti, 2014: 6–7). Sexual violence is not limited to women, but is also widespread in respect of men, particularly IS recruits (Ahram, 2015: 68). New recruits are often sexually assaulted as a type of hazing. Often the attacks are videotaped as a way of blackmailing them should they ever seek to try to leave the organisation. Thus, rape is endemic to the Syria conflict – not just as an act of violence, but as part of the very politics that has driven the crisis.

Overall, this evidence gives rise to the claim that focusing exclusively on chemical weapons with respect to Syria has created an inappropriate hierarchy of death and harm, one within which conventional violence is unnecessarily treated as irrelevant next to chemical assault. At the most simple level of comparison, it is difficult to ignore the basic fact that approximately 1,500 people have died as a consequence of chemical assault in Syria, but that 200,000+ have been killed by conventional means within the same time frame. Of course, it could be argued that this is only the case because chemical weapons were shut down in respect of Syria. That is, if chemical weapons had been allowed to persist, then the fatality rates may be greater as Assad continued to employ them. But even then, this cannot overlook the massive fatality rate on the conventional side. As already stated in Chapter 2, this conventional violence is so extensive that it has been deemed a breach of R2P (Pattison, 2014). While R2P is far from a perfect notion in terms of its application by the international community (as professed by those who describe the distinction between US foreign policy on Libya and on Syria as hypocrisy; T. Weiss, 2014: 35), this still theoretically challenges the ideational discrimination and prioritisation of chemical arms via the taboo. In their study of the legality of the US response to chemical weapons, Jillian Blake and Aqsa Mahmud (2013: 246) conclude that the same action proposed by the US in respect of the redline could be similarly justified in respect of the conventional violence that had been carried out. Everything the US has done in response to Assad's chemical weapons violations could be justified on the same basis in terms of his conventional aggression: the rationale would be the same. Yet if this can also constitute an internationally recognised excuse for intervention – even in a situation where it is not applied – then the taboo cannot hold as an exclusive basis for action.

This situation is also problematic in respect of the legitimacy of violence. The chemical weapons taboo legitimises conventional aggression. In what effectively constitutes a case of othering, the stigmatisation of chemical weapons as intolerable logically implies that conventional weapons are (in some way) permissible, or at least insufficient to warrant major concern. To the extent that the taboo sets chemical weapons apart, this distinction creates an insinuation that conventional violence is not 'as bad'. If we consider chemical weapons to be proscribed in such a distinct way, then, in comparison, conventional weapons appear less controversial. As the evidence above suggests, however, this is not an easy claim to uphold. Indeed, it has been taken even further to argue that the perception of conventional devices as relatively more tolerable has actually promoted Assad's use of chemical weapons. That is, in not acting on conventional violence, the US made the breaking of the taboo easier, especially where the unchallenged ability to carry out conventional violence gave Assad 'a sense of untouchability and impunity' (Evans, 2014: 19). As Republican Senator Marco Rubio commented, in response to a statement by John Kerry:

> In fact, Secretary Kerry, a moment ago you said that one of the calculations that Assad used in deciding to use chemical weapons was that the U.S. wouldn't do anything about it. I understand perhaps why he made that calculation because, yes, this was a horrible incident where a thousand people died, but before this incident 100,000 people had died, snipers were used to pick off civilians, women were raped – they were going out to these villages and carrying this out, and nothing happened. So, of course he reached that calculation. (In US Cong., 2013f: 29)

Furthermore, the emphasis on chemical weapons would seem to have actually encouraged conventional violence as the lesser of two evils – a criticism that has been levelled directly against Obama. John McCain (2013: S3288) said: 'drawing a redline on chemical weapons, the President actually gave the Asad regime a green light to use every other weapon in his arsenal with impunity.' In this way, upholding the distinction of the taboo has caused greater violence at the conventional level by promoting it as acceptable, or at least tolerable when it came to issues of intervention. Ironically then, the same events that underpinned US foreign policy-makers' claims that Assad was prepared to use chemical weapons were now dismissed as a consequence of that reasoning. It was Assad's conventional massacres that had been used to demonstrate his apparent lack of compassion, which was in turn cited as evidence he did not possess the necessary values and morals to adhere to the taboo. Yet, while these actions were connected to the same behavioural traits that determined chemical weapons use, the taboo then ensured this conventional aggression was eliminated from peace efforts and foreign policy-making, specifically where this related to grounds for intervention.

In line with this book's argument concerning strategic construction, however, these distinctions cannot be divorced from the contextual nature of their use by self-interested actors. This is not merely a case where Obama deliberately focused on chemical weapons as a consequence of his entrapment within the redline (as discussed in Part I), but where both he and other actors approached the situation strategically. Within this context, it cannot be ignored that the comments quoted above from US politicians challenging Obama's focus are all by Republicans and staunch opponents of the president's foreign policy strategy. They would, therefore, possess an incentive to shape the debate on their own terms, specifically as a way of questioning Obama's competence. In this sense, these quotations also provide further evidence of the strategic manipulation of language. Critically, this is not exclusive to Syria. Even more interestingly, the same point – or perhaps 'tactic' is a more apposite word – was picked up elsewhere in respect of Libya. Republican Congressperson Ron DeSantis used this as a way of criticising Obama for the failure to act on the Benghazi scandal. The Obama administration was heavily criticised after Islamic militants attacked a US diplomatic compound in Benghazi, Libya, on 11 September 2012. During the attack, US Ambassador, Christopher Stevens, and US Foreign Service Information Management Officer, Sean Smith, were killed. The incident shocked America and was seen as a massive failing on the part of the White House. Specifically, DeSantis framed this criticism within the relative context of norms and normative expectation:

> Secretary Kerry, you spoke about how the use of this gas [in Syria] breached the norms of civilized behaviour, international norms, and that we need to enforce this norm kind of like you would enforce lessons learned by children and bullies I think that you had said ... But as I look at it, that same line of reasoning should have applied to Benghazi. The assassination of a diplomat breaches norms that were recognized probably far longer than norms against the use of sarin gas, and yet the U.S. has not acted to avenge the deaths of the four Americans, including our Ambassador, who were massacred in Benghazi. And that lack of response, I think, using the same line of reasoning, could embolden terror groups and Islamic malcontents that they can do that and that we may not respond forcefully. (In US Cong., 2013c: 69)

DeSantis's statement raises two important points. First, it supports the idea of strategic language in that the same deliberate tactic is repeatedly used. Obama's opponents could see a clear advantage in criticising his chemical weapons policy, specifically via the comparison of chemical weapons to other types of violence. Obama was being portrayed not only as a policy hypocrite (i.e. that he was prepared to intervene in certain situations, but not in others), but also as a moral hypocrite. The president was being selective in terms of normative expectation. He would be 'good' on some moral demands, such as the response to Assad's chemical weapons, but this was not universal – specifically, he was apparently happy to let the scandal of Benghazi be brushed under the carpet, as well as the vast number of conventional fatalities in Syria. Within this framework of moral understanding, Obama could be presented as cherry-picking his principles in respect of foreign policy. Unsurprisingly, this was not a flattering image, and it was one that played extremely well into the Republican strategy to undermine the president.

Despite the strategic ramifications of these statements, however, there is still relevance to them – explicitly where they highlight problems with this exclusive focus on the taboo as foreign policy. The second key point that DeSantis's speech raises is the idea that the chemical weapons taboo is not the only norm in the international system. The assassination of a diplomat is one also. Another is the rule of war that non-combatants should not be targeted in a conflict scenario. This is a point of contention for Betcy Jose (2013), who asks why the chemical weapons taboo should come before civilian immunity in respect of Syria, since so many have been killed by conventional means. Why has the taboo effectively trumped this norm? This is particularly ironic, says Jose, in that the justification of the taboo rests on the indiscriminate nature of these arms. That is, they are intolerable because they kill non-combatants. Admittedly (as Price has already demonstrated), this is only one of many ways in which the taboo is understood as intolerable, none of which are essentialist. Yet the idea of indiscriminate use has still proved fundamental to the taboo's construction, especially in respect of Syria. Consequently, it would seem inappropriate to use the issue of indiscriminate killing to uphold the taboo when civilians can be slaughtered conventionally without similar comeback. Again, the argument comes back to that idea that chemical weapons are not sufficiently distinct to warrant their exclusive taboo. The perpetuation of the idea that chemical weapons are distinguished, and deserve special treatment as such, continues to ignore the massive overlap in destructive and psychological effect between these devices and other forms of violence.

In continuing the strategic theme, this situation can also be attributed to Obama's construction of foreign policy in the wake of the redline. Obama never wanted intervention on the grounds of conventional violence. He did not even desire intervention on the grounds of chemical weapons use; the difference being that the redline meant he could not avoid the chemical issue. Consequently, where Obama was only compelled towards a more interventionist line on the grounds of his own misinterpreted redline, this encouraged a specific focus on chemical weapons use in that the taboo set convenient boundaries as to how far the president would have to engage with the conflict. Given Obama's resistance to intervention, he certainly would not condone any action beyond the bare minimum the redline had inadvertently committed him to. Why expand consideration of the issue beyond the limited scope of chemical weapons, where this would only drag him further into the quicksand of intervention? As such, the way in which the construction of the chemical weapons taboo freezes out conventional threat was a bonus. The taboo constructs chemical weapons as a priority: it says that this comes first. It demands that politicians choose one over the other (in the absence of a successful attempt by an innovating ideologist to do otherwise). Again, this is the idea of the lens: the idea that a conflict can only be viewed in terms of chemical weapons. This was complementary to Obama's aims. But even more than this, the taboo legitimised his approach. It pushed attention away from the conventional violence and authorised it as tolerable compared to the use of chemical weapons, or at least implied that it did not require any action by the US. Consequently, this entire aspect of the Syrian crisis was discounted.

Biological weapons

The line between conventional and chemical weapons is likely to remain contentious. Consensus on their separation shows little sign of emerging, not least within the stigmatising context of the taboo. Consequently, it could be argued that this discussion on conventional weapons remains insufficient to uphold the claims here on legitimacy and priority. That is, the lack of agreement over the conventional–chemical division places a large enough question mark over that argument to undermine it, at least to the extent that it is simply more theoretically convenient to adhere to the taboo as a framework of understanding. But what if this argument were not solely based on a distinction between chemical and conventional arms, where it has been suggested that these do exist in a hierarchy? What if chemical weapons were set next to weaponry considered directly comparable? In short, what if this argument were built around a comparison with a weapon also conventionally defined as a WMD? For conventional aggression is not the only threat to be sidelined in favour of chemical devices in respect of Syria. There is a further concern that has been ignored as a consequence of the taboo: bioweapons.

Chemical weapons are supposedly special, but the basis of this is effectively identical to that of the WMD concept. In terms of Syria, Obama has been more than keen to avoid this association in relation to Assad's chemical stockpiles; the previous chapter demonstrates his strategic evasion of the term as a way of downplaying expectations for intervention. As such, Obama's approach demonstrates the sheer political construction of the WMD concept and the way in which it can so easily be associated, or not, with specific weapons according to the desires of an actor. Chemical weapons are not inevitably WMD; no weapon is. In this sense then, it is possible to divorce the taboo from the concept of WMD and treat chemical weapons as distinct. And yet, this cannot escape Skinnerian convention. Chemical weapons were stigmatised long before the concept of WMD developed, and yet the taboo is heavily reliant on the association with mass destruction. The features underpinning the taboo – the incredible destruction, the indiscriminate use, the barbaric nature of effect – are the same as those of the WMD concept. In looking at the taboo on nuclear weapons, we see the exact same thing. That is, nuclear weapons are stigmatised alone, but on the same basis as that applied to the WMD concept; indeed, Nina Tannenwald (2007) says the classification of WMD was intrinsic to the taboo that would emerge around nuclear arms. Even if we do not personally agree with this classification, therefore, analysis cannot ignore the fact that this is the basis that proponents of the taboo use to uphold that concept. And this subsequently creates a contradiction over the way in which they have ignored the bioweapons threat. For example, while Hashmi and Western (quoted in the section above) insist the taboo should be upheld on the basis that chemical arms are WMD, they fail to explain why this policy should not, therefore, be extended to similarly categorised devices. If chemical and biological arms are both WMD, then the desire to maintain a focus on only one of them is flawed. If chemical weapons demand intervention because they are intolerably horrific, then what about other weapons that are similarly marked out? Or more specifically, why has the US not reacted to Assad's biological weapons programme? Biological weapons have not been used within the Syria conflict, as chemical weapons have. But they are still a major issue, one that has been considered comparable to the chemical threat in the past. So why is there disparity in US foreign policy?

The state of play concerning Syria's biological weapons programme remains largely uncertain. Diplomatically, Syria is bound by the 1925 Geneva Protocol (on the same basis as chemical weapons) and has signed, but not ratified, the 1972 Biological and Toxin Weapons Convention (BWC). As such, it is technically free to develop biological weapons, albeit on a highly tenuous political basis. The extent to which it has done so is a point of contention. Syria has an extremely strong pharmaceutical industry, and even initiated a substantial biowarfare programme in the 1980s under the reign of Assad's father, Hafez (Sanchez, 2013). Despite this, however, it is claimed that the state has yet to weaponise biological agents on a military-level scale. It is still very much a limited research programme without the necessary infrastructure for major production (Normark *et al.*, 2004: 41; Ouagrham-Gormley, 2013). Despite this, however, the presence of a major programme is accepted, and has been for some time, by actors including those directly involved within US foreign policy-making circles. Here, Syria's potential for weapons development has been upheld as a serious threat, one that may have already been realised. Some examples are listed here:

- March 1991: Director of US Naval Intelligence, Rear-Admiral Thomas Brooks (1991: 56–9), testifies to the US Congress that Syria has an offensive biological warfare capacity.
- January 1992: Director of Central Intelligence, Robert Gates (in US Cong., 1992: 11), testifies in the US Senate that Syria has developed a biological weapons programme; specifically that Syria 'apparently is seeking assistance from China and Western firms for an improved capability with biological warheads'.
- January 1993: The US Arms Control and Disarmament Agency (USACDA, 1993) reports its opinion that the probability that Syria has biological weapons is extremely high (the agency makes the same statement in numerous reports throughout the 1990s; Cordesman, 2008: 14).
- November 2001: At the BWC Review Conference, then Undersecretary of State for Arms Control and International Security Affairs, John Bolton (2001), declared: 'We [the US] believe that Syria (which has not ratified the BWC) has an offensive BW [biological weapons] program in the research

and development stage, and it may be capable of producing small quantities of agent.'

- September 2003: Congressperson Ros-Lehtinen (in US Cong., 2003) extensively cites the work of analyst Dany Shoham, of the Begin-Sadat Center for Strategic Studies, in a congressional committee meeting on Syria. Shoham (2002a, 2002b) asserts that Syria is an advanced biological threat and has the clear capacity for a major programme.
- August 2004: The US Central Intelligence Agency (CIA) denies there is any clear evidence that Saddam transferred Iraqi biological weapons stockpiles to Syria prior to the 2003 invasion, although these allegations are prominent at the time. Denials continue throughout 2005 (NTI, 2008).
- November 2004: The CIA confirms, as it does in similar reports throughout the post-9/11 decade, that 'Syria probably also continued to develop a BW capability' (USCIA, 2004: 6).
- November 2006: John Hood (2006), Assistant Secretary for International Security and Nonproliferation, said the activities of Syria (among other states) 'are of particular concern given their support for terrorism and lack of compliance with their international obligations ... we remain seriously concerned that Syria – a signatory but not a party to the BWC – has conducted research and development for an offensive BW program'.
- February 2007: Lieutenant General Michael D. Maples, US Army Director of the Defense Intelligence Agency (in USDIA, 2007:15), says: 'Syria has pursued development of a strategic deterrent principally based on ballistic missile, chemical, and, to a limited extent, biological warfare programs, as a means of countering Israel's conventional force superiority. Syria's biotechnical infrastructure is capable of supporting limited biological agent development. DIA assesses Syria has a program to develop select biological agents.'

The uncertainty surrounding the progress of the Syrian programme has left analysis open to highly subjective interpretation. It has been accepted that the potential exists, at the very least in the research and development phase. But the extent to which this has, or could be, realised in terms of weaponisation is questioned. Standing out as an important year in the debate was 2007, thanks to biowarfare expert Jill Bellamy (in Gordon, 2007). At the time, Bellamy warned that Syria possessed a sophisticated and advanced programme, one that included major pathogens: for example, anthrax, plague, tularemia, botulinum, smallpox, aflotoxin, cholera, ricin, and camelpox. Defying those who claimed the research-centric nature of the programme precluded an actual threat at that stage, Bellamy was keen to highlight it as a major risk. She argued that the US State Department and related agencies had downplayed the threat of Syria's biological strategy.

She attributed this lack of concern to the distraction of the chemical weapons issue, given that there had long been political anxiety concerning Syria as one of the main chemical threats, if not the main chemical threat, in the Middle East. This was seen as the more concrete danger. Not unreasonably, it would seem, given that Assad would eventually employ these weapons. Yet Bellamy presents this as a case in which the prioritisation of chemical violence had undermined the biological time bomb represented by Syria. Chemical weapons are important, but so is biowarfare, and one should not push the other off the political agenda. This is especially the case given that the Assad regime was robustly committed to developing the usability of bioweapons:

> A major concern is their strategic concept of use – which has gone from one of the 'special weapons' to incorporation into their 'conventional arsenal.' That is a significant shift and one that seems to have eluded the US ... This is a huge shift in thinking by the Syrian military. It means they condone the use of biological pathogens as 'offensive' weapons. NATO and the United States should be very concerned about that re-designation. (In ibid.)

Bellamy (in Gordon, 2013) repeated this warning during the civil crisis itself, particularly where the chemical threat could be taken to indicate Assad's willingness to mass manufacture, and critically employ, their biological counterparts: 'I think if we look at Syria's commitment, they are increasingly prioritizing BW, where their chemical arsenal had always been the largest in the Middle East. Bio has gained some ground. An indicator of this is their stated intent to develop an agile BW complex and to this end we are seeing a structure that reflects this goal.' Consequently, Bellamy recommended that Assad's biological ambitions should be considered with the same seriousness as his chemical capacity.

Indeed, the US took this very seriously at the start of the Syrian conflict. The credibility of the threat is reflected in the way biological weapons were originally discussed alongside chemical arms during the initial stages of the crisis. They were directly comparable, cited in the same speeches and in relation to the same risks. Biological weapons were even mentioned in the redline statement. The redline refers explicitly to chemical weapons, and yet an analysis of the entirety of Obama's response – in answer to a journalist's question – reveals that chemical warfare was not the only so-called 'mass destructive' interest on the president's mind in respect of this issue:

> I have, at this point, not ordered military engagement in the situation. But the point that you [the journalist] made about chemical *and biological weapons* is critical. That's an issue that doesn't just concern Syria, it concerns our close allies in the region, including Israel. It concerns us. We cannot have a situation where chemical or biological weapons are falling into the hands of the wrong people. (Obama, 2012e; emphasis added)

As well as adding further weight to the arguments made in Part I that Obama was never committed to the idea of chemical weapons as an exclusive foreign policy ultimatum in respect of Syria, this demonstrates that biological weapons also occupied a similar space on the political agenda at that point. Critically, it should be noted that the journalist did not mention biological weapons in their question. That is, when asked about chemical weapons, Obama himself equated them with a biological concern. This is hardly surprising, given that Obama's response mirrored the way in which both chemical and biological weaponry were consistently discussed collectively in US foreign policy discourse during the early stages of the crisis (e.g. Edward Royce in US Cong., 2012b: 1–4), and particularly in relation to the official national emergency that Obama (2012b) set on Syria. Chemical weapons did not stand out as an exclusively terrible threat, but were subsumed within a wider categorisation of violence that incorporated the biological.

This assumption gained credibility in July 2012 when Syrian Foreign Minister Jihad Makdissi officially declared that Syria would never use chemical or biological weapons inside its country unless it experienced external hostility, a statement that apparently confirmed the existence of a biological programme:

> No chemical or biological weapons will ever be used, and I repeat, will never be used, during the crisis in Syria no matter what the developments inside Syria. All of these types of weapons are in storage and under security and the direct supervision of the Syrian armed forces and will never be used unless Syria is exposed to external aggression. (In AP, 2012)

Syrian officials later discredited this statement. Yet it was still taken as evidence of a biological programme – especially since it turned out that Syria very much did have usable chemical weapons, also mentioned in the statement. Indeed, Assad made a great effort to not deny possessing bioweapons. In an interview with *Der Speigel*, in response to a question on Syria's biological capacity, he said: 'We didn't give any information in this regard because it is considered classified information' (in Lentzos, 2013). This answer has overtones of overtly refusing to kiss and tell, where it implies you did it as much as you didn't. In line with Bellamy's thinking, the desire for biological weapons – or at least, the desire to be feasibly considered a biological threat – was important. Assad clearly saw value in being labelled a biological weapons state, regardless of whether this was matched by his actual capability and stockpiling. As such, this is someone who believes that biological weapons have political importance and that they are usable devices. And the fact that states including Russia, Iran, and China have been so willing to assist with WMD technologies in the past indicates that a biological Syria is no idle threat.

Furthermore, the removal of chemical weapons via the CWC could be seen to provide a perfect incentive to focus on developing that biological weapons stockpile. It is believed that Syria accelerated both its chemical and biological programmes after Israel destroyed a clandestine Syrian nuclear reactor in September 2007 (Blair, 2012). Consequently, why would eradicating chemical weapons not have the same impact? Why wouldn't Assad once again choose to build up his WMD programme in one area (biological) once another had been degraded, if not entirely eliminated? Potential and desire have always been difficult concepts when it comes to weapons acquisition and employment. What an actor wants and what they can do have always been very distinct ideas. And yet, in the case of Syria, there is a strong foundational infrastructure, if not a feasible weapons programme. Indeed, some analysts are convinced that this has already been realised. An anonymous Middle East official has claimed that Syria is a functioning biological weapons state: 'We are worried about sarin, but Syria also has biological weapons, and compared to those, sarin is nothing. We know it, and others in the region know it. The Americans certainly know it' (in Warrick, 2013). And most famously, on 29 January 2014, James Clapper, Director of US National Intelligence (in AP, 2014a), said: 'We judge that some elements of Syria's biological warfare program might have advanced beyond the research and development stage and might be capable of limited agent production, based on the duration of its longstanding program.'

Despite this, however, biological weapons have been notably absent from negotiations on Syria. US foreign policy-makers have portrayed Assad's use of chemical weapons as the consequence of his wider determination to massacre rebels and civilians. Why then is there not a similar concern about the escalation of other forms of WMD? In particular, while great effort has been invested in encouraging Assad to accede to the CWC, why has there been no similar demand that Syria ratify its signature of the BWC? The Obama administration did not even consider this suggestion relevant to put on the table, let alone reject it for any strategic reason: for example, that asking Assad for 'too much' at this stage (eradicating both chemical and biological capabilities at the same time) might have jeopardised any deal. It did not even come up. For some, the failure to address bioweapons within the same context as chemical arms elimination was risky and constitutes a more significant threat than that posed by chemical weapons alone. Republican Senator John Cornyn (2013) wrote to Kerry following the declaration of accession to the CWC to complain that not incorporating biological weapons prohibitions as well 'would represent a gaping hole in the plan'. Of course, as a Republican, Cornyn would have an incentive to utilise this conflation of biological/chemical warfare to his own advantage; that is, a way in which to publicly undermine the opposition. Yet this still highlights a problematic disparity in respect of US foreign policy prioritisation. Both biological and chemical armaments are considered dangerous; specifically, they are considered dangerous on the same grounds. Consequently, the decision to not address this biological threat as part of the resolution process remains an ill fit with the political concern that has been applied to it.

Explicitly, Assad's biowarfare ambitions have not been merely downplayed or moderated; the issue has been written off within core US foreign policy strategising. This constitutes yet another example of the taboo's distortion of perceptions of conflict. The situation cannot be reduced to a case where chemical weapons take precedence because they have been used in Syria and biological arms have not. Moreover, to refer back to Bellamy, it is also not just that chemical weapons have been deemed a more tangible and advanced threat. If this were the explanation, then why was Obama and his administration so concerned about the scope of the biological weapons during the initial stages of the conflict, to the extent that they were treated as comparable to the chemical threat? This reveals that something more complex has governed understanding of bioweapons in respect of Syria. More specifically, that this has been caused by the focus on the taboo. Again, the lens has been applied, and has removed the bio threat from consideration. Admittedly, the realities of Assad's bioweapons threat have always been difficult to 'see'. It was, and remains, a highly uncertain threat – as such, policy-makers have never been sure what it is they were looking at, let alone how to accurately assess it. The civil conflict obscures this further: information is less accessible and, potentially, more clandestine on the part of Assad. But the additional framing of the chemical weapons taboo means the debate was not merely unclear; it was also no longer relevant. The taboo ensures that attention is paid only to chemical weapons, so all other threats are discounted. They do not even register; hence a situation in which biological weapons were initially considered a foreign policy issue in terms of the conflict, but this issue was dropped once the redline and the taboo were brought into play.

Within the context of Syria, this has caused a significant gap to emerge in terms of US foreign policy. Even where it can be argued that the biological threat is less certain, this is not the issue. The issue is that the taboo created a situation in which the debate on the possibility of biological weapons use was not even engaged with. Assad's programme may still be in its research infancy, or not, but this potential is not even considered under the conditions of the taboo. Given that chemical weapons were themselves deemed 'only' a possibility at the start of the crisis, the failure to seriously consider the role of bioweapons in Syria is difficult. Admittedly, Obama never desired to consider them. In line with the discussion of WMD in the previous chapter, and the idea that mass destructive weaponry demands international involvement in cases of their illegal possession and/or use, bringing these devices into the debate could only have increased the pressure for an intervention that the president never wanted. Again, therefore, this is evidence of strategic use. Yet this too is a further demonstration of the way in which the taboo shapes understanding. Specifically, it has forced a potentially major threat out of the foreign policy debate on Syria. Despite evidence that the threat may not be immediate, it remains a red flag as to what the US might be missing. The taboo has structured debate in ways that preclude threats even before they have a chance to be contemplated.

Stigmatisation and prioritisation

This discussion of the taboo and how it has skewed understanding of the Syria crisis is a very different picture from the one painted of the norm elsewhere within IR. Here, it is an extremely worthy and positive ideal. It is a politically valuable concept seen exclusively in terms of its 'good'. And indeed, the idea that chemical weapons are horrific and would best be eliminated is hard to argue against. Whether this is understood within the wider context of stigmatisation or not (in that they are constructed as especially vile weapons, some would say regardless of their actual capacity for destructive effect), these armaments are not nice. Not having them is better than having them. Why then does there exist such disparity between this commitment to the eradication of chemical warfare and the problems experienced in respect of Syria? The reason is that the taboo does not separate weapons elimination from the prioritisation of chemical weapons. This is not simply the case that chemical weapons are horrific, but that the level to which they are so renders them distinct from other weapons, and this distinct nature underpins the taboo itself. Conventional understanding states that the very nature of the taboo revolves around the discrete stigmatisation of these weapons. But even more than this, it states that it should be a priority concern. This can be problematic, however; Syria being an ideal example. Chemical weapons have undoubtedly constituted a horrific aspect of the conflict, but because the issue has dominated debate to such an extent it has actually skewed understanding away from the major threats at the heart of the crisis. The way in which the taboo upholds chemical weapons as special can have damaging implications for a conflict scenario, particularly one that is not determined by chemical warfare alone. The way in which the idea of chemical weapons elimination has translated into a biased and exclusionary foreign policy that builds unsustainable hierarchies of understanding has caused this. In effect, this is a difference between us saying that chemical weapons are very important and should be removed *at the same time* as dealing with political and other threats (a moral commitment), as opposed to the way the Obama administration has dealt with it and looked only at chemical weapons (a moral commitment that cancels out all other issues). The special nature of chemical weapons has meant that as soon as these weapons were used, nothing else mattered; the lens had been applied. The expression of the ideal exaggerated the focus on chemical weapons, even at the cost of losing sight of other relevant factors.

This can be understood to the point at which that prioritisation is employed as inherently proscriptive: it demands that chemical weapons take precedence. This prioritisation plays heavily into the strength of the norm. It has already been established that the chemical weapons taboo is extremely strong. Indeed, its strength is seen as a major aspect of its success. Few norms have ever achieved the international acceptance enjoyed by the taboo. Yet this normative strength is also problematic. The taboo's strength clashes with other norms, specifically in a way that presumes it will take precedence. This is not a good thing. It means that everything else is pushed aside, with no ideological challenge to this prioritisation.

Consequently, this is a less a statement on the accuracy of the taboo as a principle of eliminating chemical weapons, and more a criticism of its expression and conventional manifestation within international politics. Specifically, this is the way in which applying the taboo to a complex conflict situation can radically misrepresent and obscure understanding of it. US foreign policy has adopted this expression in full, and – while removing chemical weapons from Assad cannot be denied to be of significant import – this has been the core factor in its failure to resolve the situation in Syria (to the extent Obama ever really desired to actively engage in resolution in the first place). This is because the application of the taboo reduced the conflict purely to terms relating to chemical weapons. The other factors – the massacres, the conventional aggression – are removed from consideration. This is not an appropriate form of foreign policy. Upholding the taboo is not about expressing it in its most vehement terms, but about analysing how chemical weapons relate to conflict and how their eradication can best serve the wider picture. The idea that they should be eliminated is not contested, but the process of eradication itself should not happen in a way that so readily violates other important norms.

Conclusion

Eliminating chemical weapons is a good thing. Eliminating chemical weapons from Syria is a good thing. The problem is that these ideals are *not* good when they are expressed through the medium of a highly biased taboo. More specifically, the exclusive nature of the taboo creates hierarchies of thinking that vastly distort understanding of the role that various types of weapon play within a conflict. The focus on chemical weapons is not merely a product of US foreign policy strategy, but a case where the framework of the taboo meant those policy-makers could do little else. The taboo is not just a moral idea; it is an inherently proscriptive normative construct. It states that chemical weapons elimination is so important that it must be held up as an unconditional ideal. Eradication must be respected at all costs. Yet the act of effectively placing the taboo on a pedestal ignores all other threats. Indeed, more than this: it does not simply ignore them, but removes them from consideration. It applies a lens to the situation in which non-chemical risks cannot be seen by the policy-makers engaged in crisis resolution. This applies even to major risks, including the vast numbers of people who have been killed by conventional means and the possibility that Assad will turn to biological weapons as his next instrument of death.

Indeed, in the case of conventional aggression, this hierarchy had gone so far as to effectively legitimate Assad's killing of rebels and civilians.

This is connected to strategic use. The lens can be the unintentional product of a policy-maker choosing to apply the taboo; in adhering to this conception they become blind to the wider realities of a given situation. Yet, as this book demonstrates, the framing of debate can compromise a resource as much as an unintended construction. The pushing aside of other issues can be beneficial, not least to a president keen to avoid intervention. Or to his opponents, who see exaggerating the sidelining of non-chemical concerns as a way of making the Commander-in-Chief appear incompetent. Yet this strategic interpretation only reinforces the key argument here: that the taboo can distort a crisis, to such an extent that it precludes resolution. It forces debate into a pathway of logic that bypasses all other concerns, even where these constitute core issues at stake. As such, the taboo cannot be judged by principle alone; or that the principle should be equated with its expression. The way this principle is presently enacted creates major problems for the international system and IR as a practice. Simply applying the chemical weapons taboo regardless of the specifics of the situation as it stands does not guarantee the best outcome.

6

Escalating the crisis

THE PROBLEMATIC construction of the chemical weapons taboo can be taken even further – to argue that it is not just misrepresentative, but has made the Syria crisis worse. The difficult hierarchies and assumptions that the taboo has introduced into US policy-makers' understanding of the conflict have resulted in its violent escalation. Syria has suffered explicitly because of the reliance on the taboo as the basis of US foreign policy. In expanding the discussion laid out in the previous chapter, this chapter explores the ways in which this has occurred. First, it considers how the exclusive focus on chemical weapons has prolonged the crisis. By failing to engage with a more wide-ranging and tailored approach, and by simultaneously creating the false impression that a workable resolution was in place (when, in fact, the strategy put forward would not substantially solve anything in respect of Syria), this caused the conflict to continue. This is a situation characterised by even greater levels of aggression than seen prior to Assad's accession to the Chemical Weapons Convention (CWC). Far from addressing the violence being carried out, the taboo created an opportunity for its intensification. Yet this is not just a case of continuation as a consequence of failing to address core problems, but also one in which the CWC introduced new dynamics that actively exacerbated the conflict, especially surrounding the logistics of chemical weapons elimination. Second, this is an issue of legitimacy. Asking someone to sign an agreement on behalf of their nation makes a major statement about the role they play as a valid leader and international figurehead. Consequently, recognising Assad as the person who could approve the CWC conveyed considerable legitimacy on the dictator. This not only strengthened his position within the conflict, but also emboldened him to carry out even more extensive acts of mass violence. These have not been limited to conventional aggression, but also include the continued use of chemical weapons. Assad's ongoing employment of the chemical agent chlorine is put into context here – not only as a violation of the CWC, but also the ways in which this agreement has encouraged and facilitated Assad's engagement with chemical warfare.

The discussion then brings Part II together to draw some conclusions about the problematic nature of the taboo. Specifically, it takes on potential criticisms of this assessment. On the basis of the taboo's conventional understanding, it would be easy to dismiss the claims made here as unduly controversial, if not dangerous. Where the taboo is adopted as a necessary and worthy political concept, any contestation of it may upset. This section tackles that opinion head-on to demonstrate why it is so important to let go of conventional perceptions surrounding the taboo, or at least to recognise their destructive potential in applying the taboo to ensure that potential is not realised. It also explains how analysis can deal with a situation where the taboo is 'undermined' in this way. Does acknowledging a challenge mean, as proponents of the taboo would argue, that we would be left with a precarious gap in extreme arms control – one that opens up the international community to the uncontrolled use of chemical weapons in the future? Or can we maintain a conceptual framework in which the ideals of disarmament can still be respected (if desired), but that also accepts that the heavy prioritisation inherent to the taboo is no longer acceptable or appropriate? In effect, are we stuck with the taboo as conventionally understood? Do we simply have too much invested in it even to question it? Or can we change the taboo, especially where it is capable of doing so much damage in terms of international politics and security?

False progress

Constructing US foreign policy around the taboo has created a false illusion of progress with regard to Syria. The diplomatic activity surrounding Assad's acceptance of the CWC and the highly visible commitment to chemical weapons elimination gave the impression that US foreign policy-makers were actively working to address the civil crisis given that something was being done. Specifically, this was presented as a wider resolution process on the part of the US. Indeed, where the conflict had been effectively reduced to the question of chemical weapons use as a consequence of the taboo, a political agreement in which Syria acceded to the CWC could ostensibly be viewed as a peace process within itself. Yet, as the previous chapter demonstrates, a chemical-centric approach could not, and did not, achieve anything significant. As such, the US's prominent foreign policy activity was fundamentally irrelevant in respect of its professed aims. The idea that any real progress was being made was a fallacy. It produced the delusion that a clear plan had been put in place and taken forward, when in fact nothing of any substance was being implemented.

To consider how this myth of progress was manifest, the CWC solution was presented as a major step forward in terms of international diplomacy – not just in addressing Assad's violation of an international norm, but also as stopping the crisis. The CWC supposedly provided a basis on which US and other foreign policy actors could come together not simply for this one political deal, but also for future agreements leading to the conflict's cessation (Fitzpatrick, 2013: 107). It created the diplomatic structure necessary for expanded negotiations. Especially where it engaged the otherwise bellicose Assad in peace-driven discussions with the international community, so the chemical weapons issue apparently opened doors to new opportunities for resolution. This is evident in Obama's annual address to the UN on 24 September 2013. In discussing the Syrian crisis, he identifies the CWC as an initial stage in the peace process: 'With respect to Syria, we believe that as a starting point the international community must enforce the ban on chemical weapons.' Critically, however, this act was not merely one aspect of that process, but the catalyst for, and foundation of, everything else that was supposedly to come: 'Our agreement on chemical weapons should energize a larger diplomatic effort to reach a political settlement within Syria.' Specifically, these future efforts were also framed within the context of the taboo. This was not simply the case that the CWC would inspire new diplomatic activity, but that this activity was intrinsically driven by the taboo also. While Obama goes on to lay out the potential detail of such a settlement, therefore – one that embraces more expansive concepts such as humanitarian aid and democracy promotion – this is still inherently understood within the context of anti-chemical weapons negotiations. The two are inseparably linked, whereby the taboo constitutes the defining basis that draws them together. They cannot be divorced, and the concept of conflict resolution is constructed in a way that is not feasible without the accompanying reference to both the CWC and the taboo.

Significantly, this inability to separate the crisis from chemical warfare occurs where Syria's very destabilisation is equated with the violation of the taboo. In his UN speech, Obama depicts Syria as a situation that 'goes to the heart of broader challenges that the international community must now confront'. That challenge (only one challenge is identified, despite the plural being used) is explicitly identified as the breaking of the taboo. Minus the taboo, therefore, there is no clear basis on which to do anything about Syria. The narrative is structured in a way that always comes back to this normative expectation. Without it, Obama provides no reason as to why the international community should act on Syria; or at least he gives no grounds other than chemical weapons on which this should be addressed. In a similar vein, Obama asserts that the UN must support action against Assad where the dictator had lost all legitimacy – but specifically where that legitimacy had been forfeit as a consequence of his violation of the chemical norm, and nothing else. Going back to the ideas outlined in Chapter 4 concerning Obama's use of the taboo to justify US foreign policy, this was again a case in which Assad was considered worthy of removal explicitly because of his use of chemical weapons. Consequently, the terms of the strategic narrative irrevocably connected all US foreign policy on Syria to the taboo, without providing any opportunity to comprehend this outside the confines of that specific framework. Once again, this was a case in which the taboo dominated discourse to the extent that it pushed out all other considerations, however relevant – as it did in relation to conventional and biological threats. The lens ensured that chemical weapons were all that were seen, and that this one risk framed US foreign policy to the exclusion of everything else.

As a consequence of this, Assad's accession to the CWC came with an expectation and confidence that the Syria issue was in hand. Obama had effectively outlined a strategy stemming from the CWC to political settlement in Syria; and with the CWC in place, this process appeared to be successfully in motion. Obama (2013p) reinforced that perception by repeatedly framing the CWC as having allowed the US to 'achieve our [America's] goals' in respect of this. This is an emotive rhetorical presentation. The reference to goals implies a clear strategy (i.e. the one outlined by Obama at the UN) leading to an effective and beneficial aim. Goals, not unlike the chemical weapons taboo, are supposedly 'good' things. They represent a culmination of effort and of positive achievement. Furthermore, this also has strong overtones not merely of achievement, but of winning; that is, of gaining the outcome that the actor desires over the actions of another (i.e. Assad). Indeed, a wider analysis of Obama's (2013l) rhetoric at this time reveals his employment of a range of phrases that support this perception of accomplishment in respect of the Syria crisis: 'firm response from the international community'; 'important step'; 'number-one priority'; and 'this [joint US–Russia] agreement could end the threat these [chemical] weapons pose not only to the Syrian people, but to the world'. These are all highly motivating phrases, implying a strong and dedicated strategy if not actual realisation. As such, this gave an impression of major commitment to a US foreign policy strategy, and to the ongoing success of that strategy.

Yet this optimistic picture of diplomatic progress masked how little it could actually do for a beleaguered Syria and its civilians. The highly public pronouncement of moving forward, which Obama deliberately presented in such positive terms, distracted from the reality that it was an unworkable solution – or at least not one that applied to the extent US policy-makers indicated. On these terms, the strategy was an abject failure. Crucially, the key point here is that it was not simply an unsustainable approach; it was this approach that had led to a false impression of progress. This is a situation in which the taboo itself contributed directly to that illusion. Specifically, the way in which the taboo was held up within the strategic narrative as effectively a multipurpose solution to the Syrian problem created a false sense of security that something was being done. Moreover, who would question the taboo as a form of political progress? It has already been established that the norm is considered an explicit positive in respect of international politics. How, therefore, could diplomatic advancement on this basis be inappropriate or 'not' progress? There is simply no rhetorical or conceptual provision for the idea that the taboo can constitute a negative influence. The taboo is inevitably constructed as a 'good', and this precludes the idea that there may have been something amiss concerning its application to the Syrian crisis. Indeed, even where commentators have criticised the political focus on chemical weapons (such as J. Freedman's work cited below), this never frames that criticism within the context of the taboo. Even though the CWC and the taboo are inherently connected – not least via the strategic narrative constructed by Obama in respect of the redline – this is not recognised, because the taboo itself is effectively immune to censure. Within this framework of understanding, the taboo now exaggerated the erroneous belief that a foreign policy approach that prioritised chemical weapons elimination was working, even though the crisis was now deteriorating under these terms.

This plays into the strategic element of the taboo's use. The confusion created by this situation was beneficial for Obama in that it provided the president with a convenient tactic for avoiding intervention. Throughout this analysis, the expectation that Obama should act on Syria has been a major consideration. From those who support military intervention, and also from those who do not, Obama has experienced intense pressure to bring about a resolution, or some significant form of crisis amelioration. This criticism has plagued the president for some time, and was a persistent theme within US foreign policy debates even before chemical weapons had been used. Within this context, Obama's air strike proposition, and later his joint activity with Russia concerning the CWC, gave the impression that he *was* acting. He was engaging with the conflict. Critically, however, the CWC not only lessened the pressure to take responsibility for action (in that he appeared to be doing so), but also lowered the expectation that Obama should undertake military intervention as a consequence of that responsibility. He was not only acting, but also taking attention away from calls for direct military intervention, which he had never desired. In this sense, he was killing two birds with one stone: addressing the political pressure to act, and avoiding the intervention option by ostensibly pursuing an alternative, i.e. the CWC. Indeed, as an added benefit, the CWC proceedings allowed Obama to portray himself as something of a diplomatic hero. He had avoided the military option by succeeding at the negotiating table. For someone committed to pragmatic governance, this was especially becoming and a major incentive in pursuing Syria's CWC accession.

Yet ultimately this remained a situation in which Obama was attempting to limit his involvement. As already discussed in Part I, the redline meant he could not avoid the chemical issue – hence his appeal to the taboo and its expression via the CWC. But beyond this, Obama could use that appeal to avoid a strong interventionist stance. Explicitly, this more tentative and isolationist strategy was made feasible where the commitment on chemical arms detracted from it. If the situation looked as though it was being attended to, then Obama did not have to pursue any option he was uncomfortable with, aside from that explicitly connected to upholding the taboo. This approach ostensibly dealt with a growing criticism that was dogging his presidency and yet also avoided US 'boots on the ground'. Consequently, there was a clear incentive for Obama to play up the taboo further, where this constituted an act of strategic employment and the performance of a strategic narrative.

Prolonging conflict

Critically, however, this is not simply a case in which the taboo masked its own failure to help in Syria; it is also a situation in which the illusion of progress would exacerbate the conflict. The false impression that a resolution process was now in place prolonged the civil war. This is not a complex claim. Pursuing a strategy that was both speculative and also fundamentally incapable of solving the crisis would, logically, only result in its unaided continuation. No workable method of resolution had been enacted; therefore, the civil war would continue on its destructive course. Insofar as a taboo-based approach distracted from the problems inherent to US foreign policy strategy, the violent protraction of the crisis can be attributed to that normative expectation. Creating the conditions under which the conflict would be allowed to continue kept the aggression going, in turn leading to further deaths, casualties, and mass dislocation. And because the matter was seemingly being dealt with, there was no incentive to engage in further resolution efforts or modify the strategy in place in order to change this.

Indeed, the conventional violence experienced in Syria actually intensified after Assad's accession to the CWC. Assad's actions have been labelled 'industrial-scale killing' and likened to the acts uncovered by war crimes prosecutors at the Nuremberg trials (in O'Toole, 2014). At one level this is an issue of targeting. There has been a significant expansion in regime troops' targeting of civilian areas, including medical facilities, schools and school buses, residential areas, and other high-density targets such as bakeries (HRW, 2013b; SNHR, 2013a). Assad has demonstrated that he is now substantially more willing to strike non-combatants than he was at the start of the conflict (which he was more than prepared to do even then). At another level, this is also an issue of the types of weapon employed. One of the most prominent issues that have hit both news headlines and political agendas concerning the post-CWC Syria is the expanded use of barrel bombs by government forces. Barrel bombs are exactly that: massive conventional explosive munitions made of barrels or similarly shaped metal containers. They are well known not only for the ease and efficacy of their construction, but also for their extensive and indiscriminate destructive effect. Their use is prohibited under the terms of UN Resolution 2139 (2014) on the Syria crisis, which demanded that all parties in the conflict allow humanitarian aid into the country and its safe passage to those who require it, especially in besieged areas. This has had only a limited effect, however, as the continued use of these devices clearly indicates. A report released one year since the passage of the resolution reveals that, within that time frame, 6,163 civilians were killed in regime barrel bomb attacks, including 1,892 children and 1,720 women (HRW, 2015a). Neither the US nor the UN has reacted, largely due to the expectation that Russia and China would veto any sanctions to be imposed. In response, the Syrian Network for Human Rights (SNHR, 2013b) has stated bluntly that this inaction demonstrates that 'there is no red line'. In a similar way, Assad has also raised international concern by using cluster bombs. Syria is not a signatory of the 2008 Convention on Cluster Munitions agreement that controls employment of these armaments.

Escalation has also allegedly occurred in respect of involvement by extremist organisations. While the origins of the Syrian conflict can be found in the Arab Spring and the violent deterioration of otherwise peaceful protests against Assad's dictatorship, it has become embroiled in a complex fight between Sunni and Shiite jihadist groups (Smyth, 2015: 1–2). This study does not intend to address this complexity in full here – that is another book in itself. But it is enough to state here that the Syrian crisis is now characterised by the involvement of Islamic extremist factions. These have vastly expanded and complicated the conflict, explicitly where this relates to the level of violence and the continuation of fighting. Syria is no stranger to jihadist organisations: al-Qaeda has a long-standing connection with Syria (Jones, 2013: 54–5), and has even been supported by Assad in the past (O'Bagy, 2012: 6). Yet the emerging crisis has created new opportunities for extremist groups in the region. This applies even to those organisations that had a presence in Syria long before the Arab Spring, of which al-Qaeda was initially at the fore (Hoffman, 2013: 636, 643–5; Jenkins, 2013: 3–4; Turner, 2015: 209–10). Syria was seen as a chance to strengthen and regroup within al-Qaeda, particularly after the hard campaign surrounding the 2003 Iraq invasion. Dynamics within al-Qaeda would soon see this situation splinter and intensify, however, specifically in relation to the development of al-Qaeda affiliate group, Jabhat al-Nusra (Byman, 2014: 453–6; Cheterian, 2015: 112), and also IS, which emerged out of al-Qaeda in Iraq and would eventually split from the organisation (Hashim, 2014; Stern and Berger, 2015; Weiss and Hassan, 2015). IS in particular has also sought to exploit the turmoil of Syria, especially in terms of its aims to establish a caliphate (Holbrook, 2015: 93–4). This would happen on a much more aggressive and violent scale than seen in relation to al-Qaeda and other extremist groups now in the region, both Sunni and Shiite. IS has acquired a reputation for extreme violence, which is considered not just an expression of aggression but a strategy in itself (Neer and O'Toole, 2014), and was one of the reasons for the split from al-Qaeda, who found their abusive tactics intolerable (Zelin, 2014: 3). As such, the combination of group rivalry and greater levels of destruction has increased the scale of the conflict. At the most basic level of measurement, this relates to the sheer number of extremist and foreign fighters entering the war zone (Cragin, 2015: 311–12). As Charles Lister (2014: 88) says: 'the Syrian jihad has become a truly international phenomenon, with at least 15,000 foreign nationals from at least 90 countries having emerged in combat in the country since 2011. This represents a rate of foreign-fighter influx into a civil conflict that is unprecedented in modern history.' He adds that this 'poses a very real immediate and long-term threat to regional and international security'. As such, this development towards Islamic extremism in the country constitutes a major feature of the Syria crisis, especially in terms of its escalation.

This has been directly attributed to the CWC negotiations. Specifically, this is the claim that pursing this diplomatic option wasted time, which created a temporal opportunity for extremist groups to establish themselves within the conflict. As Ros-Lehtinen said (in US Cong., 2013b: 2): 'The delayed response also allowed for extremist groups and al-Qaeda affiliates to move in to coopt the movement, setting up the bloody conflict that we see every day.' Kinzinger (in US Cong., 2013g: 4) expresses the same sentiment, explicitly where it attaches that delay to the US strategy based on chemical weapons elimination:

> I supported President Obama earlier this year in limited U.S. military strikes as a punishment for chemical weapons use, but in solving a larger crisis the simple fact is we waited too long. We waiting too long to exert U.S. influence in the region, thus creating a power vacuum and leaving open the door for al-Qaeda, Hezbollah, Iran and Russia to fill this void. All groups that I certainly do not want to exert more influence in the Middle East.

This is clearly speculative and based on counterfactual reasoning. A counterfactual is an imagined alternative scenario: 'what if' certain factors governing the outcome of a specific event were different? In this case, what if the US had not become so focused on the CWC and that time had been spent on actions that would have precluded the rise of extremist organisations in the country? While counterfactuals are useful to analysis, therefore, it must also be recognised that they are not based on empirical fact. Because of this speculative nature, it is difficult to unequivocally connect the taboo to the conflict's exacerbation on these grounds, and it is not presented here as anything other than conjecture, and at worst Republican propaganda. Yet these accusations still raise important issues concerning what might have occurred had the US not pursued the CWC as a lone solution. In combination with the concept of false progress outlined above, this questions the validity of the CWC approach. It is certainly not an absolute statement, but it is also not unfeasible to ask: would we have seen extremist involvement (or at least this high degree of extremist involvement) if the CWC had not been prioritised above all other concerns? Would Syria now be so violently complex if that one option had not come with the conceptual expectation that it alone would be sufficient, at least as the initiation of a wider resolution? The empirical basis of these questions may be circumspect, but this does not make them invalid in terms of whether there is analytic value in asking them, particularly when asking them in relation to the taboo.

Critically, this is not to suggest that the US – or indeed anyone else in the international system – was required to act on behalf of Syria and take responsibility for resolving the crisis, specifically beyond the limited issue of chemical weapons elimination. What is demonstrated, however, is that the adoption of the taboo as the basis of US foreign policy created a situation in which the conflict was allowed to continue and intensify. This is because policy-makers had no clear idea of what was actually happening in Syria, or what could be done to address it, or that there was anything to address. Or indeed, that they could understand what they would be prepared to do. If you do not know what is required of a specific situation, you cannot make a reasoned judgement as to how far you are willing to go in order to achieve it. In effect, perception had become so skewed as a consequence of the taboo that accurate policy-making could not take place. The ideational framing associated with the taboo meant that the decisions surrounding the CWC were not clear, and this has prolonged the US's toleration of the conflict as well as the conflict itself. To reiterate again, this is not to lay the burden of resolving Syria at the feet of the US. This is explicitly not the expectation here. But it is to say that the conceptual structure put in place by US foreign policy-making vastly distorted understanding of the crisis to the extent that resolution and/or crisis mitigation became unfeasible.

The downside of elimination

The chemical weapons taboo also made things worse on the ground by introducing new dynamics of conflict. In particular, the sheer practicalities of eliminating Assad's chemical stockpiles had a major impact in terms of escalation. At one level this is again the prolonging of the conflict, in that getting rid of chemical weapons is an extremely complex process that takes time to carry out. This applies even in the case of Syria, where the elimination process was severely compressed in order to be completed in the relatively short nine-month time frame allotted to it. As such, it plays into all those ideas already identified above in terms of how a protracted conflict has exacerbated the wider situation. At a further level, however, this created issues surrounding the geopolitical structure of the conflict, in particular making the opposition observe a controversial agreement that Assad – not the rebels – had signed. This in itself is problematic: several members of the opposition resisted the CWC solution because eliminating chemical weapons would remove the deterrent they constituted against Israel (Van Tets, 2014). Although there was a massive outcry from the opposition over Ghouta and other chemical attacks, the CWC solution was still far from a universally accepted agreement given these other considerations. And yet the opposition was expected to comply fully with the elimination procedure – hardly the best basis for moving forward. And this also created difficulty in that the agreement entailed highly disruptive provisions, which would undercut the opposition position while strongly benefiting Assad's. Brian Jenkins (in US Cong., 2013g: 44), Senior Advisor to the President of the RAND Corporation, said in a congressional hearing:

> Assad's agreement to get rid of the chemical weapons in a certain sense is a strategy that helps the Assad regime survive, because it is a major logistics enterprise to both protect and move those weapons and to ultimately dismantle or disarm them. Doing that in the midst of a conflict is very, very difficult, and so there is going to be extreme pressure on the rebel forces to not interfere with the disarmament process. In other words, it is a way in which we are obliged to accept the legitimacy of the Assad regime and the primacy of it and to lean on the rebels to allow the disarmament process to take place.

Legitimacy issues aside for the moment, the CWC was a tactical boon for the Syrian dictator. In particular, the logistics of chemical weapons elimination allowed regime troops unprecedented access to areas controlled by the opposition (McDonnell, 2013). Syria had declared a total of 23 locations, consisting of some 41 facilities – not all of them in areas then under government control (Trapp, 2014: 15). In fact, many of these locations were technically then within opposition territory. Because Assad's troops were tasked with protecting the convoys responsible for transporting Syria's chemical stockpiles from these facilities to their place of destruction, government forces could enter opposition areas that they would have otherwise been unable to. As well as being highly intimidating and appearing to favour Assad over the opposition, the Joint Agreement effectively demanded that the rebels permit their enemy access – an entitlement that they did not have reciprocally in terms of government-held areas. This undermined the opposition in relation to their tactics and also their geographical position. Assad was all too aware of this advantage and took it, carrying out even more violent attacks as a consequence. Michael Weiss (2014) describes this as a situation where Assad used the CWC provisions to wage a scorched-earth campaign, ostensibly to clear areas such as the Damascus highway for the delivery of the weapons for their eventual disposal. But this was little more than a cover for an increasingly brutal strategy against his opponents. Specifically, it was now a campaign that could be carried out behind enemy lines under the guise of cooperation with the Organisation for the Prohibition of Chemical Weapons (OPCW). Consequently, this conferred considerable power on the government and gave it a significant advantage in the field.

This problem was also seen in the pressure placed on the opposition to negotiate ceasefires within their own areas of occupation. These agreements were supposed to ensure the safe transit of chemical weapons and agent stockpiles (Cumming-Bruce, 2013). These have not proven easy to secure, given that agreeing to a ceasefire would severely undercut the opposition's security. Not least where enemy forces were now allowed access into opposition areas, there was little incentive for rebels to additionally sacrifice military options for attack in response. You do not have to be a realist to see that such a policy would challenge every instinct and survival option of those in opposition. This was made worse by the fact that the Joint Agreement failed to adequately detail how a chemical weapons elimination programme should be carried out, specifically in an active war zone (Horner, 2013: 31). The agreement did not sufficiently clarify what this would entail or the problems that could emerge from it – not least in terms of exacerbating the conflict and the levels of violence enacted as part of it. The US had assumed that elimination would be a 'good' thing. Yet this expectation concealed the problematic nature of the taboo's realisation. As already discussed above, this is not the type of issue typically considered in respect of the taboo. Chemical weapons are abhorrent and intolerable; ergo, their elimination must be a positive. In this way, the simplicity of the taboo's understanding masks a whole world of difficulties associated with its application. The taboo has ramifications (such as the practical demands of elimination), and not all of them are beneficial. But this potential for danger gets lost in the certainty that the taboo can only do good. As such, these negative issues are allowed to fester unaddressed and, as in the case of Syria, this can escalate a crisis – the very crisis the taboo was supposed to address.

Conferring legitimacy

As Jenkins signals above, the taboo-based approach is also problematic in that it unnecessarily legitimised Assad. This is specifically the case where the US has effectively recognised Assad as the legitimate Syrian state authority by asking him (of all those laying claim to leadership within Syria) to accede, on behalf of the country, to the CWC. This has been extremely detrimental in terms of relations with the opposition. Major factions within the opposition have rejected the CWC agreement on that basis that it favours and legitimises Assad (Zanders and Trapp, 2013). This is a situation that has not only undermined the chemical weapons elimination process, but conflict resolution more widely. Yet this has not merely upset the balance between the US and the opposition, but has actively empowered Assad in ways that have then exacerbated the crisis. There are two aspects to this: (a) confirming Assad's position as national leader despite the presence of a recognised opposition, and (b) conferring on him all the benefits of joining a legitimate normative regime.

Establishing Assad as leader

Asking Assad to accede to the CWC reaffirmed his position as figurehead and the national leader of Syria, despite the challenge posed to this by the opposition and continued anti-government civilian unrest. Identifying Assad as the person authorised to commit Syria to an international agreement reinforced his otherwise contested political standing. Recognition by, and consent to govern through, the international community is essential in establishing state legitimacy (Oppenheim, 1905: 116; Crawford, 2006); the signing of treaties/agreements is an act that both demonstrates and enables sovereignty (Krasner, 1999: 16; Steinberg, 2004: 331; Carcano, 2006: 53). While the exact criteria for state recognition (and indeed non-recognition) remains the subject of ongoing debate, the definition of the state as a legitimate body has long been assumed to include the 'capacity to enter into relations with other States', as cited in the 1933 Montevideo Convention on the Rights and Duties of States. Within this context, the external recognition of a specific leadership is important in ascertaining *who* has the right to exert that authority on the global stage (Fowler and Bunck, 1996; Murphy, 1999: 545). Simply put, the national leader signs on behalf of their country – and by looking to Assad as that signatory for accession to the CWC, this accepted and strengthened his regime. It was he who was singled out and treated as ruler. No other person or forum was recognised as having the legitimacy to bring Syria to the negotiating table on the CWC, or even as possessing a rightful interest in the process.

This is hardly surprising, perhaps. Assad was in charge prior to the rebellion, and without any clear usurping of that position he could still lay claim to state ownership, however tacit or disputed by the civil conflict. He had won the 2014 presidential election as incumbent, and the process of election can be seen as a valid entitlement to sovereign power and international endorsement (Reisman, 1990: 869), even where this is not achieved on strictly democratic grounds (Murphy, 1999). And indeed, the 2014 election were far from democratic: the word 'farce' would be a more accurate description given the extensive vote-rigging, violent intimidation, and forced disenfranchisement that characterised it (AP, 2014b). Yet even ruling out that election on those grounds, this was still a case in which Assad was the one with the chemical weapons stockpiles and the person who had used them. As such, he was the target for elimination measures. Committing Syria to the CWC via other political channels would have almost certainly proved futile in removing chemical armaments from the country, even if this approach were considered politically feasible. Assad would simply have claimed he was not subject to CWC provisions if it was not his 'name' on the agreement. Consequently, elimination could not have been achieved without full-scale military intervention – an option Obama had ruled out, or at least was doing all he could to avoid. Realistically then, Assad had to be the focus. But whatever the legality or practicality of recognising Assad as national leader in respect of the CWC, that selection sent an extremely strong political message, concerning not only the extent and security of Assad's position, but also the civil crisis more generally. While it was never intended as a statement of support for Assad's rule, this was effectively the outcome. It said that Assad was still legitimately in charge. It said he still enjoyed all the powers of legitimacy and sovereignty within the international context. His position was not merely secure: it had been publicly reaffirmed, and by the US, no less. As such, this was a slight against the very concept of an opposition and the rebellion against Syria's dictatorship.

This was an extremely ill fit with Obama's previous rejection of Assad's position, as well as US attempts to delegitimise the Syrian government. In 2012, Obama announced that the US now recognised the Syrian National Coalition as a de facto Syrian administration, specifically where this was intended as a 'move that further saps the legitimacy of president Bashar al-Assad's rule' (McGreal, 2012). Obama stated: 'We've made a decision that the Syrian Opposition Coalition is now inclusive enough, is reflective and representative enough of the Syrian population, that we consider them the legitimate representative of the Syrian people in opposition to the Assad regime.' Admittedly, this proved more symbolic than anything else. Chris McGreal, a journalist reporting on this presidential statement, says that the announcement could be seen as simply a way of placating the opposition after they had openly berated Obama for failing to sufficiently support them. It certainly did not come with any substantive commitment in terms of military backup, or an agreement that the opposition could call on the US for military support. As such, Joshua Freedman (2013) concludes that the failure to fully enact this recognition of the opposition meant that 'Assad remains the only legally recognised government in Syria'. Consequently, there is a clear disparity here between Obama's diplomatic offer to Assad as regards the CWC and his attempts to wrest state recognition away from the dictator.

Furthermore, for someone who had banked much of his foreign policy on the belief that the Assad regime had forfeit all legitimacy, Obama's extending of the hand of diplomacy in this specific way was a highly contradictory move. Obama wanted to avoid military action and resolve the crisis through non-violent means, and saw the CWC route as an opportunity for achieving this. But recognising Assad as a political equal in order to do so was contrary to US foreign policy aims more generally, where these relied explicitly on delegitimisation. Critically, this situation had implications not just for US foreign policy, but for the entire international community and especially the OPCW. Within this context, Freedman (2013) goes so far as to argue that this approach was so unacceptable that the OPCW should have rejected the US–Russia joint request with regard to Syria's accession to the convention:

To allow President Bashar al-Assad to sign the convention on behalf of Syria endorses his position as the leader of the country, a move which is not only symbolically important for Assad himself, but also affirms the coveted legal status which separate his regime from those in the opposition ... it allows Assad to engage in the quintessential act of statecraft, reaffirming himself as Syria's only legally recognised government.

He adds:

By denying Syria's accession to the Chemical Weapons Convention under Assad's tutelage, the OPCW would have been able to dent Assad's legal right to behave as the Government of Syria in the international arena. It should have embraced this possibility.

The reasoning here is clear: if the aim was to delegitimise Assad, Obama (and others) should not have engaged in a strategy that accomplished the very opposite, i.e. one that reaffirmed Assad as the main actor in respect of Syrian leadership. You do not empower the person you wish to diminish or simply let collapse.

This explains Assad's preparedness to accede. Obama hailed this willingness as a major diplomatic achievement; and yet – once again – the claim to progress concealed the fact that there was very little to negotiate or to convince Assad of. On the contrary, there was every incentive for Assad to comply. The CWC did nothing for Syria, but it did everything for its otherwise waning dictator. What Assad gained from this agreement would more than make up for the loss of his chemical weapons, whose effect, in turn, could more than be made up for in terms of more conventional violence. The importance of recognition and legitimacy to Assad should not be understated. Assad came to the negotiating table in an extremely precarious position: the civil crisis was continuing to weaken his regime, and the US, although now seeking to consult directly with him, had elsewhere acknowledged the opposition. Consequently, the effective reversal of that policy in recognising Assad was a major coup. Even as a pragmatic gesture, it was a significant boost to the regime.

In understanding this importance, it is worth going back to debates on African states' use of recognition and sovereignty to establish their position in the 1980s. In discussing their search for stability and power, Robert Jackson and Carl Rosberg (1986: 2) demonstrate that external recognition proved more important to state survival than any other factor, including factors such as geopolitical security, military power, and economic strength. More than any of these considerations closely associated with state viability, it was the recognition of statehood by the international community that was the most significant dynamic in keeping these states feasible. In a similar vein, it has been argued elsewhere that international recognition has proved especially important for the survival of authoritarian regimes (Masahiro, 2009: 5). Together with the concept of state sovereignty, this has been employed as an essential way of asserting a regime's power on the global stage, even where that power is limited or the regime in question has been subject to condemnation by the international community. Whatever weakness or political fraction has been experienced, authoritarian states have exploited their position as a 'rightful' and recognised member of the international political system in order to maintain their status. Within this context, it can be seen just how critical Obama's act of chemical diplomacy was with regard to Syria. Recognition was important in that it gave Assad back so much of what he had lost – power, legitimacy, and authority (both internal and external). This was not simply an agreement to remove chemical weapons from Syria, but a high-profile signal and default acceptance that Assad was still in charge. Recognition is an extremely powerful tool to have, one that goes to the very heart of regime survival. The US was effectively handing this to Assad and, in doing so, making any resolution of the Syrian crisis even more difficult.

While not inviting Assad to accede to the CWC would not have stopped the Syrian conflict, granting him legitimacy as a consequence of accession not only unnecessarily strengthened his regime but also undermined wider US foreign policy ambitions towards delegitimisation. Not only was Assad now more of a problem, but also the US had severely limited its foreign policy options in dealing with this. In particular, it limited the diplomatic options open to the US (given that Obama had actively sought to take military options out of consideration wherever possible). Giving Assad greater diplomatic leverage as a legitimate figure meant that the US had relatively less. Yet the CWC took away the potential resort to military responses as well, whether Obama wished to exploit them or not. Although not explicitly stated in the Joint Agreement, it was accepted that Assad's accession came with the unofficial promise that the US would not enact air strikes against the government. Air strikes were an option that Obama had demonstrated his willingness to take, having at this stage announced his intention to go to Congress for approval to do so. Indeed, it was a useful tactic in bringing not only Assad into diplomatic engagement with the US, but also Russia – where Putin was otherwise a thorn in America's side. Now this was another option that was off the table. Consequently, Obama had sacrificed a range of foreign policy options in dealing with Assad. The US had simultaneously both empowered Assad and reduced its ability to address that situation in one easy step.

Adherence and concession

The CWC solution also conferred legitimacy via Assad's ostensible adherence to the taboo itself. As Emilie Hafner-Burton *et al.* (2008: 116) have already discussed in relation to human rights norms more generally, the taboo grants legitimacy via its own legitimacy: 'Exactly because human rights norms are among the most legitimate standards in the world, subscribing to them has great legitimating value for nation-states. The subscribing sovereign gains, or claims, legitimacy in the eyes of superior sovereigns, peers, internal and external competitors, and internal subordinate groups and interests.' Accepting the terms of the taboo (as with upholding the taboo against violation) is considered a highly credible and ethical act of international diplomacy. Once again, this is the idea of the taboo as a 'good' thing; and specifically, as the above quotation demonstrates, adherence to the taboo is a 'good' itself. Anyone who publicly observes the taboo can enjoy the approval of the international community – even, apparently, where they continue to pursue conventional massacre on a significant scale. There are few more persuasive ways for a pariah to gain/regain international acceptance than openly embracing core norms held by that community, of which the chemical weapons taboo is one of the most prominent. Compliance is awarded a proverbial gold star, especially where compliance comes from a state with a poor normative record concerning previous behaviour. Everyone loves a convert.

This is also the case where that new compliance exists as a concession, as it was in the case of Assad. That is, there was pressure from the international community to comply, and in doing so Assad secured himself a sense of legitimacy in return. This process has been already been modelled by Ayse Zarakol (2014), who analyses the ways in which specifically Western pressure can influence the uptake of norms by non-Western states. She terms that pressure 'stigmatization', using this concept to demonstrate the methods by which the West effectively demonises non-Western states for not openly employing certain normative expectations. In order to overcome this, norm adoption takes place within the non-Western state in order to ensure acceptance within the international political system. In the case of Syria, Obama had vehemently stigmatised Assad for failing to comply with the chemical weapons taboo. In shifting government policy towards adoption via CWC accession, therefore, Assad was moving himself from an illegitimate to a legitimate status with respect to international politics. This is the legitimacy Assad was now benefiting from. Indeed, immediately after the accession agreement was announced, Assad began to enjoy better relationships with many previously unfriendly states. For example, in terms of key players in the region, the president of Turkey, Recep Tayyip Erdogan, demonstrated significantly more accommodating behaviour towards Assad after the CWC was put into force in Syria (Ma'oz, 2014: 53).

Yet Assad's strategy addressed an even deeper need with respect to legitimacy than improved relations. Not least where Obama had so emphatically used Assad's violation of the taboo to demonstrate the Syrian dictator's evil and immoral character – whereby this set Assad apart as being worthy of greater forms of involvement on the part of the US, for example, air strikes – so there was every incentive for Assad to reverse that foreign policy narrative through his compliance with the taboo. For this was not just the case that accession took options such as air strikes off the table, but it also removed the very ideational basis on which they were then being justified. That is, if Assad could signal that he was not of the character that would engage in norm violation – indeed, that he was actually willing to officially comply with the terms of the taboo, as expressed via the CWC – then there was no foundation on which Obama could intervene. Insofar as Obama had utilised this as his excuse for engagement in Syria and as the basis of his strategic narrative, then removing that as a consequence of accession would protect Assad from any escalation on the part of the US. As analyst Ramzy Mardini said, Assad's accession 'made a dent in the interventionist narrative that he's an uncontrollable madman who can't recognise diplomacy if it hit him in the face ... That growing reality is favouring Assad, not the opposition' (in McDonnell, 2013). Assad was now the man who was willing to make concessions. Specifically, these were concessions on issues at the heart of international politics with regard to Syria; or rather, had been constructed as such as a consequence of the taboo and its application to the crisis. Consequently, this was a tactical move by Assad. And it was one that would benefit him significantly in terms of gaining legitimacy, and in gaining ground within the conflict itself.

Conferring legitimacy on the basis of perceived concession raised two problems surrounding the crisis's escalation. First, it not merely granted Assad legitimacy as the supposedly rightful leader of Syria, but it also allowed the dictator to paint himself in a relatively positive light: as a moderate and a compromiser. Admittedly, this would prove somewhat temporary thanks to Assad's continued use of chemical weapons (discussed below). But at this initial stage, the situation gave him a certain kudos within the international system, and more specifically in respect of any further negotiations related to the conflict. This was an ace in his hand that he could potentially play further down the line. Should he face any proposition by the US for increased concessions, Assad could simply point to his apparent sacrifice over the CWC as evidence that he had already committed to so much – and so why should he give more? It gave him an unnecessary diplomatic advantage with regard to the US (where it was the US that would bear the burden of that advantage – the other party in the Joint Agreement, Russia, already enjoyed the best of relations with Assad and so this would not matter). Although still an international pariah, therefore, Assad was now a recognised national leader with a not-inconsiderable amount of goodwill behind him. Specifically, this was an element of goodwill that came directly from the taboo. That is, it was his ostensible adherence to the taboo that effectively forced other states to recognise him as having carried out a positive act. Once more, this is the idea that the taboo is considered solely within the context of the 'good', in that any compliance must also be seen in these terms. With this in mind, it is worth noting that the accession agreement was constructed in way that did not involve any element of punishment. In being prepared to make such a concession, Assad did not even receive a slap on the wrist for engaging in chemical warfare: 'The Russian-American agreement on Syria is not only a victory for Putin, but for Assad, who had paid no price for using chemical weapons' (Kaufman, 2014: 456). Crucially, this is not to say Assad was rehabilitated in respect of international relations – far from it. And the legitimacy he was granted was accidental as opposed to intentional. That is, the US did not intend to confer legitimacy, but did so as an unintended by-product of pursuing the taboo. Yet the taboo came with additional consequences that would ultimately empower Assad and make the conflict worse as a result. As Stephen Rademaker, an adviser with the Bipartisan Policy Center (in US Cong., 2013h: 70–1), said:

> It will be interesting to see how historians look back on this current – the last few months of what happened in Syria and how they explain or interpret the sequence of events. But I worry that the historical judgement will be that President Assad very cleverly decided to use chemical weapons against his civilian population, killed about 1,500 people, and the consequence of that was he was able to remain in power, that he pivoted and he focused attention of the international community on the existence of his chemical weapons, he volunteered to get rid of them, but as a practical matter the price of his cooperation in getting rid of those chemical weapons had to be that he would remain in power.

Second, the way this strategy was tied to the chemical weapons taboo (a) limited the conditions Assad had to meet in order to gain legitimacy, and (b) secured that legitimacy against the degrading impact of any other norm violation. In relation to the first half of this statement, the way the taboo reduced the crisis to chemical warfare meant this was the only concern Assad had to address in order to 'qualify' for legitimacy. This was the only objection that Obama had officially made against him. Yes, the president had recognised the other terrible acts Assad had carried out in addition to chemical warfare, including conventional massacre. Yet these had never been made a condition of intervention, or even the US's engagement with Assad more generally. These were known offences, but they were never on the table in a political or diplomatic sense. Consequently, this meant that adherence to the taboo was the only thing Assad had to do to comply – a concession already known to be no major sacrifice for the dictator. And once Assad had achieved legitimacy on these highly limited grounds, he was empowered. Importantly, this was a case in which that empowerment meant Assad could now engage in other acts of reprehensible behaviour and it would not undermine the legitimacy he had secured. This explains the intensification of conventional aggression. Where the taboo took the focus (whatever limited focus there had been) off Assad's acts of conventional assault, so there was even less pressure on him to stop or curtail this strategy of violence. In fact, he could now carry it out on a much greater scale because he was not to be held to account for these actions. Where Assad had effectively removed the chemical issue by acceding to the CWC, then there would be no further reason for the US or the international community to become involved, since it had never been part of the bargain. To use Zarakol's model: where there was no stigmatisation process around the issue of non-chemical warfare – that is, the US did not care about Assad's breaking of taboos against conventional harm, including crimes against humanity, and so did not apply pressure for the (re)adoption of those norms – then this was off the resolution agenda. And with US attention clearly secured on chemical weapons as a consequence of the exclusionary nature of the taboo, this was not likely to change.

In effect, then, the taboo protected Assad's legitimacy in that – as long as he did not use chemical devices – he could use any other weaponry and this would not undermine his newly strengthened position. The way in which the taboo's lens forces other threats out of consideration saw this limited and controversial legitimacy safeguarded because no other form of aggression could challenge that authority within this very specific context. While UN Secretary General, Ban Ki-moon (in UN 2013d), was keen to clarify that the CWC agreement was 'not a licence to kill with conventional weapons' and that 'a red light for one form of weapons did not mean a green light for others', this has not been the case (Rosen, 2014). Instead, as Jonathan Stevenson (2014: 130) argues, in 'publicly casting Assad as a rational compromiser, the crisis has provided him with greater political cover for using conventional military force against the opposition'. This new legitimacy emboldened Assad to continue and now escalate the massacre. It gave him a new opportunity to exert both his power in respect of the civil crisis and his position as leader – using violent means in order to do so. As such, the taboo facilitated a situation that, very far from helping the conflict, would only serve to intensify it further.

Legitimacy without compliance

Yet this argument surrounding conventional violence does not go far enough. The intensification of such aggression is not the only way the conflict has worsened under the terms of the taboo. Specifically, Assad has not complied with the CWC and regime troops have continued to employ tactics of chemical warfare, explicitly the use of chlorine. Chlorine is associated with water purification, sanitation, and the manufacture of medicines – all extremely important in war-torn and besieged Syria, where the inability to decontaminate water has been labelled 'an indirect weapon of mass destruction' (Sparrow, 2015: 40). Chlorine also has a dark side, however, and has an infamous reputation as the first chemical weapon to be used during the First World War (Shea, 2013: 5). A greenish-yellow gas, it is a choking agent that kills by causing respiratory failure and pulmonary oedema (Anderson, 2012: 65). It asphyxiates victims by damaging the lungs and suffocating them to death. Admittedly, chlorine is not seen as one of the most dangerous chemicals, or the most effective on the battlefield; there are allegations that al-Qaeda in Iraq abandoned chlorine as a weapon because the destructive effects were so inadequate that they were not considered worth the effort (Stewart, 2014). Despite this, however, chlorine has been used in an ongoing strategy of chemical attacks carried out since Syria's accession to the CWC.

This is a strategy that brings the increasing concern over barrel bombs into the equation, since this has proved to be the government's preferred method of delivering chlorine. A UN Human Rights Council (UNHRC, 2014a: 8–9) report details an eyewitness account of a major attack in April 2014 on Kafr Zeita – an opposition-held town in north-west Syria, located within Hama Governorate. Following the breakdown of a ceasefire between government and rebel forces in the area, the former launched a series of strikes that included barrel bombs filled with chlorine agent. The report describes the first of these assaults, during which three people were killed:

> On 11 April 2014, at 6.00pm, he [the witness] heard a warship helicopter hovering. A few minutes later the helicopter dropped several barrels on the western part of Kafr Zeita. The first barrel bomb was dropped about 400 metres away from where he was. It resulted in a massive explosion with yellowish fumes. The yellowish fumes were moving eastward with the wind and smelled like chlorine. Meanwhile armed group fighters started screaming from mosque minarets and on the radio that this was a chemical attack and that people should take necessary precautions. The fumes and the smell of chlorine caused a state of panic and terror among the people ... Ambulances rushed to the impact site and transferred dozens of victims who were suffering from suffocation and had difficulty breathing.

The government initially blamed Islamic rebel group Jabhat al-Nusra for the strikes, although this claim has been widely discounted due to the agent's dispersal by helicopter (HRW, 2014). Weapons delivery by aircraft has seen the finger of blame point towards Assad, since the regime was the only faction within the conflict to possess aircraft. As soon as allegations of the attack surfaced, the OPCW opened a fact-finding investigation into the incident. This reported later that year, in September, and concluded that its mission had found 'compelling confirmation' that chlorine had been used (OPCW, 2014). More specifically, it stated that the agent had been employed 'systematically and repeatedly' – not just at Kafr Zeita, but against the villages of Talmanes and Al Tamanah, also in the north of the country. In response to the OPCW findings, Secretary of State John Kerry (2014) said: 'The Assad regime must know that it will be held to account for such use in the international community.' Assad clearly knew otherwise. The incident passed without any condemnation on the part of the US or any other member of the international political system, let alone any measure in retribution for the strikes. Far from being held to account, Assad was not even seriously rebuked for his actions.

Chlorine hit the headlines again in March the next year, following a major strike on Sarmin village at Idlib (HRW, 2015b; MSF, 2015). Chlorine was not new to the area; the village had previously been targeted around the same time as Kafr Zeita in 2014 in response to similar losses by regime forces against the opposition there. Yet the 2015 attack stands out because of its scale, and particularly the killing of an entire family that included three very young children (AI, 2015). It also exposed over 100 people to chlorine, the vast majority of whom were civilians. A civil defence worker described the scene (ibid.):

> The smell was horrible. We evacuated people. We were told that a family lives in the basement. Three of us went downstairs. I took one breath and then when I took the second my throat burned, my eyes started burning. We didn't have masks. We don't have special clothes. I couldn't proceed. I was holding my breath but couldn't hold it further. I saw a woman on the stairs. She was blue and was not breathing. We evacuated her and a minute later the next team went in and evacuated the family. They were wearing masks – that is why they were able to go all the way down. They evacuated the father, mother and three babies. They all died.

Syrian medical worker, Dr Mohamed Tennari, who was working at a local field hospital during the strike, later gave eyewitness testimony to the UN Security Council. Tennari (in Editorial, 2015) confirmed that Idlib was a chlorine attack, commenting that: 'I have never seen children die in a more obscene manner.' His testimony made the news because he reduced some Council members to tears when he showed them videos of the scene (Nichols, 2015). One in particular detailed the failed attempts by medical staff to resuscitate the small children killed in the strike, aged one, two, and three years old. US Ambassador to the UN, Samantha Power, said it was an 'extremely unusual and very emotional meeting'. She added: 'If there was a dry eye in the room I didn't see it.' Somewhat ironically, only ten days before the Idlib attack took place, the Council had adopted Resolution 2209, in which the use of chlorine as a weapon was 'condemned in the strongest terms' (UN, 2015b). Starting as it meant to go on, however, this statement clearly had little impact and, even after Tennari's emotive testimony, the resolution would fail to contribute anything in terms of stopping the chlorine assaults (Edwards and Cacciatori, 2015). Indeed, Obama expressly went out of his way to avoid addressing the chlorine issue. He achieved this strategically by suggesting that chlorine is not actually a weapon and, therefore, irrelevant to any redline commitment or CWC violation:

> It is true that we've seen reports about the use of chlorine in bombs and that have the effect of chemical weapons. Chlorine itself, historically, has not been listed as a chemical weapon, but when it is used in this fashion can be considered a prohibited use of that particular chemical. And so we're working with the international community to investigate that. (Obama, 2015)

The logic is clear: if chlorine is not a weapon, the redline cannot apply. Once again, Obama was being an innovating ideologist. He selectively redefined the terms of debate in order to uphold his interests against intervention.

Assad has routinely denied the use of chlorine. In an interview on 17 April 2015 with Swedish newspaper *Expressen*, he repudiated the attacks, dismissing the accusations as 'propaganda ... to demonize the president, [and] to demonize the state' (Kenner, 2015). A few days later he told television station *France 2* that there was no proof of chlorine use at Idlib – a claim that drew on the wider idea that chlorine is not sufficiently destructive to be worth the bother: 'This is another fake narrative by the western governments ... The regular armaments that we have are more influential than chlorine, so we don't need it anyway. We didn't use it. We don't need to use it. We have our regular armaments, and we could achieve our goals without it. So, we don't use it. No, there's no proof' (in Ross and Malik, 2015). Yet the allegations and the evidence continue. The Security Council itself has officially documented many of these strikes: in a 2015 report, the organisation noted further chemical attacks in Idlib and also in the villages of Janoudieh, Kansafrah, and Kafr Batiekh (UN, 2015c: 2). The situation is now that reports are coming in 'almost daily' concerning the regime's use of chlorine (Kaszeta, 2015). Indeed, chlorine has now earned a reputation as the 'chemical weapon of choice' by Assad forces (Corder, 2015). This is highly concerning. Although these have been relatively limited attacks to date, it is worth considering that this is the same situation that previously led to the more extensive chemical attack at Ghouta. Prior to this major strike, Assad had carried out smaller attacks – where, with hindsight, this was a case of him testing the US and the international community as to what he could get away with in regard to chemical warfare. When no retribution came, even despite Obama's declaration of the redline, Assad was emboldened to authorise the greater strike at Ghouta. With this in mind, are these smaller chlorine attacks also Assad's testing of the international political waters? With the CWC now technically in place, is Assad trying to see how far he can push it without comeback? And if so, is this is the start of yet another build-up to more devastating chemical assaults in the future?

This behaviour fits in with Zarakol's analysis. For while she identifies stigmatisation as a transformative pressure on non-Western states to comply with Western ideals, she also demonstrates that this process of norm adoption can be an illusion. She draws a line between internalisation and socialisation; that is, between the recognition of a norm and its absolute acceptance in terms of a state's behaviour. A norm can exist within the context of the state's thinking, but compliance is a separate matter. Simply adopting a norm is not sufficient guarantee that it will be adhered to, not least in the face of other state interests that may be seen as more critical than normative expectations. As Zarakol (2014: 313) says: 'Normative judgements may be simultaneously internalised and publicly rejected. Emulation and non-compliance are at times often two sides of the same coin.' Critically, this is not a case in which states necessarily do not wish to 'do good', but where other factors influence. This is particularly identified as a case where non-Western states may be uncomfortable with Western-centric normative ideals. In this situation, compliance cannot be assumed, even if a given state proclaims its commitment. Rebecca Adler-Nissen (2014: 143) takes this even further to argue that 'states are not passive objects of socialization, but active agents'. That is, the nature of the state may preclude socialisation of a norm and open up the possibility that it will be rejected at some point, where it conflicts with the construction of the state as an active agent in its own right.

In effect, stigmatisation does not ensure that a norm will be upheld, specifically where adoption is dependent only on a desire to overcome stigmatisation and not actual normative commitment. This creates a highly fragile situation in that the recognition of a norm is conditional. It is hardly surprising then that when other self-interested pressures are introduced into the equation, this commitment can fall apart, partially or completely. This goes back again to the work of Hafner-Burton *et al.* (2008), who analyse why states with poor human rights records ratify human rights treaties at a similar rate to states with positive records. They show that the act of ratification is especially attractive where the legitimacy associated with joining that regime is valuable, and this constitutes a highly effective way to overcome stigmatisation. But they also demonstrate that these states have no real commitment to those treaties, where they do not possess either the normative socialisation or the resources to comply. Indeed, they highlight that such actors frequently go on to violate the agreements they commit to because there is no genuine acceptance of the norm in question. But the signing of a treaty in itself is so low-cost and so beneficial in the short term that they see a significant advantage in doing so.

Consequently, Assad's non-compliance is unsurprising. A disappointment perhaps, but no shock. The benefits for Assad associated with CWC accession indicate that it was an act of self-interest, not norm socialisation. There were major advantages in overcoming stigmatisation, but it was essentially the only motive in Assad's actions. It was about bowing to US and Russian diplomatic pressure as opposed to any intrinsic acceptance of the taboo. Once Assad faced new military pressure on the ground – specifically opposition advances in key geopolitical locations – he abandoned the taboo and instead resorted to extreme tactics in order to halt the rebel progress. Simply put, talk is cheap. To employ another cliché: once push came to shove, Assad was more than willing to renege on diplomatic concessions in order to reassert his military position within the crisis. As such, there is ironically little difference between his motivation in acceding to the CWC and his use of the weapons that it bans. The CWC was a vehicle for strengthening his power at a time when it was waning in respect of the wider conflict. Chemical weapons have now been used to re-establish his status on the ground against rebel advances. Assad has only ever fought for his regime's survival. Why then expect him to do any less? All he has done in terms of the taboo is live up to his reputation. Within this context, the taboo was not an approach that would achieve anything beyond symbolism. And, as the continued use of chlorine indicates, this was false symbolism at best.

Yet again, this demonstrates the extensive problems with the taboo. Specifically, the failure to comprehend the crisis outside this highly biased framework has caused not only the continuation of the crisis, but also its escalation. The taboo has introduced a way of understanding the crisis that has actively worsened the situation, including where it has engendered new dynamics of conflict that would not have arisen in the absence of the taboo as the basis of US foreign policy. Consequently, the taboo is not (always) beneficial for peace and conflict resolution, despite a perception of it as lessening the risks of mass violence. While the idea at the centre of taboo – that chemical weapons should be prohibited – is geared towards a concept of security, its application to complex scenarios that extend beyond the issue of chemical warfare leads to the distortion of political understanding. This in turn jeopardises how appropriate the response to a given situation will be, and also exaggerates the extent to which a response is taking place. Both of these mistakes can result in the escalation of that situation. This is made worse by the fact that preconceptions of the taboo as a 'good' disguise its damaging nature. Policy-makers pursue the taboo because of the illusion that it is a positive; indeed, it is an idea they feel obligated to fight for and protect at all costs. In fact, they risk causing greater destruction and political difficulty, specifically where this is understood as establishing the taboo as the priority basis for foreign policy activity. The taboo may look like an effective response, but, applied incorrectly and indiscriminately, it is little more than political snake oil.

The importance of being taboo

The idea that the chemical weapons taboo is a negative influence is controversial. The taboo is held up as an essential aspect not only of extreme arms control, but also – as seen in Syria – international security more generally. As such, any challenge to it is viewed as dangerous. It is unsurprising then that critics of the taboo are few and far between. The only real opponent has been John Mueller (2013), who argues for the taboo's conceptual abandonment. But even here, he bases his argument on the idea that chemical weapons are not sufficiently destructive to warrant a taboo. This is less a criticism of the taboo itself, and more a hark back to those arguments that chemical weapons are not distinct enough to be set apart from conventional weaponry, such as where this relates to their classification as WMD. Within this context, this is not a direct challenge to the taboo itself, or to the way in which it is engrained and expressed within international political discourse. Indeed, there exists an inherent barrier against such criticism. Since the idea of banning chemical weapons is so important, why would anyone risk being seen to oppose it? Specifically in respect of Syria, there is no incentive to criticise Obama in a situation where he was ostensibly uphold-ing this all-important prohibition on chemical warfare as a noble and moral act. To do so is to be seen to threaten one of the most valuable and respected norms of international politics. Within this context, criticism is dismissed as unneces-sarily undermining the taboo and the arms control regime that has developed around it.

Yet this book maintains that both academics and practitioners must reject these conventional perceptions of the taboo insofar as they are causing signif-icant damage in respect of international politics, and explicitly in the case of Syria. By assuming that the taboo must be held up as a priority regardless, this precludes context – a situation that can create severe problems and exacerbate insecurity. Not least where norm compliance is not guaranteed (as demonstrated by Assad's continued resort to tactics of chemical warfare), this is a poor basis on which to construct foreign policy. Indeed, on the issue of non-compliance, it is also worth noting that it is not limited to 'rogue' actors such as Assad. The US has hardly been the best role model in terms of norm adherence and has frequently used chemical weapons in violation of its own CWC commitments (Joyce, 2015: 349). As such, it is difficult to maintain that this is a necessary concept, where that necessity translates into immunity from criticism. In a simi-lar vein, it is difficult to uphold it on the basis that chemical weapons are distinct. As already demonstrated throughout this book, while chemical weapons are capable of terrible destructive effects, this is very far from secure as an essential-ist distinction from other types of weaponry. Consequently, the basis of the taboo is not sufficiently solid to state that it should be upheld regardless, specifically on such exclusionary and prioritised terms.

Crucially, this is not to suggest the taboo is unimportant; as demonstrated by Obama's response to Assad's use of chemical weapons, the drive to control and eliminate chemical weapons constitutes a decisive pressure within international politics and should be acknowledged as such. It is also not to suggest that the elimination of chemical weapons from Syria would never constitute a stabilis-ing move. Nor is it to call for the concept's total abandonment as an underly-ing principle: chemical weapons are horrific and the world would undoubtedly be a better place without them, at least as it currently stands. Yet this cannot overcome the problems associated with the taboo as conventionally expressed. Specifically, the way in which the taboo prioritises the chemical threat – to the exclusion of all other interests and considerations – is detrimental to the wider realities of international conflict. Consequently, this conventional understand-ing must be treated with significantly more care, and should not be allowed to create distortions in policy-makers' comprehension of conflict. The hierarchies that it produces may, for some, reflect the extensive threat these weapons pose, but here this is identified as a misrepresentation, one that can engender dev-astating consequences if not recognised as such. A commitment to weapons elimination may be a positive, but applying it on such exclusive terms can actually exacerbate a conflict/political scenario and prevent its resolution. In short, too much is invested in the taboo.

Is this investment so great that we can no longer walk away from it? As this book argues: no, at least theoretically. Looking at the taboo as a construct of convention provides the basis for changing it. The stigmatisation/prioritisation model certainly constitutes the predominant understanding of the taboo, as well as the arms control regime built upon it. But this is still convention. It is still social construction. And as we know from Skinner, so there is scope to change and modify this expression of chemical weapons elimination if it is our desire. Moreover, the arguments that this would cause the chemical arms control regime to come crashing around our ears are exaggerated. Specifically, the aim of removing chemical weapons is not dependent on ensuring its priority status, where this causes all other threats to be pushed aside. There is nothing to suggest that asking Assad to accede to the CWC was contingent on ignoring all other aspects of the conflict. While the fact that it did so was a great incentive to Assad in acceding to the CWC (a highly negative development in respect of the Syrian conflict), this has proved a major sacrifice to make on the part of the US to secure an agreement on the elimination of chemical weapons. Consequently, there are ways of ensuring that chemical weapons eradication can be upheld as of critical importance without employing a qualifying notion of stigmatisation that prioritises these arms to such an extent that they are all policy-makers see. Recognising that this conventional understanding creates major problems does not negate either the ideal of chemical weapons elimination or the ambitions of the taboo in carrying it out. It also does not necessarily undermine the belief in the horrific – although not distinctively horrific – nature of these weapons for those who would wish to uphold the taboo (although, as Mueller and others demonstrate, some would be more than happy to abandon this perception of chemical weapons as particularly destructive, where such a claim is seen as unrepresentative). As such, the barriers to conceptual change are largely illusory.

Admittedly, this argument is made with the caveat that such a conceptual transformation is only theoretically possible. Reality, as is so often the case, is very different. It is still up to international actors to adopt this process of change. Yet, as the discussions detailing the taboo's strategic use here indicate, this may be more difficult than amending the terms of the taboo. The concept as it stands provides great conceptual value to policy-makers, as seen in Obama's employment of it to control US foreign policy in Syria in relation to intervention. Changing the taboo would necessitate actors giving up a concept that may hold significant value for them as a strategic resource. Consequently, this potentially precludes whether actors would engage in conceptual change regardless of whether or not it is possible (this is the case in respect of the WMD concept;

see Bentley, 2012). But again, this does not overcome the evidence here that the taboo's current expression, as based around an unworkable form of prioritisation, is hurting other aspects of security discourse to the extent that it is actively detrimental. The taboo is at the centre of some extremely questionable acts of foreign policy-making. And an unsustainable appeal to upholding that taboo cannot excuse it any longer.

Conclusion

We have to talk...

International relations (IR) and the chemical weapons taboo need to break up. While on the surface the connection between the two is extremely strong, the way in which that relationship is conventionally structured is far from healthy. Syria in particular is the sign that something is not working. Specifically, as Syria descends even further into greater levels of violence, the role that the taboo has played in this aggressive escalation cannot continue to be overlooked. Despite the illusion of the taboo as an unequivocal 'good', the evidence demonstrates otherwise. Instead, its employment as the basis of US foreign policy has not only caused the crisis's protraction by failing to put in place, or even to recognise the need for, a more appropriate and relevant response, but also intensified the war itself. The framing of US foreign policy within the exclusionary conceptual structure of the taboo has led policy-makers to misinterpret the core issues in Syria, to such a degree that the provisions introduced have actually made things worse, both politically and in terms of fighting on the ground.

Accepting the taboo means accepting a very specific and complex logic of how conflict should be addressed. While the taboo is often portrayed as simply upholding the need to eliminate chemical weapons, this is not the case. Assuming that the taboo can be reduced to eradication only is naive. Instead, that understanding goes far beyond this relatively abstract aim, where it creates certain implications for its application to actual crisis scenarios. Actors may try to present the taboo as being so important that it must be protected at all costs, regardless of such implications. But to construct that ideal in such a non-contextualised framework is problematic and masks the very real difficulties that the taboo can foster in respect of non-chemical threats. This is not to accuse proponents of the taboo of being unrealistic, or to suggest that they have to face the real world and abandon their ideals. It is, however, to argue that the way in which this principle of elimination is conventionally expressed is harmful to security. If applied to situations that are not exclusively defined by a chemical threat, then the taboo cannot be the only answer. This does not preclude the need to consider chemical elimination a must, but states that, if other threats apply, then the taboo cannot be allowed to completely override their consideration as it does now. Its expression must be made with more care, otherwise it risks distorting international political thinking. Consequently, IR needs to walk away from it and establish a new relationship with the taboo. Any conversation surrounding that split is likely to be difficult and contentious, but this is a debate that cannot be ignored. If Syria shows us anything, it is that IR cannot rely on such a problematic conception of the chemical weapons taboo any more.

Conclusion

O BAMA'S FOREIGN policy on Syria put the chemical weapons taboo front and centre of international politics. This has always been a prominent feature of international discourse. But now, where the taboo constituted (a) an imperative for, and justification of, US foreign policy, and (b) the basis of key diplomatic negotiations, so the norm came to dominate the entire crisis. As such, this would seem to substantiate the inherent claim behind the taboo, i.e. that chemical weapons are so offensive that possession and use cannot be tolerated. Furthermore, that violation cannot take place without a significant and norm-driven response from the international community, and especially from its hegemon. This view, however, is far too simplistic. Specifically, it ignores two core dynamics of the taboo's use (where these map onto the two parts to this book):

1 In contrast to the accepted understanding of taboos as fundamentally static, they are actually used in very strategic and manipulative ways that shape policy in line with an actor's self-interest.
2 Despite an entrenched assumption within International Relations (IR) that the chemical weapons taboo is a positive, it can have an extremely detrimental impact on conflict resolution – one that can severely escalate and prolong a crisis scenario.

In relation to the first overlooked feature of use, the taboo has been erroneously reduced to a static restraint on actors. It governs them; it is not something over which they have control. Yet the evidence presented here demonstrates that this is very far from the case. Obama has used the taboo for his own gain. More explicitly, he has selectively employed ideas conventionally associated with the taboo as an innovating ideologist. This is not to suggest that Obama does not genuinely respect and adhere to the chemical weapons taboo. Indeed, the way in which the taboo creates behavioural and conceptual pressures can be seen in the way Obama's redline statement was misinterpreted; expectations surrounding the taboo were so engrained that they were applied regardless of Obama's intention.

But the fact that Obama did not mean to express the taboo in this exact way, and that he would subsequently manipulate the terms of the taboo's conventional understanding in order to realise his own foreign policy ambitions, proves that this normative constraint is not absolute. The taboo is as much a resource for the strategic construction of political discourse as a behavioural guide. By exploiting the very ideals of the taboo, Obama constructed discourse in ways that pushed US foreign policy in a very specific and self-interested direction. He embraced the principles of Skinner, which argue that actors who manipulate existing language and concepts are more likely to get what they want.

Consequently, this book directly contests static constructivist interpretations of language to argue that taboos are significantly more agency-centric in their use than assumed. Language may shape rhetorical and political behaviour as convention, but beyond this there exists significant opportunity for manipulation, calculated application, and strategic redefinition. As such, this book is a call for a new recognition of agency within IR analysis. This is particularly important with respect to Syria – where the taboo has constituted a central element of that conflict – because it demonstrates that the crisis cannot be reduced to absolute normative belief. Indeed, such a reduction has led to major misunderstandings in how the crisis is comprehended and addressed. Yet this championing of agency goes far beyond Syria to influence how we see all forms of taboo, as well as norms and language more widely. Current frameworks of understanding are far too restrictive in their analysis and ignore the very extensive and highly creative ways in which actors exert agency over the norms and behaviours they engage with, to the extent that they can manipulate and even change them. Critically, this is not merely a drawing on of existing ideas and language, but their deliberate manipulation for the purposes of shaping policy in ways beneficial to an actor. Within this context, Skinner provides an ideal starting point for bringing this new perspective into analysis. He shows that, even in a world of linguistic convention, there is still an opportunity for strategic construction. His work provides a model for taking IR's comprehension of language forward to explore exactly how far actors can play with rhetoric, concepts, and ideas in order to get, if not precisely what they want, at least the best out of a situation.

In terms of the second claim, this is the assertion that the chemical weapons taboo is not as 'good' as we thought. While both academics and practitioners have been brought up to believe that the taboo is an unequivocal positive, this is not the case. In fact, the taboo is capable of doing significantly more harm than good – exacerbating and escalating the crisis situations it is supposed to solve or mitigate. When it is applied to situations in which the scenario in question is not about, or only about, chemical threat, the application of the taboo skews understanding to such an extent that it actually makes things worse. Specifically, it is the conceptual structure of the taboo that causes this problem. The way in which the taboo is held up as a necessary value within international politics that must be maintained and protected at all costs, and the way in which it upholds chemical weapons as distinct from other modes of violence, create a problematic hierarchical prioritisation of the chemical threat – one that forces all other issues out of consideration. This in turn jeopardises policy-makers' ability to carry out an appropriate and effective response. Far from the positive that the taboo is portrayed as, its inappropriate and indiscriminate application makes it a political liability.

Critically, this does not dispute the first claim. That is, the problems with the taboo are largely connected to conventional understandings of what that normative expectation is and means. It is because policy-makers slavishly adhere to these ideas that unsustainable biases and hierarchies of understanding in response to international issues are created. As such, this would seem to support the idea of taboos as an intrinsic restraint. Yet this book has never questioned that convention is important, or that every use of language is strategic. What it does is open up analysis to the possibilities associated with strategic use. Indeed, Obama was strategic even when it came to convention in respect of Syria. And it was fundamentally because of his strategic adherence to the taboo that these ideas would become so prominent in respect of US foreign policy on this issue. Those ideas of the taboo that have proved so problematic were also very valuable to a president who wanted to avoid intervention. The way in which the taboo dominated discussion was beneficial at the time in that it removed the pressure to intervene on other grounds – specifically conventional massacre and evidence of crimes against humanity. Once again, the innovating ideologist comes to the fore.

Constructivist frameworks within IR have accepted that taboos are a construction, but this study shows that this has failed to appreciate exactly what this means and how this influences the way actors think. In particular, the way in which the debate has failed to criticise the chemical weapons taboo is a red flag. Regardless of how important the taboo is deemed to be, the idea that debate has not engaged in any meaningful criticism of the concept is worrying. It suggests that there are expectations surrounding taboos and norms that are precluding a full analysis of this. Analysts are, of course, entitled to draw any conclusion they wish. But the current nature of the debate suggests that insufficient consideration is being put into drawing those conclusions, particularly where they relate to normative ideas. The claims made in this book are controversial, and many will not agree with them. But at least they are being made. This in itself is progress in a debate that is, at present, too afraid to challenge what is too often perceived to be un-challengeable.

REFERENCES

Adler-Nissen, R. (2014) 'Stigma Management in International Relations: Transgressive Identities, Norms, and Order in International Society', *International Organization* 68(1): 143–76.

AFP (2014a) 'Syria "May Be Able to Produce Biological Weapons" ', *Telegraph*, 29 January. Available: www.telegraph.co.uk/news/worldnews/middleeast/syria/10605512/Syria-may-be-able-to-produce-biological-weapons.html.

Ahram, A. (2015) 'Sexual Violence and the Making of ISIS', *Survival* 57(3): 57–78.

AI (2012) ' "I Wanted to Die": Syria's Torture Survivors Speak out', Amnesty International. Available: www.amnestyusa.org/research/reports/i-wanted-to-die-syria-s-torture-survivors-speak-out.

AI (2015) 'Syria: Evidence of a Fresh War Crime as Chlorine Gas Kills Entire Family', Amnesty International. Available: www.amnesty.org/en/latest/news/2015/03/syria-war-crime-chlorine-gas-attack.

Al Arabiya (2012) 'Top Syrian General Declares Defection on Al Arabiya', 25 December. Available: http://english.alarabiya.net/articles/2012/12/25/257059.html.

Al Jazeera Syria Live Blog (2012) 'Gas Used in Homs Leaves Seven People Dead and Scores Affected, Activists Say', *Al Jazeera*, 24 December. Available: http://blogs.aljazeera.com/topic/syria/gas-used-homs-leaves-seven-people-dead-and-scores-affected-activists-say.

Allin, D. (2014) 'Obama and the Middle East: The Politics, Strategies and Difficulties of American Restraint', *Adelphi Series* 54(447–8): 165–84.

Anderson, P. (2012) 'Emergency Management of Chemical Weapons Injuries', *Journal of Pharmacy Practice* 25(1): 61–8.

AP (2012) 'Syrian Regime Makes Chemical Warfare Threat', *Guardian*, 23 July. Available: www.theguardian.com/world/2012/jul/23/syria-chemical-warfare-threat-assad.

AP (2014b) 'Bashar al-Assad Wins Re-election in Syria as Uprising against Him Rages on', *Guardian*, 4 June. Available: www.theguardian.com/world/2014/jun/04/bashar-al-assad-winds-reelection-in-landslide-victory.

Archer, T. (2004) 'The Emperor Has Some Clothes on: Fairy Tales, Scary Tales and Weapons of Mass Destruction', UPI Working Papers, Finnish Institute of International Affairs: 1–40.

Arquilla, J. and Rondfelt, D. (2001) 'What Next for Networks and Netwars', in J. Arquilla and D. Rondfelt (eds) *Networks and Netwars: The Future of Terror, Crime and Militancy* (Santa Monica, CA: RAND): 311–62.

Austin, J. L. (1975) *How to Do Things with Words* (Oxford: Oxford University Press).

Behre, A. (2005) 'Politicizing Indiscriminate Terror: Imagining an Inclusive Framework for the Anti-Landmines Movement', *The Journal of Environmental Development* 14(3): 375–93.

Bellamy van Aalst, J. and Guitta, O. (2013) 'Syria's Real Threat: Biological Weapons', *National Interest*, 19 September. Available: http://nationalinterest.org/commentary/syrias-real-threat-biological-weapons-9093.

Benshoof, J. (2014) 'The Other Red Line: The Use of Rape as an Unlawful Tactic of Warfare', *Global Policy* 5(2): 146–58.

Bentley, M. (2012) 'The Long Goodbye: Beyond an Essentialist Construction of WMD', *Contemporary Security Policy* 33(2): 384–406.

Bentley, M. (2014a) 'Strategic Taboos: Chemical Weapons and US Foreign Policy', *International Affairs* 90(5): 1033–48.

Bentley, M. (2014b) *Weapons of Mass Destruction and US Foreign Policy: The Strategic Use of a Concept* (London: Routledge).

Bentley, M. (2015) 'The Problem with the Chemical Weapons Taboo', *Peace Review* 27(2): 228–36.

Bergoffen, D. (2009) 'Exploiting the Dignity of the Vulnerable Body: Rape as a Weapon of War', *Philosophical Papers* 38(3): 307–35.

Berman, S. (2001) 'Ideas, Norms, and Culture in Political Analysis', *Comparative Politics* 33(2): 231–50.

Bjorkdahl, A. (2002) 'Norms in International Relations: Some Conceptual and Methodological Reflections', *Cambridge Review of International Affairs* 15(1): 9–23.

Blair, C. (2012) 'Fearful of a Nuclear Iran? The Real WMD Nightmare Is Syria', *Bulletin of the Atomic Scientists*, 1 March. Available: http://thebulletin.org/fearful-nuclear-iran-real-wmd-nightmare-syria.

Blake, J. and Mahmud, A. (2013) 'A Legal Red Line? Syria and the Use of Chemical Weapons in Civil Conflict', *UCLA Law Review Discourse* 61: 244–60.

Bolton, J. (2001) 'Remarks to the 5th Biological Weapons Convention RevCon Meeting, Geneva, Switzerland, November 19, 2001'. Available: http://2001-2009.state.gov/t/us/rm/janjuly/6231.htm.

Braut-Hegghammer, M. (2013) 'Red Lines Matter: Why We Should Care about Syria's Chemical Weapons', *Foreign Affairs*, 7 May. Available: www.foreignaffairs.com/articles/139369/malfrid-braut-hegghammer/red-lines-matter.

Brenner, G. (2010) 'To Speak or Not to Speak: The Taboo of Communication', *Journal of Gay and Lesbian Mental Health* 14(3): 230–9.

Brooks, T. (1991) 'Statement of Rear Admiral Thomas A. Brooks, USN, Director of Naval Intelligence, before the Seapower, Strategic, and Critical Materials Subcommittee of the House Arms Services Committee on Intelligence Issues', 7 March.

Brown, C. (2004) 'Do Great Power Have Great Responsibilities? Great Powers and Moral Agency', *Global Society* 18(1): 5–19.

Bush, G. H. W. (1991) 'Radio Address to the Nation on the Persian Gulf Crisis', in *1991 Public Papers of the Presidents of the United States, Book I* (Washington, DC: US Government Printing Office): 10–11.

Bush, G. W. (2010) *Decision Points* (London: Virgin Books).

Byman, D. (2014) 'Buddies or Burdens? Understanding the Al Qaeda Relationship with Its Affiliate Organizations', *Security Studies* 23(3): 431–70.

Cannon, P. (2012) 'A Feminist Response to Rape as a Weapon of War in Eastern Congo', *Peace Review* 24(4): 478–83.

Carcano, A. (2006) 'End of the Occupation in 2004? The Status of the Multinational Force in Iraq after the Transfer of Sovereignty to the Interim Iraqi Government', *Journal of Conflict and Security Law* 11(1): 41–66.

Chesterman, S. (2011) '"Leading from Behind": The Responsibility to Protect, the Obama Doctrine, and Humanitarian Intervention after Libya', *Ethics & International Affairs* 25(3): 279–85.

Cheterian, V. (2015) 'ISIS and the Killing Fields of the Middle East', *Survival* 57(2): 105–18.

Chulov, M. (2014) 'Syria Wiping Neighbourhoods off the Map to Punish Residents – Rights Group', *Guardian*, 30 January. Available: www.theguardian.com/world/2014/jan/30/syria-neighbourhoods-residents?CMP=fb_gu.

Chumley, C. (2013) 'Islamic Cleric Decrees It OK for Syrian Rebels to Rape Women', *Washington Times*, 3 April. Available: www.washingtontimes.com/news/2013/apr/3/islamic-cleric-decrees-it-ok-syrian-rebels-rape-wo.

Cirincione, J. (2007) *Bomb Scare: The History and Future of Nuclear Weapons* (New York: Columbia University Press).

Clinton, W. (1998) 'Videotaped Remarks on Expansion of United Nations Security Council Resolution 986 Concerning Iraq', in *1998 Public Papers of the Presidents of the United States, Book I* (Washington, DC: US Government Printing Office): 261–2.

Cooper, N. (2011) 'Humanitarian Arms Control and Processes of Securitization: Moving Weapons along the Security Continuum', *Contemporary Security Policy* 32(1): 134–58.

Corder, M. (2015) 'Full Circle: Chlorine Now Chemical Weapon of Choice in Syria', *Seattle Times*, 20 April. Available: www.seattletimes.com/nation-world/full-circle-chlorine-now-chemical-weapon-of-choice-in-syria.

Cordesman, A. (2008) 'Syrian Weapons of Mass Destruction: An Overview', Center for Strategic and International Studies.

Cornyn, J. (2013) 'Cornyn Demands Disarming Syria of Bioweapons', personal website, 13 September. Available: www.cornyn.senate.gov/public/index.cfm?p=InNews&ContentRecord_id=06ce0978-8b0b-4d2b-8547-c0adbc851734.

Cragin, R. (2015) 'Semi-Proxy Wars and U.S. Counterterrorism Strategy', *Studies in Conflict and Terrorism* 38(5): 311–27.

Crawford, J. (2006) *The Creation of States in International Law*, 2nd edn (Oxford: Oxford University Press).

Crocker, C. (2015) 'The Strategic Dilemma of a World Adrift', *Survival* 57(1): 7–30.

Cumming-Bruce, N. (2013) 'Watchdog Says Syria Has Been Cooperative on Weapons', *New York Times*, 9 October. Available: www.nytimes.com/2013/10/10/world/middleeast/syria-chemical-weapons.html?_r=1.

Dardagan, H. and Salama, M. (2013) 'Stolen Futures: The Hidden Toll of Child Casualties in Syria', Oxford Research Group.

Darke, D. (2014) *My House in Damascus: An Inside View of the Syrian Revolution* (London: Haus Publishing).

De Graaf, B., Dimitriu, G., and Ringsmose, J. (2015) 'Shaping Societies for War: Strategic Narratives and Public Opinion', in B. De Graaf, George Dimitriu, and Jens Ringsmose (eds) *Strategic Narratives, Public Opinion, and War* (London: Routledge): 3–14.

Democracy Now! (2013) 'Syrian Activist on Ghouta Attack', 23 August. Available: www.democracynow.org/2013/8/23/syrian_activist_on_ghouta_attack_i.

Diab, M. (1997) 'Syria's Chemical and Biological Weapons: Assessing Capabilities and Motivations', *The Nonproliferation Review* 5(1): 104–11.

Dimitriu, G. R. (2011) 'Winning the Story War: Strategic Communication and the Conflict in Afghanistan', *Public Relations Review* 38(2): 195–207.

Doty, R. (1996) *Imperial Encounters: The Politics of Representation in North–South Relations* (Minneapolis: University of Minnesota Press).

Dowty, A. (2001) 'Making "No First Use" Work: Bring All WMD inside the Tent', *The Nonproliferation Review* 8(1): 79–85.

Drezner, D. (2011) 'Does Obama Have a Grand Strategy? Why We Need Doctrines in Uncertain Times', *Foreign Affairs* 90(4): 57–68.

Easterbrook, G. (2002) 'Term Limits: The Meaningless of "WMD"', *New Republic* 227(1): 22–5.

Editorial (2015) '"Barbarism" with Chlorine Gas Goes Unchecked in Syria', *Washington Post*, 20 June. Available: www.washingtonpost.com/opinions/barbarism-with-chlorine-gas-goes-unchecked-in-syria/2015/06/20/dcb8eb0c-16a2-11e5-8 9f3-61410da94eb1_story.html.

Edwards, B. and Cacciatori, M. (2015) 'Chlorine Attacks Continue in Syria with No Prospect of Assad Being Brought to Account', *The Conversation*, 8 April. Available: http://theconversation.com/chlorine-attacks-continue-in-syria-with-no-prospect-of-assad-being-brought-to-account-39209.

Enia, J. and Fields, J. (2014) 'The Relative Efficacy of the Biological and Chemical Weapon Regimes', *The Nonproliferation Review* 21(1): 43–64.

Epstein, C. (2008) *The Power of Words in International Relations: Birth of an Anti-Whaling Discourse* (Cambridge, MA: MIT Press).

Epstein, C. (2013) 'Theorizing Agency in Hobbes' Wake: The Rational Actor, the Self, or the Speaking Subject?', *International Organization* 67(2): 287–316.

Evans, G. (2014) 'The Consequences of Non-Intervention in Syria: Does the Responsibility to Protect Have a Future?', in R. Murray and A. McKay (eds) *Into the Eleventh Hour: R2P, Syria and Humanitarianism in Crisis* (Bristol: E-IR): 18–25.

Farer, T. (2013) 'Syria: The Case for Staggered Decapitation', in N. Hashemi and D. Postel (eds) *The Syria Dilemma* (Cambridge, MA: MIT Press): 131–44.

Fitzpatrick, M. (2013) 'Destroying Syria's Chemical Weapons', *Survival* 55(6): 107–14.

Fowler, M. and Bunck, J. (1996) 'What Constitutes the Sovereign State?', *Review of International Studies* 22(4): 381–404.

Frankenberg, G. (2008) 'Torture and Taboo: An Essay Comparing Paradigms of Comparative Law', *American Journal of Comparative Law* 56(2): 403–22.

Freedman, J. (2013) 'Don't Let Assad Sign the Chemical Weapons Convention on Syria's Behalf', *Al Jazeera*, 29 September. Available: www.aljazeera.com/indepth/opinion/2013/09/don-let-assad-sign-chemical-weapons-convention-syria-behalf-201392981058347857.html.

Freedman, L. (2006) 'The Transformation of Strategic Affairs', *The Adelphi Papers* 45(379): 5–93.

Freedman, L. (2013) 'Disarmament and Other Nuclear Norms', *The Washington Quarterly* 36(2): 93–108.

Freedman, L. (2015) 'The Possibilities and Limits of Strategic Narratives', in B. De Graaf, George Dimitriu, and Jens Ringsmose (eds) *Strategic Narratives, Public Opinion, and War* (London: Routledge): 17–36.

Friedman, D. (2012) 'Biological and Chemical Weapons Arms Control in the Middle East', *The Nonproliferation Review* 19(3): 401–11.

Gallagher, A. (2014) 'Syria and the Indicators of a "Manifest Failing"', *The International Journal of Human Rights* 18(1): 1–19.

Goertz, G. and Diehl, P. (2012) 'Towards a Theory of International Norms: Some Conceptual and Measurement Issues', *Journal of Conflict Resolution* 36(4): 634–64.

Gordon, J. (2007) 'Syria's Bio-Warfare Threat: An Interview with Dr. Jill Dekker', *New English Review*, December. Available: www.newenglishreview.org/Jerry_Gordon/ Syria's_Bio-Warfare_Threat:_an_interview_with_Dr._Jill_Dekker.

Gordon, J. (2013) 'The Danger of Syria's Bio-Warfare Complex Should Assad Fall: An Interview with Dr. Jill Bellamy van Aalst', *New English Review*, January. Available: www.newenglishreview.org/custpage.cfm/frm/130225/sec_id/130225.

Greenberg, D. (1990) *The Construction of Homosexuality* (Chicago, IL: University of Chicago Press).

Greenwood, P. (2013) 'Rape and Domestic Violence Follow Syrian Women into Refugee Camps', *Guardian*, 25 July. Available: www.theguardian.com/world/2013/jul/25/ rape-violence-syria-women-refugee-camp.

Guillemin, J. (2005) *Biological Weapons: From the Invention of State-Sponsored Programs to Contemporary Bioterrorism* (New York: Columbia University Press).

Hachiguan, N. and Shorr, D. (2012) 'The Responsibility Doctrine', *The Washington Quarterly* 36(1): 73–91.

Hafner-Burton, E., Tsutsui, K., and Meyer, J. (2008) 'International Human Rights Law and the Politics of Legitimation', *International Sociology* 23(1): 115–41.

Hajer, M. (1997) *The Politics of Environmental Discourse: Ecological Modernization and the Policy Process* (Oxford: Clarendon).

Haldane, J. (1925) *Callinicus: A Defence of Chemical Weapons* (London: Kegan Paul).

Hamid, S. (2013) 'Syria Is Not Iraq: Why the Legacy of the Iraq War Keeps Us from Doing the Right Thing in Syria', in N. Hashemi and D. Postel (eds) *The Syria Dilemma* (Cambridge, MA: MIT Press): 19–27.

Hansen, L. (2000) 'Gender, Nation, Rape: Bosnia and the Construction of Security', *International Feminist Journal of Politics* 3(1): 55–75.

Hansen, L. (2006) *Security as Practice: Discourse Analysis and the Bosnian War* (London: Routledge).

Hashim, A. (2014) 'The Islamic States: From al-Qaeda Affiliate to Caliphate', *Middle East Policy* 21(4): 69–83.

Hashmi, S. and Lee, S. (2004) 'Introduction', in S. Hashmi and S. Lee (eds) *Ethics of Mass Destruction: Religious and Secular Perspectives* (Cambridge: Cambridge University Press): 1–15.

Hashmi, S. and Western, J. (2013) 'A Taboo Worth Protecting: Chemical Weapons Are Indiscriminate – And That's Why They Should Be Outlawed', *Foreign Affairs*, 9 September. Available: www.foreignaffairs.com/articles/139913/sohail-h-hashmi-and-jon-western/a-taboo-worth-protecting.

Hawkins, V. (2014) 'Beheadings and the News Media: Why Some Conflict Atrocities Receive More Coverage than Others', *Conflict Trends* 4: 3–9.

Hazelgrove, S. (2013) 'Obama's Syria Dilemma Showed That for Foreign Policy to Be Successful, the Management of Information Is Just as Important as the Substance of Ideas', *LSE Blog*, 29 October. Available: http://blogs.lse.ac.uk/usappblog/2013/10/29/obama-syria-ideas-management.

Hersh, S. (2014) 'The Red Line and the Rat Line', *London Review of Books*, 17 April. Available: www.lrb.co.uk/v36/n08/seymour-m-hersh/the-red-line-and-the-rat-line.

Higgins, R. (2002) 'Weapons of Mass Destruction: Rhetoric and Realities', International Security Information Service: 1–10.

Hoffman, B. (2013) 'Al Qaeda's Uncertain Future', *Studies in Conflict and Terrorism* 36(8): 635–53.

Hogger, H. (2014) 'Syria: Hope or Despair?', *Asian Affairs* 45(1): 1–8.

Hoijer, B. (2004) 'The Discourse of Global Compassion: The Audience and Media Reporting of Human Suffering', *Media, Culture and Society* 26(4): 513–31.

Holbrook, D. (2015) 'Al-Qaeda and the Rise of ISIS', *Survival* 57(2): 93–104.

Holmes, O. and Solomon, E. (2013) 'Alleged Chemical Attack Kills 25 in Northern Syria', *Reuters*, 19 March. Available: www.reuters.com/article/2013/03/19/us-syria-crisis-chemical-idUSBRE92I0A220130319.

Homolar, A. (2012) 'Multilateralism in Crisis? The Character of US International Engagement under Obama', *Global Security* 26(1): 103–22.

Hood, J. (2006) 'Remarks to the Sixth Biological Weapons Convention Review Conference, Geneva, Switzerland, November 20, 2006'. Available: http://2001-2009.state.gov/t/isn/rls/rm/76446.htm.

Horner, D. (2013) 'Syria Meets Key Chemical Arms Deadline', *Arms Control Today* 43(9): 30–1.

HRW (2012a) 'Torture Archipelago: Arbitrary Arrests, Torture, and Enforced Disappearances in Syria's Underground Prisons since March 2011', Human Rights Watch. Available: www.hrw.org/report/2012/07/03/torture-archipelago/arbitrary-arrests-torture-and-enforced-disappearances-syrias.

HRW (2012b) 'Syria: Sexual Assault in Detention', Human Rights Watch. Available: www.hrw.org/news/2012/06/15/syria-sexual-assault-detention.

HRW (2013a) 'Attacks on Ghouta: Analysis of Alleged Use of Chemical Weapons in Syria', Human Rights Watch. Available: www.hrw.org/report/2013/09/10/attacks-ghouta/analysis-alleged-use-chemical-weapons-syria.

HRW (2013b) 'Death from the Skies: Deliberate and Indiscriminate Air Strikes on Civilians', Human Rights Watch. Available: www.hrw.org/report/2013/04/10/death-skies/deliberate-and-indiscriminate-air-strikes-civilians.

HRW (2014) 'Syria: Strong Evidence Government Used Chemicals as a Weapon', Human Rights Watch. Available: www.hrw.org/news/2014/05/13/syria-strong-evidence-government-used-chemicals-weapon.

HRW (2015a) 'Syria: New Spate of Barrel Bomb Attacks – Government Defying UN Resolution', Human Rights Watch. Available: www.hrw.org/news/2015/02/24/syria-new-spate-barrel-bomb-attacks.

HRW (2015b) 'Syria: Chemicals Used in Idlib Attacks – Security Council Should Act Decisively to Establish Responsibility', Human Rights Watch. Available: www.hrw.org/news/2015/04/13/syria-chemicals-used-idlib-attacks.

Huber, D. (2015) 'A Pragmatic Actor: The US Response to the Arab Uprising', *Journal of European Integration* 37(1): 57–75.

Iaquinta, K. (2011) 'Surprising U.S. Foreign Policy Continuity under Obama', *The Brazilian Economy* 3(4): 33–6.

International Conference of American States (1933) 'Montevideo Convention on the Rights and Duties of States', 26 December.

IRC (2013) 'Syria: A Regional Crisis – The IRC Commission on Syrian Refugees', International Rescue Committee. Available: www.rescue.org/resource-file/syria-regional-crisis-irc-commission-syrian-refugees-january-2013.

Jackson, R. and Rosberg, C. (1986) 'Sovereignty and Underdevelopment: Juridical Statehood in the African Crisis', *The Journal of Modern African Studies* 24(1): 1–31.

Jalabi, R. (2013) 'Critics Question Catholic Nun's "Alternative Story" on Syria Civil War', *Guardian*, 5 December. Available: www.theguardian.com/world/2013/dec/05/catholic-nun-mother-agnes-syria-civil-war.

James, E. (2012) *Fifty Shades of Grey* (London: Arrow).

Jefferson, C. (2014) 'Origins of the Norm against Chemical Weapons', *International Affairs* 90(3): 647–61.

Jenkins, B. (2013) 'The Role of Terrorism and Terror in Syria's Civil War', RAND Corporation.

Jones, S. (2013) 'Syria's Growing Jihad', *Survival* 55(4): 53–72.

Jose, B. (2013) 'Civilians vs. Chemicals: Protecting the Right Norm in Syria', *Foreign Affairs*, 26 September. Available: www.foreignaffairs.com/articles/139959/betcy-jose/civilians-vs-chemicals.

Joyce, C. (2015) 'Dulce et Decorum: The Unique Perception of Chemical Warfare and the Enforcement of the Geneva Protocol in the 21st Century', *McGeorge Global Business and Development Law Journal* 28: 331–57.

Kahf, M. (2014) 'The Syrian Revolution, Then and Now', *Peace Review* 26(4): 556–63.

Kaldor, M. (2013) 'A Humanitarian Strategy Focused on Syrian Civilians', in N. Hashemi and D. Postel (eds) *The Syria Dilemma* (Cambridge, MA: MIT Press): 147–59.

Kaszeta, D. (2015) 'Why Chlorine Gas Has Returned in Syria and Iraq', *Cicero*, 15 April. Available: http://ciceromagazine.com/features/why-chlorine-gas-has-returned-in-syria-and-iraq.

Katzenstein, P. (1996) 'Introduction: Alternative Perspectives on National Security', in P. Katzenstein (ed.) *The Culture of National Security: Norms and Identity in World Politics* (New York: Columbia University Press): 1–32.

Kaufman, R. (2014) 'Prudence and the Obama Doctrine', *Orbis* 58(3): 441–59.

Kaufmann, C. (2004) 'Threat Inflation and the Failure of the Marketplace of Ideas', *International Security* 29(1): 5–48.

Kaye, B. and Sapolsky, B. (2009) 'Taboo or Not Taboo? That Is the Question: Offensive Language on Prime-Time Broadcast and Cable Programming', *Journal of Broadcasting and Electronic Media* 53(1): 22–37.

References

Kazemzadeh, M. (2010) 'The Emerging Obama Doctrine', *American Foreign Policy Interests* 32(3): 194–5.

Kellner, D. (2007) 'Bushspeak and the Politics of Lying: Presidential Rhetoric in the "War on Terror" ', *Presidential Studies Quarterly* 37(4): 622–45.

Kennedy, P. (1987) *The Rise and Fall of the Great Powers: Economic Change and Military Conflict from 1500–2000* (New York: Random House).

Kenner, D. (2015) 'They Were Just Struggling to Breathe', *Foreign Policy*, 17 April. Available: http://foreignpolicy.com/2015/04/17/they-were-just-struggling-to-breathe-syr ia-chlorine-gas-attacks.

Kerry, J. (2014) 'State Dept. on OPCW Report and Ongoing Concerns with Chemical Weapons Use in Syria', Press Statement, US Embassy, 21 September. Available: http:// london.usembassy.gov/midest505.html.

Kitchen, N. (2011) 'The Obama Doctrine: Détente or Decline?', *European Political Science* 10(1): 27–35.

Krasner, S. (1999) *Sovereignty: Organized Hypocrisy* (Princeton, NJ: Princeton University Press).

Krebs, R. R. and Jackson, P. T. (2007) 'Twisting Tongues and Twisting Arms: The Power of Political Rhetoric', *European Journal of International Relations* 13(1): 35–66.

Krebs, R. R. and Lobasz, J. K. (2007) 'Fixing the Meaning of 9/11: Hegemony, Coercion, and the Road to War in Iraq', *Security Studies* 16(3): 409–51.

Legagnoux, M. (2014) 'The Silent Crime of Systematic Mass Rape in Syria', *Borgen*, 24 August. Available: www.borgenmagazine.com/silent-crime-systematic-mass-rape-syria.

Lele, A. (2011) 'Challenges for the Chemical Weapons Convention (CWC)', *Strategic Analysis* 35(5): 752–6.

Lentzos, F. (2013) 'Syria and Bioweapons: The Need for Transparency', *Bulletin of the Atomic Scientists*, 21 November. Available: http://thebulletin.org/syria-and-bioweapons-n eed-transparency.

Levesque, J. and Choussudovsky, M. (2013) 'The Ghouta Chemical Attacks: US-Backed False Flag? Killing Syrian Children to Justify "Humanitarian" Military Inter- ven- tion', *Global Research*, 25 September. Available: www.globalresearch.ca/the-ghouta-chemical-attacks-us-backed-false-flag-killing-children-to-justify-a -humanitarian-military-intervention/5351363.

Lewis, C. S. (1996 [1944]) *Perelandra* (New York: Scribner).

Lister, C. (2014) 'Assessing Syria's Jihad', *Survival* 56(6): 87–112.

Lumar, A., Hessini L., and Mitchell, E. (2009) 'Conceptualising Abortion Stigma', *Culture, Health and Sexuality* 11(6): 625–39.

McCain, J. (2013) 'Syria', *Congressional Record – Senate*, 9 May: S3288–9.

McDonnell, P. (2013) 'Push to Eliminate Syria's Chemical Weapons May Extend Assad's Rule', *Los Angeles Times*, 15 October. Available: http://articles.latimes.com/2013/ oct/15/world/la-fg-syria-assad-20131015.

Macfarlane, A. (2004) 'All Weapons of Mass Destruction Are Not Equal', *MIT Center for International Studies Audit of the Conventional Wisdom* 5(8): 1–5.

McGreal, C. (2012) 'US to Formally Recognise Syrian Opposition', *Guardian*, 12 December. Available: www.theguardian.com/world/2012/dec/12/us-formally-recognise-syrian-opposition.

McHugo, J. (2014) *Syria: From the Great War to the Civil War* (London: Saqi).

McKinnon Doan, H. and Morse, J. (2009) 'The Last Taboo: Roadblocks to Researching Menarche', *Health Care for Women International* 6(5–6): 277–83.

Mahmood, M. and Chulov, M. (2013) 'Syrian Eyewitness Accounts of Alleged Chemical Weapons Attack in Damascus', *Guardian*, 22 August. Available: www.theguardian.com/world/2013/aug/22/syria-chemical-weapons-eyewitness.

Ma'oz, M. (2014) 'The Arab Spring in Syria: Domestic and Regional Developments', *Dynamics of Asymmetric Conflict: Pathways Towards Terrorism and Genocide* 7(1): 49–57.

Martin, S. (2004) 'Weapons of Mass Destruction: A Brief Overview', in S. Hashmi and S. Lee (eds) *Ethics of Mass Destruction: Religious and Secular Perspectives* (Cambridge: Cambridge University Press): 16–42.

Masahiro, M. (2009) 'Sovereignty and International Law', paper presented at The State of Sovereignty: 20th Anniversary Conference, International Boundaries Research Unit, 1–3 April, Durham University.

Meger, S. (2012) 'Rape in Syria: A Weapon of War or Instrument of Terror?', *The Conversation*, 16 September. Available: http://theconversation.com/rape-in-syria-a-weapon-of-war-or-instrument-of-terror-8816.

Miles, T. (2014) 'U.N. Aided 38,000 Victims of Syrian Gender-Based Violence in 2013', *Reuters*, 8 January. Available: www.reuters.com/article/2014/01/08/us-syria-crisis-rape-idUSBREA0711R20140108.

Milliken, J. (1999) 'The Study of Discourse in International Relations: A Critique of Research and Methods', *European Journal of International Relations* 5(2): 225–54.

Minogue, K. (1988) 'Method in Intellectual History: Quentin Skinner's Foundations', in J. Tully (ed.) *Meaning and Context: Quentin Skinner and His Critics* (Cambridge: Polity Press): 176–93.

Miskimmon, A., O'Loughlin, B., and Roselle, L. (2013) *Strategic Narratives: Communication Power and the New World Order* (New York: Routledge).

Miskimmon, A., O'Loughlin, B., and Roselle, L. (2014) 'Strategic Narrative: A New Means to Understand Soft Power', *Media, War & Conflict* 7(1): 70–84.

Mohamed, A. (2011) 'Clinton, Citing Syrian Boy, Sees "Total Collapse"', *Reuters*, 31 May. Available: www.reuters.com/article/2011/06/01/us-syria-usa-boy-idUSTRE74U5P920110601.

Mohammed, A. and Osborn, A. (2013) 'Kerry: Syrian Surrender of Chemical Arms Could Stop U.S. Attack', *Reuters*, 9 September. Available: www.reuters.com/article/2013/09/09/us-syria-crisis-kerry-idUSBRE9880BV20130909.

Mother Agnes de la Croix, A. M. (2013) 'The Chemical Attacks on East Ghouta Used to Justify Military Right to Protect Intervention in Syria', Institut International pour la Paix la Justice et les Droit de l'Homme.

MSF (2015) 'Syria: MSF-Supported Hospital Treats Victims of Chlorine Gas Attack', MSF Press Release, 18 March. Available: www.doctorswithoutborders.org/article/syria-msf-supported-hospital-treats-victims-chlorine-gas-attack.

Mueller, J. (2013) 'Erase the Red Line: Why We Shouldn't Care about Syria's Chemical Weapons', *Foreign Affairs*, 30 April. Available: www.foreignaffairs.com/articles/139351/john-mueller/erase-the-red-line.

References

Murphy, J. (2003) '"Our Mission and Our Moment": George W. Bush and September 11th', *Rhetoric and Public Affairs* 6(4): 607–32.

Murphy, S. (1999) 'Democratic Legitimacy and the Recognition of States and Governments', *The International and Comparative Law Quarterly* 48(3): 545–81.

Murray, D. (2013) 'Military Action But Not as We Know It: Libya, Syria and the Making of an Obama Doctrine', *Contemporary Policy* 19(2): 146–66.

Natarajan, K. (2014) 'Digital Public Diplomacy and a Strategic Narrative for India', *Strategic Analysis* 38(1): 91–106.

Neer, T. and O'Toole, M. (2014) 'The Violence of the Islamic State of Syria (ISIS): A Behavioral Perspective', *Violence and Gender* 1(4): 145–56.

Nichols, M. (2015) 'Syria Gas Attack Video Moves U.N. Security Council Envoys to Tears', *Reuters*, 16 April. Available: www.reuters.com/article/2015/04/16/us-mideast-crisis-syria-un-idUSKBN0N72SY20150416.

Nitkitin, M., Kerr, P., and Feickert, A. (2013) 'Syria's Chemical Weapons: Issues for Congress', Congressional Research Service, 12 September.

Norheim-Martinsen, P. (2011) 'EU Strategic Culture: When the Means Becomes the End', *Contemporary Security Policy* 32(3): 517–34.

Normark, M., Lindblad, A., Norqvist, A., Sanstrom, B., and Waldenstrom, L. (2004) 'Syria and WMD: Incentives and Capabilities', Swedish Defence Research Agency.

NTI (2008) 'Syria Biological Chronology', Nuclear Threat Initiative.

Nye, J. (1990) 'Soft Power', *Foreign Policy* 80: 153–71.

O'Bagy, E. (2012) 'Jihad in Syria: Middle East Security Report 6', Institute for the Study of War.

Obama, B. (2006) *The Audacity of Hope: Thoughts on Reclaiming the American Dream* (New York: Random House).

Obama, B. (2009a) 'President's Weekly Address: September 26', *CPD*. Available: www.gpo.gov/fdsys/pkg/DCPD-200900751/pdf/DCPD-200900751.pdf.

Obama, B. (2009b) 'Statement on the Situation in North Korea', *CPD*. Available: www.gpo.gov/fdsys/pkg/DCPD-200900400/pdf/DCPD-200900400.pdf.

Obama, B. (2011a) 'Presidential Study Directive PSD 10: Creation of an Interagency Atrocities Prevention Board and Corresponding Interagency Review'. Available: www.whitehouse.gov/the-press-office/2011/08/04/presidential-study-directive-mass-atrocities.

Obama, B. (2011b) 'President's News Conference with Prime Minister David Cameron of the United Kingdom in London', *CPD*. Available: www.gpo.gov/fdsys/pkg/DCPD-201100389/pdf/DCPD-201100389.pdf.

Obama, B. (2012a) 'Address before a Joint Session of Congress on the State of the Union', *CPD*. Available: www.gpo.gov/fdsys/pkg/DCPD-201200048/pdf/DCPD-201200048.pdf.

Obama, B. (2012b) 'Message to the Congress on Continuation of the National Emergency with Respect to the Actions of the Government of Syria', *CPD*. Available: www.gpo.gov/fdsys/pkg/DCPD-201200352/pdf/DCPD-201200352.pdf.

Obama, B. (2012c) 'Remarks at the Veterans of Foreign Wars National Convention in Reno, Nevada', *CPD*. Available: www.gpo.gov/fdsys/pkg/DCPD-201200590/pdf/DCPD-201200590.pdf.

Obama, B. (2012d) 'Remarks at the Nunn–Lugar Cooperative Threat Reduction Symposium', *CPD*. Available: www.gpo.gov/fdsys/pkg/DCPD-201200924/pdf/DCPD-201200924.pdf.

Obama, B. (2012e) 'President's News Conference: August 20, 2012', *CPD*. Available: www.gpo.gov/fdsys/pkg/DCPD-201200656/pdf/DCPD-201200656.pdf.

Obama, B. (2012f) 'President's News Conference: November 14, 2012', *CPD*. Available: www.gpo.gov/fdsys/pkg/DCPD-201200886/pdf/DCPD-201200886.pdf.

Obama, B. (2013a) 'President's News Conference with Prime Minister Benjamin Netanyahu of Israel', *CPD*. Available: www.gpo.gov/fdsys/pkg/DCPD-201300168/pdf/DCPD-201300168.pdf.

Obama, B. (2013b) 'President's News Conference: April 30, 2013', *CPD*. Available: www.gpo.gov/fdsys/pkg/DCPD-201300283/pdf/DCPD-201300283.pdf.

Obama, B. (2013c) 'Remarks to the United Nations General Assembly in New York City', *CPD*. Available: www.gpo.gov/fdsys/pkg/DCPD-201300655/pdf/DCPD-201300655.pdf.

Obama, B. (2013d) 'Remarks Prior to a Meeting with King Abdullah II of Jordan', *CPD*. Available: www.gpo.gov/fdsys/pkg/DCPD-201300277/pdf/DCPD-201300277.pdf.

Obama, B. (2013e) 'Remarks Prior to a Meeting with President Toomas H. Ilves of Estonia, President Andris Berzins of Latvia, and President Dalia Grybauskaite of Lithuania', *CPD*. Available: www.gpo.gov/fdsys/pkg/DCPD-201300583/pdf/DCPD-201300583.pdf.

Obama, B. (2013f) 'Address to the Nation on the Situation on Syria: September 10, 2013', *CPD*. Available: www.gpo.gov/fdsys/pkg/DCPD-201300615/pdf/DCPD-201300615.pdf.

Obama, B. (2013g) 'President's News Conference with Prime Minister John Fredrik Reinfedlt of Sweden', *CPD*. Available: www.gpo.gov/fdsys/pkg/DCPD-201300599/pdf/DCPD-201300599.pdf.

Obama, B. (2013h) 'Remarks on the Situation in Syria: August 31, 2013', *CPD*. Available: www.gpo.gov/fdsys/pkg/DCPD-201300596/pdf/DCPD-201300596.pdf.

Obama, B. (2013i) 'Remarks Prior to a Meeting with Congressional Leaders on the Situation in Syria', *CPD*. Available: www.gpo.gov/fdsys/pkg/DCPD-201300598/pdf/DCPD-201300598.pdf.

Obama, B. (2013j) 'President's News Conference in St. Petersburg, Russia', *CPD*. Available: www.gpo.gov/fdsys/pkg/DCPD-201300606/pdf/DCPD-201300606.pdf.

Obama, B. (2013k) 'President's Weekly Address: September 14, 2013', *CPD*. Available: www.gpo.gov/fdsys/pkg/DCPD-201300627/pdf/DCPD-201300627.pdf.

Obama, B. (2013l) 'Remarks on the National Economy', *CPD*. Available: www.gpo.gov/fdsys/pkg/DCPD-201300631/pdf/DCPD-201300631.pdf.

Obama, B. (2013m) 'President's Weekly Address: September 7, 2013', *CPD*. Available: www.gpo.gov/fdsys/pkg/DCPD-201300611/pdf/DCPD-201300611.pdf.

Obama, B. (2013n) 'President's News Conference with Prime Minister Recep Tayyip Erdogan of Turkey', *CPD*. Available: www.gpo.gov/fdsys/pkg/DCPD-201300338/pdf/DCPD-201300338.pdf.

Obama, B. (2013o) 'President's News Conference with Chancellor Angela Merkel of Germany', *CPD*. Available: www.gpo.gov/fdsys/pkg/DCPD-201300438/pdf/DCPD-201300438.pdf.

Obama, B. (2013p) 'Statement on the Framework Agreement between Russia and the United States on the Elimination of Chemical Weapons in Syria', *CPD*. Available: www.gpo.gov/fdsys/pkg/DCPD-201300628/pdf/DCPD-201300628.pdf.

Obama, B. (2014) 'Address before a Joint Session of the Congress on the State of the Union', *CPD*. Available: www.gpo.gov/fdsys/pkg/DCPD-201400050/pdf/DCPD-201400050.pdf.

Obama, B. (2015) 'The President's News Conference at Camp David, Maryland', *CPD*. Available: www.gpo.gov/fdsys/pkg/DCPD-201500363/pdf/DCPD-201500363.pdf.

O'Hagan, J. (2013) 'War 2.0: An Analytical Framework', *Australian Journal of International Affairs* 67(5): 555–69.

Olsen, S. H. (1973) 'Authorial Intention', *British Journal of Aesthetics* 13(3): 219–31.

OPCW (2014) 'OPCW Fact Finding Mission: "Compelling Confirmation" That Chlorine Gas Used as Weapon in Syria', OPCW Press Release, 10 September. Available: www.opcw.org/news/article/opcw-fact-finding-mission-compelling-confirmation-that-chlorine-gas-used-as-weapon-in-syria.

Oppenheim, L. (1905) *International Law: A Treatise, Volume 1* (London: Longmans, Green and Co.).

O'Toole, G. (2014) 'Syria's Regime's "Industrial-Scale Killing"', *Al Jazeera*, 22 January. Available: www.aljazeera.com/indepth/features/2014/01/syria-regime-industrial-scale-killing-2014122102439158738.html.

O'Tuathail, G. (2002) 'Theorizing Practical Geopolitical Reasoning: The Case of the United States' Response to the War in Bosnia', *Political Geography* 21(5): 601–28.

Ouagrham-Gormley, S. (2013) 'Bioweapons Alarmism in Syria', *Bulletin of the Atomic Scientists*, 4 October. Available: http://thebulletin.org/bioweapons-alarmism-syria.

Owen, W. (1920) 'Dulce et Decorum Est'. Available: www.warpoetry.co.uk/owen1.html.

Pamment, J. (2014) 'Strategic Narratives in US Public Diplomacy: A Critical Geopolitics', *Popular Communication: The International Journal of Media and Culture* 12(1): 48–64.

Panofsky, W. K. H. (1998) 'Dismantling the Concept of "Weapons of Mass Destruction"', *Arms Control Today* 28(3): 3–8.

Parekh, B. and Berki, R. N. (1973) 'The History of Ideas: A Critique of Q. Skinner's Methodology', *Journal of the History of Ideas* 34(2): 163–84.

Patrick, S. (2011) 'Libya and the Future of Humanitarian Intervention', *Foreign Affairs*, 26 August. Available: www.foreignaffairs.com/articles/68233/stewart-patrick/libya-and-the-future-of-humanitarian-intervention.

Pattison, J. (2010) *Humanitarian Intervention and the Responsibility to Protect: Who Should Intervene?* (Oxford: Oxford University Press).

Pattison, J. (2014) 'The Case for Criteria: Moving R2P forward after the Arab Spring', in R. Murray and A. McKay (eds) *Into the Eleventh Hour: R2P, Syria and Humanitarianism in Crisis* (Bristol: E-IR): 26–32.

PBS (2013) 'President Obama: "I Have Not Made a Decision" on Syria', 28 August. Available: www.pbs.org/newshour/bb/white_house-july-dec13-obama_08-28.

References

Peresin, A. and Cervone, A. (2015) 'The Western Muhajirat of ISIS', *Studies in Conflict and Terrorism* 38(7): 495–509.

Perry, S., King, S., and Wolf, F. (2013) 'Investigating Benghazi', Congressional Record – House, 12 September: H5533–40.

Pinheiro, P. (2015) 'Statement by Mr. Paulo Sergio Pinhiero, Chair of the Independent International Commission of Inquiry on the Syrian Arab Republic'. Available: www.ohchr.org/EN/NewsEvents/Pages/DisplayNews.aspx?NewsID=15843&LangID=E.

Pita, R. and Domingo, J. (2014) 'The Use of Chemical Weapons in the Syrian Conflict', *Toxics* 2(3): 392–402.

Price, R. (1995) 'A Genealogy of the Chemical Weapons Taboo', *International Organization* 49(1): 73–103.

Price, R. (1998) 'International Norms and the Mines Taboo: Pulls Towards Compliance', *Canadian Foreign Policy Journal* 5(3): 105–23.

Price, R. (2013) 'No Strike, No Problem: The Right Way to Nurture a Norm', *Foreign Affairs*, 5 September. Available: www.foreignaffairs.com/articles/139903/richard-price/no-strike-no-problem.

Proudman, C. (2013) 'War Rape: The Forgotten Pandemic Sweeping Syria', *Independent*, 21 January. Available: www.independent.co.uk/voices/comment/war-rape-the-forgotten-pandemic-sweeping-syria-8460566.html.

Quester, G. (2005) 'If the Nuclear Taboo Gets Broken', *Naval War College Review* 58(2): 71–91.

Quinn, A. (2011) 'The Art of Declining Politely: Obama's Prudent Presidency and the Waning of American Power', *International Affairs* 87(4): 803–24.

Ramsey, M. (2011) 'Dirty Hands or Dirty Decisions? Investigating, Prosecuting and Punishing Those Responsible for Detainees in Counter Terrorism Operations', *The International Journal of Human Rights* 15(4): 627–43.

Reisman, W. (1990) 'Sovereignty and Human Rights in International Law', *The American Journal of International Law* 84(4): 866–76.

Reuters (2013) 'U.S. Plays Down Media Report That Syria Used Chemical Weapons', 16 January. Available: www.reuters.com/article/2013/01/16/us-syria-usa-chemical-idUSBRE90F00P20130116.

Robinson, J. P. (2004) 'WMD: What Is Mass Destruction?', *Falmer*, Summer: 12–14.

Rogin, J. (2013) 'Secret State Department Cable: Chemical Weapons Used in Syria', *Foreign Policy*, 15 January. Available: http://foreignpolicy.com/2013/01/15/exclusive-secret-state-department-cable-chemical-weapons-used-in-syria.

Rosen, A. (2014) 'How the Assad Regime Benefitted from Gassing Its Own People', *Business Insider*, 21 August. Available: www.businessinsider.com/how-assad-benefited-from-ghouta-2014–8?IR=T.

Ross, A. and Malik, S. (2015) 'Syrian Doctors to Show the US Evidence of Assad's Use of Chemical Weapons', *Guardian*, 16 June. Available: www.theguardian.com/world/2015/jun/16/syria-assad-regime-is-weaponising-chlorine-us-congress-to-hear.

Roth, K. (1998) 'Sidelined on Human Rights: America Bows out', *Foreign Affairs* 77(2): 2–6.

References

Russia Today (2013) 'At Least 25 Dead in Syrian "Chemical" Attack as Govt and Rebels Trade Blame', 19 March. Available: https://rt.com/news/syria-rebels-chemical-aleppo-479.

Sanchez, R. (2013) 'Syria's Neighbours Fear Biological Weapons Attack', *Telegraph*, 5 September. Available: www.telegraph.co.uk/news/worldnews/middleeast/syria/10289468/Syrias-neighbours-fear-biological-weapons-attack.html.

Sechser, T. (2011) 'Militarized Compellent Threats, 1918–2001', *Conflict Management and Peace Science* 28(4): 377–401.

Shachtman, N. and Lynch, C. (2013) 'The Fog of Chemical War: After Eight Months of Allegations, Why Do We Know So Little about Syria's Nerve Gas Attacks?', *Foreign Policy*, 19 August. Available: http://foreignpolicy.com/2013/08/19/the-fog-of-chemical-war.

Shea, D. (2013) 'Chemical Weapons: A Summary Report of Characteristics and Effects', Congressional Research Service, 13 September.

Shoham, D. (2002a) 'Guile, Gas and Germs: Syria's Ultimate Weapons', *Middle East Quarterly*, Summer: 53–61.

Shoham, D. (2002b) 'Poisoned Missiles: Syria's Doomsday Deterrent', *Middle East Quarterly*, Fall: 13–20.

Shoham, D. (2005) 'Image vs. Reality of Iranian Chemical and Biological Weapons', *International Journal of Intelligence and CounterIntelligence* 18(1): 89–141.

Sislin, J. (1998) 'A Convergence of Weapons', *Peace Review* 10(3): 455–61.

Skidmore, D. (2012) 'The Obama Presidency and US Foreign Policy: Where's the Multilateralism?', *International Studies Perspectives* 13(1): 43–64.

Skinner, Q. (1969) 'Meaning and Understanding in the History of Ideas', *History and Theory* 8(1): 3–53.

Skinner, Q. (1970) 'Conventions and the Understanding of Speech Acts', *The Philosophical Quarterly* 20(79): 118–38.

Skinner, Q. (1971) 'On Performing and Explaining Linguistic Action', *The Philosophical Quarterly* 21(82): 1–21.

Skinner, Q. (1972) 'Motives, Intentions and the Interpretations of Texts', *New Literary History* 3(2): 393–408.

Skinner, Q. (1974) 'Some Problems in the Analysis of Political Thought and Action', *Political Theory* 2(3): 277–303.

Skinner, Q. (1975) 'Hermeneutics and the Role of History', *New Literary History* 7(1): 209–32.

Skinner, Q. (1988) 'A Reply to My Critics', in J. Tully (ed.) *Meaning and Context: Quentin Skinner and His Critics* (Cambridge: Polity Press): 231–88.

Skinner, Q. (2002) 'Introduction: Seeing Things Their Way', in Q. Skinner (ed.) *Visions of Politics, Volume 1* (Cambridge: Cambridge University Press): 1–7.

Sluka, J. (2008) 'Terrorism and Taboo: An Anthropological Perspective on Political Violence against Citizens', *Critical Studies on Terrorism* 1(2): 167–83.

Smith, M. (2006) 'Pragmatic Micawberism? Norm Construction on Ballistic Missiles', *Contemporary Security Policy* 27(3): 526–42.

Smithson, A. (2013) 'A Phony Farewell to Arms', *Foreign Affairs*, 1 October. Available: www.foreignaffairs.com/articles/139970/amy-e-smithson/a-phony-farewell-to-arms.

Smyth, P. (2015) 'The Shite Jihad in Syria and Its Regional Effects', The Washington Institute for Near East Policy.

SNHR (2013a) 'Report on the Expanded and Systematic Usage of Scud Missiles by Forces Loyal to the Syrian Government', Syrian Network for Human Rights. Available: http://sn4hr.org/public_html/wp-content/pdf/english/Reporte-of-scud-missiles-by-Syrian-government.pdf.

SNHR (2013b) 'There Is No Red Line: The Syrian Regime Violates UN Security Council's Resolution 2118 More than 27 Times', Syrian Network for Human Rights. Available: http://sn4hr.org/public_html/wp-content/pdf/english/There%20Is%20No%20Red%20Line.pdf.

Soderback, F. (2004) 'The Tattoo Taboo', *Jewish Quarterly* 51(2): 13–14.

Sparrow, A. (2015) 'Syria: Death from Assad's Chlorine', *New York Review of Books* 62(8): 40–2.

Stein, J. (2010) 'Taboos and Regional Security Regimes', *Journal of Strategic Studies* 26(3): 6–81.

Steinberg, R. (2004) 'Who Is Sovereign?', *Stanford Journal of International Law* 40: 329–45.

Stern, J. (1999) *The Ultimate Terrorists* (Cambridge, MA: Harvard University Press).

Stern, J. and Berger, J. (2015) *ISIS: The State of Terror* (London: William Collins).

Sterner, E. (2014) 'Dictators and Deterrence: Syria's Assad, Chemical Weapons, and the Threat of U.S. Military Action', *Comparative Strategy* 33(5): 407–23.

Stevenson, J. (2014) 'The Syrian Tragedy and Precedent', *Survival* 56(3): 121–40.

Stewart, S. (2014) 'Evaluating Ebola as a Biological Weapon', Security Weekly, 23 October. Available: www.stratfor.com/weekly/evaluating-ebola-biological-weapon.

Strategic Comments (2012) 'Unease Grows over Syria's Chemical Weapons', *Strategic Comments* 18(5): 1–3.

Strategic Comments (2013a) 'Syria Crisis Highlights Importance of Chemical Weapons Convention', *Strategic Comments* 19(3): iv–vi.

Strategic Comments (2013b) 'Strategic Syria Chemical Plan Faces Multiple Challenges', *Strategic Comments* 19(6): vii–viii.

Strategic Survey (2014) 'The Levant', *Strategic Survey* 114(1): 179–200.

Sunstein, C. R. (2007) *Worst-Case Scenarios* (Cambridge, MA: Harvard University Press).

Susskind, Y. (2015) 'What Will It Take to Stop ISIS Using Rape as a Weapon of War?', *Guardian*, 17 February. Available: www.theguardian.com/global-development/2015/feb/17/disarm-isis-rape-weapon-war.

Svendsen, A. (2014) 'Sharpening SOF Tools, Their Strategic Use and Direction: Optimising the Command of Special Operations amid Wider Contemporary Defence Transformation and Military Cuts', *Defence Studies* 14(3): 284–309.

Syria Direct (2013) 'Adra Attack Aftermath', 29 May. Available: http://syriadirect.org/main/37-videos/509-adra-attack-aftermath.

Tannenwald, N. (2007) *The Nuclear Taboo: The United States and the Non-Use of Nuclear Weapons Since 1945* (Cambridge: Cambridge University Press).

Tertrais, B. (2014) 'Drawing Red Lines Right', *The Washington Quarterly* 37(3): 7–24.

Thrall, A. T. (2009) 'Framing Iraq: Threat Inflation in the Marketplace of Ideas', in J. K. Cramer and A. T. Thrall (eds) *American Foreign Policy and the Politics of Fear: Threat Inflation Since 9/11* (London: Routledge): 174–91.

Trahan, J. (2015) 'Defining the "Grey Area" Where Humanitarian Intervention May Not Be Fully Legal, But It Is Not the Crime of Aggression', *Journal on the Use of Force and International Law* 2(1): 42–80.

Trapp, R. (2014) 'Elimination of the Chemical Weapons Stockpile of Syria', *Journal of Conflict and Security Law* 19(1): 7–23.

Trenin, D. (2012) 'Syria: A Russian Perspective', *SADA*, 28 June. Available: http://carnegieendowment.org/sada/index.cfm?fa=show&article=48690&solr_hilite=.

Tucker, J. (2006) *War of Nerves* (New York: Pantheon Books).

Turner, J. (2015) 'Strategic Differences: Al Qaeda's Split with the Islamic State of Iraq and al-Sham', *Small Wars and Insurgencies* 26(2): 208–25.

Turner, J. and Maryanski, A. (2009) *Incest: Origins of the Taboo* (Boulder, CO: Paradigm).

UN (2013a) ' "We Face a Race against Time", Secretary-General Tells Council on Foreign Relations, Urging Collective Action to Address Crisis in Syria, Threat of Climate Catastrophe', UN Press Release, 13 February. Available: www.un.org/press/en/2013/sgsm14808.doc.htm.

UN (2013b) 'United Nations Mission to Investigate Allegations of the Use of Chemical Weapons in the Syrian Arab Republic'. Available: https://unoda-web.s3.amazonaws.com/wp-content/uploads/2013/12/report.pdf.

UN (2013c) 'Report of the United Nations Mission to Investigate Allegations of the Use of Chemical Weapons in the Syrian Arab Republic on the Alleged Use of Chemical Weapons in the Ghouta Area of Damascus on 21 August 2013'. Available: www.un.org/disarmament/content/slideshow/Secretary_General_Report_of_CW_Investigation.pdf.

UN (2013d) 'Security Council Requires Scheduled Destruction of Syria's Chemical Weapons, Unanimously Adopting Resolution 2118 (2013)', UN Press Release, 27 September. Available: www.un.org/press/en/2013/sc11135.doc.htm.

UN (2014) 'Syria – Humanitarian Assistance, Resolution 2139', United Nations.

UN (2015a) 'Daily Press Briefing by the Office of the Spokesperson for the Secretary-General', UN Press Release, 15 January. Available: www.un.org/press/en/2015/db150115.

UN (2015b) 'Adopting Resolution 2n209 (2015), Security Council Condemns Use of Chlorine Gas as Weapon in Syria', UN Press Release, 6 March. Available: www.un.org/press/en/2015/sc11810.doc.htm.

UN (2015c) 'Implementation of Security Council Resolutions 2139 (2014), 2165 (2014) and 2191 (2014)', UN Security Council.

UNHRC (2014a) 'Selected Testimonies from Victims of the Syrian Conflict', UN Human Rights Council.

UNHRC (2014b) 'Report of the Independent International Commission of Inquiry on the Syrian Arab Republic', UN Human Rights Council.

UNHRC (2015) 'Report on the Independent International Commission of Inquiry on the Syrian Arab Republic', UN Human Rights Council.

USACDA (1993) 'Adherence to and Compliance with Arms Control Agreements and the President's Report to Congress on Soviet Non-Compliance with Arms Control Agreements, January 14, 1993', Washington, DC: US Government Printing Office.

References

USCIA (2004) 'Unclassified Report to Congress on the Acquisition of Technology Relating to Weapons of Mass Destruction and Advanced Conventional Munitions, 1 July Through 31 December 2003'.

US Cong. (1992) 'Weapons Proliferation in the New World Order: Hearing before the Committee on Governmental Affairs, United States Senate, One Hundred Second Congress, Second Session, January 15, 1992', Washington, DC: US Government Printing Office.

US Cong. (2003) 'Syria: Implications for U.S. Security and Regional Stability – Hearing before the Subcommittee on the Middle East and Central Asia of the Committee on International Relations, House of Representatives, One Hundred Eighth Congress, First Session, September 16, 2003', Washington, DC: US Government Printing Office.

US Cong. (2012a) 'Syria: The Crisis and Its Implications – Hearing before the Committee on Foreign Relations, United States Senate, One Hundred Twelfth Congress, Second Session, March 1 2012', Washington, DC: US Government Printing Office.

US Cong. (2012b) 'When Regimes Fall: The Challenge of Securing Lethal Weapons – Hearing before the Subcommittee on Terrorism, Nonproliferation, and Trade of the Committee on Foreign Affairs, House of Representatives, One Hundred Twelfth Congress, Second Session, July 19 2012', Washington, DC: US Government Printing Office.

US Cong. (2012c) 'Next Steps in Syria: Hearing before the Committee on Foreign Relations, United States Senate, One Hundred Twelfth Congress, Second Session, August 1 2012', Washington, DC: US Government Printing Office.

US Cong. (2012d) 'The Situation in Syria: Hearing Before the Committee on Armed Services, United States Senate, One Hundred Twelfth Congress, Second Session, March 7, 2012', Washington, DC: US Government Printing Office.

US Cong. (2012e) 'Syria: U.S. Policy Options – Hearing before the Committee on Foreign Relations, United States Senate, One Hundred Twelfth Congress, Second Session, April 19, 2012', Washington, DC: US Government Printing Office.

US Cong. (2013a) 'Crisis in Syria: The U.S. Response – Hearing before the Committee on Foreign Affairs, House of Representatives, One Hundred Thirteenth Congress, First Session, March 20, 2013', Washington, DC: US Government Printing Office.

US Cong. (2013b) 'A Crisis Mismanaged: Obama's Failed Syria Policy – Hearing before the Subcommittee on the Middle East and North Africa of the Committee on Foreign Affairs, House of Representatives, One Hundred Thirteenth Congress, First Session, June 5 2013', Washington, DC: US Government Printing Office.

US Cong. (2013c) 'Syria: Weighing the Obama Administration's Response – Hearing before the Committee on Foreign Affairs, House of Representatives, One Hundred Thirteenth Congress, First Session, September 4, 2013', Washington, DC: US Government Printing Office.

US Cong. (2013d) 'Syria: Hearing before the Committee on Foreign Relations, United States Senate, One Hundred Thirteenth Congress, First Session, October 31 2013', Washington, DC: US Government Printing Office.

US Cong. (2013e) 'Examining the Syrian Refugee Crisis: Hearing before the Subcommittee on the Middle East and North Africa of the Committee on Foreign Affairs, House of

Representatives, One Hundred Thirteenth Congress, First Session, September 19, 2013', Washington, DC: US Government Printing Office.

US Cong. (2013f) 'The Authorization of Use of Force in Syria: Hearing before the Committee on Foreign Relations, United States Senate, One Hundred Thirteenth Congress, First Session, September 3, 2013', Washington, DC: US Government Printing Office.

US Cong. (2013g) 'Terrorist Groups in Syria: Hearing before the Subcommittee on Terrorism, Nonproliferation, and Trade of the Committee on Foreign Affairs, House of Representatives, One Hundred Thirteenth Congress, First Session, November 20, 2013', Washington, DC: US Government Printing Office.

US Cong. (2013h) 'Establishing a Syrian War Crimes Tribunal? Joint Hearing before the Subcommittee on Africa, Global Health, Global Human Rights, and International Organizations and the Subcommittee on the Middle East and North Africa of the Committee on Foreign Affairs, House of Representatives, One Hundred Thirteenth Congress, First Session, October 30, 2013', Washington, DC: US Government Printing Office.

US Cong. (2014a) 'The Humanitarian Crisis in Syria: Views from the Ground – Hearing before the Subcommittee on the Middle East and North Africa of the Committee on Foreign Affairs, House of Representatives, One Hundred Thirteenth Congress, Second Session, May 21, 2014', Washington, DC: US Government Printing Office.

USDIA (2007) 'Current and Projected National Security Threats to the United States', Defense Intelligence Agency. Available: www.investigativeproject.org/documents/testimony/268.pdf.

USDNI (2011) 'Acquisition of Technology Relating to Weapons of Mass Destruction and Advanced Conventional Munitions, Covering 1 January to 31 December 2011', Unclassified DNI Report to Congress.

USDOD (1997) 'Proliferation: Threat and Response', US Department of Defense.

Van Tets, F. (2014) 'Syria's Chemical Weapons', *Independent*, 23 March. Available: www.independent.co.uk/news/world/middle-east/syrias-chemical-weapons-a-third-of-the-most-dangerous-weapons-have-been-destroyed-including-all-mustard-gas-ahead-of-final-un-deadline-9211052.html.

Walsh, N. E. and Walsh, W. S. (2003) 'Rehabilitation of Landmine Victims: The Ultimate Challenge', *Bulletin of the World Health Organization* 81(9): 665–70.

Walt, S. (2013) 'Types of Weapons Assad Uses Shouldn't Affect U.S. Policy', *New York Times*, 26 August. Available: www.nytimes.com/roomfordebate/2013/08/26/is-an-attack-on-syria-justified/type-of-weapons-assad-uses-shouldnt-affect-us-policy.

Walzer, M. (2006 [1977]) *Just and Unjust Wars: A Moral Argument with Historical Illustrations* (New York: Basic Books).

Warrick, J. (2013) 'As Syria Deteriorates, Neighbors Fear Bioweapons Threat', *Washington Post*, 4 September. Available: www.washingtonpost.com/world/national-security/as-syria-deteriorates-neighbors-fear-bioweapons-threat/2013/09/04/ed5b47e0-10ad-11e3-85b6-d27422650fd5_story.html.

Webster, H. (1942) *Taboo: A Sociological Study* (Stanford, CA: Stanford University Press).

References

Weiss, M. (2014) 'The Unraveling: How Obama's Syria Policy Fell Apart', *Politico*, 2 January. Available: www.politico.com/magazine/story/2014/01/how-obamas-syria-policy-fell-apart-101704_Page5.html#.VcODzxYnjwx.

Weiss, M. and Hassan, H. (2015) *ISIS: Inside the Army of Terror* (New York: Regan Arts).

Weiss, T. (2014) 'Military Humanitarianism: Syria Hasn't Killed It', *The Washington Quarterly* 37(1): 7–20.

Wheeler, N. (2010) *Saving Strangers: Humanitarian Intervention in International Society* (Oxford: Oxford University Press).

Wimsatt, W. and Beardsley, M. (1946) 'The Intentional Fallacy', *The Sewanee Review* 54(3): 468–88.

Wolfe, L. (2013) 'Syria Has a Massive Rape Crisis', *The Atlantic*, 18 June. Available: www.theatlantic.com/international/archive/2013/04/syria-has-a-massive-rape-crisis/274583.

Zanders, J. and Trapp, R. (2013) 'Ridding Syria of Chemical Weapons: Next Steps', *Arms Control Today* 43(9): 8–14.

Zarakol, A. (2014) 'What Made the Modern World Hang Together: Socialisation or Stigmatization?', *International Theory* 6(2): 311–32.

Zawaiti, H. (2014) 'Sexual Violence as a Weapon of War in the Ongoing Syrian Conflict: Testimony Before the Subcommittee on International Human Rights of the Standing Committee on Foreign Affairs and International Development of the House of Commons, 2nd Session, 41st Parliament, The Parliament of Canada, Ottowa'.

Zelin, A. (2014) 'The War between ISIS and Al-Qaeda for Supremacy of the Global Jihadist Movement', Washington Institute for Near East Policy.

INDEX